SANIA SHARAWI LANFRANCHI is a freelance interpreter, and has worked for international, regional and national organisations, including the Library of Alexandria and the Egyptian Ministry of Foreign Affairs. She holds postgraduate degrees in both English Literature and Arabic Literature from the American University in Cairo.

To my sister Malak

Casting off the Veil

THE LIFE OF
HUDA SHAARAWI
EGYPT'S FIRST FEMINIST

SANIA SHARAWI LANFRANCHI
Edited by Dr John Keith King

I.B.TAURIS
LONDON · NEW YORK

Published in 2012 by I.B.Tauris & Co. Ltd
6 Salem Road, London W2 4BU
175 Fifth Avenue, New York NY 10010
www.ibtauris.com

Distributed in the United States and Canada Exclusively by Palgrave Macmillan,
175 Fifth Avenue, New York NY 10010

ISBN 978 1 84885 719 3

A full CIP record for this book is available from the British Library
A full CIP record for this book is available from the Library of Congress
Library of Congress catalog card: available

Typeset in Goudy by Dexter Haven Associates Ltd, London

Printed and bound by CPI Group (UK) Ltd, Croydon, CR0 4YY

Contents

List of illustrations

Acknowledgements

The great West-African writer Hampâté-Bâ said that the death of an old man is like a library set on fire. It is true that oral history is as vital to human experience as written history. I therefore wish to address posthumous thanks and gratitude to Céza Nabarawi, Hawa Idris, Huria Idris-Shafik and her husband Hasan Shafik, to Sherifa Lutfi Mehrez, to Eva Habib al-Masri, to Doria Shafik, to Suza Khulusi, to Jazbia Saad al-Din, to Fathia Abd al-Raziq, and to my mother Munira Asim, for their willingness to speak openly about their lives and experience with me since my early adolescence. Their memories were added to the discoveries I otherwise made in my grandmother's mansion. I wish to thank posthumously Gabrielle Rousseau-Fahmi, Jeanne Marquès, Mary Kahil and all the women who regularly came to the house and sat with the family long after Huda Shaarawi's demise, for all the stories they passed on to me. My memory takes me to Dame Margery Corbett-Ashby and her wonderfully spontaneous granddaughter Charlotte, with whom I spent some time when they came to Cairo. Dame Margery entertained me much later in Horsted Keynes, where we talked for long hours about my grandmother and she honoured me by calling herself my 'English grandmother'. I similarly wish to thank Dr John Von B. Rodenbeck and Dr Afaf Lutfi al-Sayid for their precious advice on the manuscript, as well as Dr Malak Badrawi for bringing some invaluable references to my attention, and Dr Aida Graff for a providential addition to my sources. Thanks are also due to Maria Marsh for following this book in in its various phases, and very special thanks to Gretchen Ladish and Robert Hastings for their exacting contribution and for having turned a history book into a work of art. I wish to thank Dr Margot Badran for her charming translation of Huda Shaarawi's memoirs, which my grandmother asked her faithful secretary, Abd al-Hamid Fami Mursi, to write for her. Dr Badran also showed a passionate interest in the history of Egyptian and Arab feminists in her other works, and should be thanked for fulfilling the difficult task of writing extensively on the subject. Last but not least, I wish to thank all my sisters and brothers for sharing their memories with me and my children for their unfailing support and enthusiastic interest in my family's history.

Note on transliteration

Arabic words are usually transliterated, or rather romanised, according to the Western language in which the story is written. The French pronunciation and spelling, for example, are different from the English.

I have adopted a transliteration system mostly based on the use of the three Arabic vowels – the letter 'aleph' and the 'fatha' are conveyed by a; the letter 'yaa' and the 'kasra' are conveyed by 'i', and the letter 'wow' and the 'damma' are conveyed by 'u'. Furthermore, 'q' replaces 'k' to convey the guttural 'Qaf' in Arabic. This unfortunately means that the letter 'y' is not used at all.

In older times, in both daily life and in the magazine *L'Égyptienne*, as well as other publications, the French spelling of names was adopted, so that Huda Shaarawi's full name was Hoda Chaaraoui and Asim, up to the present day, is usually spelt 'Assem'. The same system has been followed in this book for all the names of Arab characters, places or institutions. The Arabic *'ayn* and the *hamza*, represented by ' and ', respectively, have been deleted when possible (for example, Ali or Umar). All long vowels have been omitted. No distinction is made between the Arabic consonants zein and za, which are both transliterated as 'z', or sad and sin, which are both transliterated as 's'. My goal throughout has been to simplify the spelling of Arabic words and to eliminate diacritical marks in order to avoid confusing readers unfamiliar with Arabic. Well-known geographical place names (such as Cairo) and words with familiar spellings (such as pasha) have been retained, but less well known place names and words have been transliterated in accordance with the rules I have adopted. In the odd case, where a quotation from a text has used a certain form for a proper name, or where I know the person's preference in spelling his name, I have retained it. Ains and hamzas have been included in titles of books and in quotations, but all other diacritical marks have been omitted. The *ta' marbuta* of words in a construct state is written as 't' at the end of the word.

1

Childhood in a conservative home

Huda Shaarawi was born on 23 June 1879. Her name at birth was Nur al-Huda Sultan. Her father, Muhammad Sultan Pasha, who was 55 when his daughter came into the world, was a man of substantial influence in Egyptian society and political life. An Egyptian from Minya, in Upper Egypt, where he had extensive estates, he was an extremely rich man accustomed to deference. In the way Egyptians have of conferring nicknames on important people, Sultan Pasha was widely referred to as the 'King' of Upper Egypt. Wilfrid Blunt, an English resident who knew Egypt well and was a sympathiser with the Egyptian nationalist cause, observed that Sultan Pasha 'was a proud man of great wealth and importance and used to being given the first place everywhere'.[1] Huda's mother, Iqbal, by contrast, was of Circassian origin, the daughter of a family from the Shapsigh tribe of Dagestan. Her origins were both obscure and romantic, and she was scarcely 20 when Huda was born. Huda's brother Umar was born two years later, in 1881.

Iqbal's own story was a romantic one. She was a proud and reticent woman who had been brought to Egypt as a child, and Huda only gradually pieced together her tale, learning much when she eventually

1

met her mother's brothers. Iqbal's father, reputedly a tribal chieftain, had been killed by the Russians during the Russian invasion of the Caucasus, and his widow, Aziza, had fled to Istanbul with her remaining family, including Iqbal. As refugees, the family suffered terrible hardship. One son died, and Iqbal's baby sister was abducted by her wet nurse. When Iqbal was nine, Aziza decided to send her for safety to Egypt, a country she had never visited, under the protection of an Egyptian friend who was travelling to Cairo. It can only be imagined what an act of blind faith this was, and how much Aziza must have feared for her daughter's welfare. The intention was to place Iqbal under the care of a man Huda later came to understand from her own uncles' accounts was her mother's maternal uncle, Yusuf Sabri Pasha, an officer in the Egyptian army and a member of Egypt's Turco-Circassian elite. It happened, however, that Yusuf Sabri Pasha was absent on military duty in the Sudan. His wife, described as a freed slave of a member of the royal family, who was no doubt herself of Circassian origin, reacted badly to Iqbal's arrival, refusing to receive her and declaring that her husband had no family in the Caucasus. Iqbal was therefore taken instead by her escort to the house of his own trusted friend, Ali Bey Raghib. Raghib Bey and his family cared for her. She was brought up with their daughter and learned to speak Arabic as well as Turkish. Yusuf Sabri Pasha evidently remained in contact with her, however, and she grew up to regard him and his family as her kin. Iqbal came to feel a special bond with Yusuf Sabri Pasha's daughter, Munira Sabri, who was her cousin. When she was of a suitable age, Raghib Bey's family set about finding a wealthy husband for the Circassian girl for whom they had cared. Iqbal had grown into an extremely beautiful young woman, and it was a stroke of good fortune for her that Sultan Pasha was seeking just such a woman as a consort.[2] His first wife, Hasiba, had born him a son, Ismail, who had sadly died not long before, and she had evidently lapsed into depression.

Out of compassion for his new young wife, who sometimes brooded sadly and wept when memories of her distant family flooded back to her, Sultan Pasha investigated Iqbal's family's whereabouts in Turkey. He discovered that Ahmed Idris and Yusuf Idris, Iqbal's brothers, were settled in the little Turkish port of Bandirma, on the southern shore of the Sea of Marmara. Aziza, with whom she had lost touch, was also still alive and well. Sultan invited the two brothers and Iqbal's mother, Huda's grandmother, to come to Cairo. The brothers now spoke Turkish, even between themselves. They brought with them their memories of the past, and Huda eagerly questioned her uncle Yusuf about the history of her Circassian family. She found his tales captivating, and her imagination was further stimulated by the fact that the stories were about her ancestors. Yusuf told her the history of his father, Sharaluqa Gwattish, who had been the chief from the Shapsigh tribe, whose home was on the Caspian Sea coast. Like the hero of the Caucasus, Hadji Murad, who was immortalised in fiction by Leo Tolstoy, Gwattish had fought against the Russians and had lost his life in a desperate battle against the Russian invaders. The family's flight to Turkey was part of the chaotic exodus that followed the Russian conquest of the Caucasus.[3] Soon after her marriage, Iqbal met a Circassian woman in Cairo named Jazb Ashiq, with whose story her own seemed to have much in common, and with whom she struck up an instinctive friendship. This was unusual for Iqbal, who was somewhat reserved. It was apparently concluded by the two women, who exchanged information about their lives, that this was Iqbal's long-lost baby sister, abducted in Turkey, so that Huda in due course grew up calling Jazb Ashiq 'Auntie'. Iqbal took Jazb Ashiq into her household.

Sultan Pasha began his career in government service as a local administrator in the province of Minya. Thanks to his ability and personal wealth, he rose to the position of Director of the Inspectorate for Upper Egypt, which gave him a foothold in national political life. He became widely known, and eventually achieved the position of President of the Consultative Chamber of Delegates ('Majlis Shura al-Nuwwab'). He was an advocate of constitutional rule in Egypt and, with his associates, had plans for wide-ranging reform.[4] In addition to his political friends, he was acquainted with Jamal al-Din al-Afghani and with al-Afghani's disciple, Muhammad Abduh, who had become the Grand Mufti of Egypt under Khedive Tawfiq. Sultan Pasha shared Muhammad Abduh's enlightened ideas and beliefs, even in relation to banking and insurance. In 1879, the year of Huda's birth, together with his friend Umar Lutfi Pasha, another powerful official within Khedive Tawfiq's establishment, Sultan Pasha drew up a plan to create a National Bank in Egypt, based on local rather than foreign capital, a project that paved the way for later similar efforts.[5]

There was nothing in Muhammad Sultan Pasha's life that pointed to a tragic destiny. In common with the Khedive, however, and the wealthy landed class which ruled the country, he was obliged to accept the financial and political control exercised by Western countries in Egypt, and in particular by Britain, that had arisen as the consequence of the debt contracted by Tawfiq's predecessor, Khedive Ismail, during the building of the Suez Canal. The creation by the British and French Governments of the Caisse de la Dette to administer Egypt's repayments, together with the presence of the British and French financial controllers, who together supervised Egypt's fiscal affairs, had resulted in what was in effect an economic occupation of the country. Most decisions related to financial issues were referred to the two foreign financial controllers, who had the ultimate say. Egypt's economy had in effect been hijacked by the obligation to service the debt, and its rulers were tricked into a false situation that prevented them from governing effectively. This situation resulted in discontent within the country and the army, so that the effectiveness of the autocratic khedivial style of rule came to be questioned, not least by the local population. In February 1881, Egyptian-born officers of the Egyptian army, led by Colonel Ahmad Urabi, demanded constitutional rule from the Khedive, as well as greater opportunities for their own preferment, distinct from the Turco-Circassian elite which ran Egypt's army as well as so much else in Egypt. When this happened, Sultan Pasha's first instinct was to lend them his support. His roots, after all, lay with the Egyptian people, and he believed that Egypt was ready for constitutional or parliamentary rule.

The story of what ensued was recounted to Huda when she was still a child by Qallini Fahmi Pasha, her father's former secretary, who was also a friend of the family.[6] Sultan Pasha and other Egyptian political figures initially lent their support to Urabi and his fellow officers, but Sir Edward Malet, the British Consul, and Sir Auckland Colvin, the Khedive's financial adviser, had repeatedly warned them that a revolution would provoke British wrath, and would certainly result in dire retribution. The implication was that the only way to save the country was to bring about the defeat of Urabi. Britain sent a fleet to Alexandria and threatened mayhem if Urabi and the other Egyptian officers continued with their plan to force Khedive Tawfiq from the throne. Sultan Pasha's change of heart sprang from his fear that a massacre might take place with the British warships off the Alexandria coast.[7] He realised that a military intervention in Egypt by the invincible army of the British Empire might lead to the country's occupation, leading to a passage from Ottoman to British hegemony. In the last resort, he believed his ultimate allegiance was to the Khedive, as Viceroy of the Ottoman Sultan, and therefore to the Ottoman Empire itself. Instinct and political beliefs therefore led him to back the Khedive and conform to the advice that was being issued by the British, and to turn against Urabi and the other officers whom he had previously supported. In May 1882, when matters came to a head, Sultan Pasha took the Khedive's side against Urabi. In the words of Wilfrid Blunt, who sympathised with the justice of Urabi's case, Sultan Pasha 'was partly cajoled, partly frightened by Malet into declaring himself in favour of the British demands, and threw in his lot finally with the Court party against his former associates'.[8] This caused anger against him, and while Sultan Pasha was in Alexandria, an Urabist mob attacked his property in Cairo. Blunt copied into his diary a statement from the *Observer* newspaper, according to which 'Sultan Pasha went... to the Khedive to make terms between him and Arabi...' Blunt's comment was,

The papers all say that he and the Chamber have sided against Arabi with the Khedive, but I will not believe that till I hear further. What is likely is that Sultan Pasha has been put out, at the Chamber being invoked without a legal summons, and at an inconvenient time of the year. The army has had too much influence in the Ministry not to have made itself enemies. There is probably jealousy, but I do not believe in more. The whole thing has probably been encouraged by Colvin and Malet and the Circassians have been encouraged by the idea of Turkish intervention. They have ordered ships to Alexandria, which, if I am not mistaken, will have the effect of uniting all once more against the Europeans.[9]

Meanwhile, Sir Edward Malet had promised Sultan Pasha and others that, though the British would never on any terms allow Urabi and his friends to rule the country in the Khedive's place, they would withdraw their forces immediately after the crisis. However, Malet never provided Sultan Pasha with a written memorandum setting out the British Government's position, as Sultan Pasha had asked. Nevertheless, Sultan Pasha, in typically oriental fashion, relied on the British Consul's word of honour and his integrity, not suspecting that he might have been manipulated. His sincere belief was that the British forces would not remain in the country after winning their battle. He was, of course, to be gravely disappointed. After the crisis, Sultan Pasha was never the same man again. It was generally believed in the family and in other circles that Sultan Pasha bitterly blamed himself when he realised that Malet's promises of immediate evacuation after the Khedive's victory over Urabi were false, and that the British, who had purported to intervene in Egypt to support the Khedive's rule, would maintain indefinitely their occupation of the country.

Wilfrid Blunt quotes Abd al-Salam al-Muilhi, a member of Egypt's Parliament in 1882 and previously a good friend of Sultan Pasha, who gave an account of how Sultan Pasha was viewed by the pro-Urabi partisans after the crisis. Al-Muilhi said of himself that

he had been an intimate friend and partisan of Sultan Pasha's, and had been one of those who joined Sultan in his quarrel with Urabi, but they were all very sorry now for not having held together; and he did not approve Sultan's conduct during the war. Sultan had been deceived by Malet, who induced him to act as he did on the basis of a distinct promise that the rights of the

Egyptian Parliament would be respected. Malet made this promise verbally, and Sultan asked to have it in writing, but was dissuaded from insisting by the Khedive, who assured him that the English agent's words were as good as his. The old man, when he found out after the war how much he had been deceived, took it to heart and died expressing a hope that Urabi would forgive him, and that his name would not be handed down to posterity as the betrayer of his country.[10]

Soon after the crisis, Sultan Pasha developed an incurable illness. He died two years later, in 1884, aged not quite sixty, during what was intended to have been a recuperative stay in the Austrian city of Graz. He reportedly looked like a man of ninety. The family believed he had died of a broken heart following his political disappointments. The British Government, as a result of its victory over the Urabists, succeeded in securing its hold on the Suez Canal as its own gateway to Asia. In fact, an Anglo–French agreement dividing the suzerain states of the Turkish Empire between themselves had already been signed.

Before his death, Sultan Pasha had nominated Ali Shaarawi, the son of his sister – a major landowner in the Minya region and a very wealthy man in his own right – to be the legal guardian of Huda, Umar and his other children, and the trustee of his estate. The Shaarawi fortune was based on lands acquired by Ali's father, Hasan Shaarawi, who had been a village 'umda' (mayor) near Minya. Ali managed his estates, and was embarking on a career in politics, but after the death of Sultan Pasha he also found time to fulfil his duties as guardian by paying regular visits to the family of his late uncle. Sultan Pasha's two widows, however, continued to run the house from day to day with the assistance of the body of retainers left by Sultan Pasha, prominent among whom was Said Agha, the principal eunuch. Lala Said, as he was affectionately known, was the family's senior servant, whose duty was to keep the women safe. At the age of just 25, Iqbal was, in effect, left at the helm of the family mansion, a fine house Sultan Pasha had built for himself in Jami Sharkas Street.[11] Having lost her own father and now her husband, she was haunted by the thought of death, and felt vulnerable and frightened, though she strove not to show it. She had been exposed to a hazardous life at a tender age, and had adopted a philosophical and serious attitude to life. In her mid-twenties, she was a beautiful woman, as the family remembered her, tall and slender with skin like porcelain, hazel eyes and fine features. Her Circassian origin was evident, and her straight back and haughty gait proclaimed her breeding. Thanks to her connection with Sultan Pasha, she moved in elevated circles. Huda herself in later life had shadowy memories of being taken as a small child by her mother to the palace to meet the wife of the Khedive Tawfiq.

Huda was therefore to grow up in a home devastated by mourning and ravaged by the echoes of the political conflicts of the era. At the age of five, she lived in a house where the furniture, the chandeliers, and especially the mirrors were covered with black cloth. The adult women in the house wore black. Iqbal, still distraught after her husband's death, was ordered by the doctor to rest. Sultan Pasha's first wife, Hasiba, fared even worse. Eight years earlier, before the marriage between Sultan Pasha and Iqbal, despair at the early death of her son Ismail had turned her into an invalid. She had two daughters, Luza and Nissim, but remained unconsoled for her son's loss. Now, the demise of her husband seemed to sever her last link with the departed boy. As to Huda, she was as a child unaware that the death of Sultan Pasha had been an event of political significance and had left a gap in Egypt's public life. For her, what she had lost was a father. She missed his presence in the house, and yearned for his familiar smell and touch. At a very young age, she was forced to face up to the realisation that her beloved father, who had never failed to embrace and reassure her when she needed comfort, was gone forever. She felt his absence heavily. She missed going to his room every morning with her little brother Umar, two years younger than she, sickly, and needing particular care. She missed her father's steady arms, his warm voice, his self-containment and quietness, and the daily tide of visitors who visited the house, which felt too large and too empty in his absence.

Huda was therefore aware at an early age that death took people away, never to be seen again. Though she never met her half-brother Ismail, she loved her stepmother Hasiba, whom she considered her personal friend. She knew how much Hasiba missed Ismail. For hours, Huda would nestle near the bedridden woman in her large bed. She called her 'Ummi al-Kabira', which meant 'my big mother'. She was too young to realise that she was in the exceptional situation of enjoying the care of two mothers, or that these two women, who had been the joint spouses of one man, were miraculously amicable towards one another. Hasiba had lost her son, her health and her husband, but had transferred her affection to Iqbal and her two children as well as caring for her own two daughters. Her rage at her loss had apparently worked itself out, and she seemed now to be waiting patiently in the company of her extended family for the moment when death would remember her. Huda often sought her mother's permission to spend the night in Hasiba's bed, which she loved. Hasiba had a pacifying influence over her, and they both loved the fresh air, keeping the windows open all night, especially in summer. This was of course entirely out of the question in the room she shared with her sickly little brother. Hasiba also taught her to drink cold milk with the rich cream that settled on top of it after it was boiled. They would drink the milk and soak their bread in it, while they baked chestnuts on the fire in the hearth. On summer days, they woke up to the song of the birds in the trees outside the window, and Huda felt happy and fulfilled. Iqbal was at the time obsessed by her young son's fragile health, and was therefore happy more often than not to leave Huda in Hasiba's affectionate company.[12] When Huda complained that her mother's favourite was Umar, Hasiba would explain that it was merely because, as a boy, he was destined to maintain the family name. As he was a fragile child he therefore had to be paid special attention.[13] Though jealous of Umar, Huda nevertheless came to love him dearly.

As the time of mourning came to an end, Huda enjoyed the routine of life in the great house, which stood in what was then the new part of

Cairo, an area of boulevards and gardens between the traditional heart of the city and the Nile. The house was a hive of activity, with the battalion of maids and servants and slaves who kept it in order, with the friends and visitors who came regularly and the pedlars and beggars who were constantly at the gate. The traditions and religious feasts were always enthusiastically celebrated. The family, like all well-to-do Egyptian families that formed part of upper-class society, had its established circle of friends and acquaintances. Many of the Pasha's old friends continued to visit the family, or invited them to their homes. The children often went to play under supervision in Qattawi Pasha's garden, between Suliman Pasha Street and Sharifain Street, and their social life meant that Huda was able to make friends with girls of good families of her own age. Qattawi Pasha was a Jewish aristocrat from Minya, who also possessed a mansion in the neighbourhood. One visitor to the house was Sheikh Ali al-Laithi, a man famous for his sense of humour and poetic talent, who lived in the khedivial palace and was the Viceroy's court poet. The only visitor to the house with whom Huda was sometimes ill at ease, despite his wide knowledge and culture, was Zubair Pasha, a powerful Sudanese man whose money came from the trade in slaves and whose manners were sometimes rough and uncouth.

Before his death, Sultan Pasha had held a weekly literary salon in his home, regularly attended by these men and others. Their father's love of literature and poetry had meant that Huda and Umar spent their earliest years in a house where culture ranked as highly as politics. Even after Sultan Pasha's death, the two women who now ruled the household maintained the tradition he had laid down. They too were open-minded and oriented towards culture, although their own lives, restricted by the limitations placed upon women, inevitably constricted them and conditioned their attitude towards gender and gender differences. The household was, of course, wealthy, and the two children grew up in blissful ignorance of poverty and its drawbacks. Their problems, if any, were of an emotional rather than a practical nature, as is often the case with people who do not have to worry about money.

Both continued to suffer enormously from their father's absence, and Huda, despite Hasiba's consolations, went on resenting through much of her childhood her mother's preoccupation with her delicate younger brother. She persistently misinterpreted Iqbal's apprehensive solicitude towards Umar as an unreasonable bias against her, and everything she experienced in the harem reinforced this idea. Friends, family members, teachers, servants and slaves tended to discriminate between girls and boys, and Huda's young mind was early in life accustomed to draw conclusions from people's individual attitudes and actions. She was a clever child, and instinctively shunned those who appeared not to pay proper respect to her or her intellect.

Huda soon came to prize intellectual achievement and education above everything, and felt her life would become a misery if her thirst for learning were to be denied. She decided she hated being a girl because her femininity deprived her of knowledge and sports. But she was able to compensate for this. As well as being clever, she was also a strong child, and enjoyed being outdoors as much as sitting with her books, climbing trees and walls, and planting trees in the garden. She spent her time happily playing in the open in the afternoon while poor Umar was obliged to rest in bed. She learned to read and write Ottoman Turkish, and Umar's Arabic teacher, Shaikh Ibrahim,[14] agreed to teach her to memorise the Qur'an. Like her brother, she read the Holy Book and learned it by heart when she was nine, though, as she later remarked, this did not mean she had gained a grammatical knowledge of Arabic since the Qur'an, which has the vowels marked, was the only Arabic book she could read correctly. Written classical Arabic differs from spoken Egyptian Arabic, with which, of course, Huda was perfectly familiar, and its grammar and pronunciation must be learned for full literacy.

Huda was eager to read Arabic correctly, and sometimes bought books of dubious quality from pedlars and vendors in the street. She felt a yearning to learn more Arabic and to study the complexities of Arabic syntax and grammar. She also inveigled Umar's Arabic teacher into giving her lessons, and was frustrated when Said Agha instructed the

Arabic teacher to stop teaching her Arabic grammar, because, as he mockingly said, 'It will be of no use to her during her lifetime, and she will never be a lawyer anyway'.[15] Classical Arabic was regarded as primarily a language for men and scholars. Upper-class girls such as Huda, though they spoke Arabic every day, were expected to concentrate more on the feminine accomplishments of literacy in Turkish, and increasingly in French, as this was the era when knowledge of the French language was becoming essential for any Egyptian of cultural attainments. Although she loved Said Agha for his unshakeable attachment to her family and herself, Huda hated him with all her heart for obstructing the development of her intellect. Nonetheless, Huda took great pleasure in the French that she soon began to learn.

She began to visit her late father's library in secret to read the books he had treasured. Huda was able to open the door with a key whose hiding place was known to her, and spent time alone inside the deserted room that had been preserved almost as a shrine to her father. Meanwhile Fardus and Yasmine,[16] the two little Egyptian girls who were brought up with her and were part of the household, kept guard in case Said Agha or anyone else passed by. Huda would gaze at her father's crowded book shelves, remembering how much his books had mattered to him. She recalled how he would sit for long hours reading, and how eager he always was to extend his knowledge of all aspects of life, the world, history, the cultural heritage of his people and how to further and preserve it. He had always kept chocolates in the library for the children in case they went to him there, and Huda had come to associate books with chocolates in her childish mind. Even after his death, she found a few traces of melted chocolate that lingered evocatively on the shelves.

Another consolation she found was in music. Huda's French teacher was also a pianist, and after Huda declared her love of music her French teacher was allowed also to give her piano lessons.[17] She had already acquired a piano, somewhat reluctantly, without realising how much she would come to love it. A pony had been given to Huda's brother

Umar at the suggestion of his doctor, who wanted him to have some open-air activity. Huda loved the idea of a pony, and asked if she could have one too, but her mother persuaded her instead to have a piano, which would be more ladylike. She agreed, thinking that she could borrow the pony from Umar when she wanted, and therefore have the best of both worlds.[18] In fact, she took to the piano with zeal, willingly practising for hours. She found great comfort in playing the piano, which she continued to do until the end of her life.

Muhammad Sultan Pasha's keenness to expand his experience had led him to befriend a number of foreigners in addition to his Egyptian acquaintance. He had, for example, admitted to his circle a French irrigation engineer, a M. G. Richard, whose wife came to play an important part in Huda's youth. Sultan Pasha had consulted M. G. Richard regarding improvements to the irrigation system in his plantations, and after his death Mme Jeanne Richard continued to be a friend of the family. Both Huda and Umar enjoyed the company of this affectionate and intelligent companion, and thus grew up with no mistrust of foreigners, to whom they had become accustomed early. Surrounded by people of diverse origins, they developed the habit of looking for the human qualities in others, rather than relying on social or ethnic distinguishing marks. They were serious children who, as the descendants of a powerful public man, set store by the virtues of self-possession and composure. This tended to curb Huda's sense of humour, though Umar's irrepressible wit was sometimes not to be contained.

Jeanne Richard was a slender brunette with wide brown eyes and jet-black hair. Her salient quality was charm, as was the case with many of the French women who lived in foreign lands at the time. This acquaintance with the Richards was the first, for Huda, in a long list of personal friendships, both with foreigners and Egyptians. The Richards needed money, and it was for this reason that Iqbal often asked the young woman to keep the children company when she was away from home, travelling to Upper Egypt or sometimes to Turkey. When Iqbal visited her husband's tomb in Minya, for example, Mme Richard would generally take charge of the two children in Cairo.[19]

This led, however, to conflict in the household, and made it necessary for Huda to assert herself, realising for perhaps the first time her ability to influence people. A maid and companion Iqbal happened to have at the time, a woman named Futunat, had a sharp tongue and made it clear she disliked Mme Richard. She was not especially fond of Huda, and was antagonistic to anyone in the house who appeared to be Huda's friend. Yasmine and Fardus eventually ran away because of her hostility. Futunat openly displayed her resentment of Mme Richard, whom Huda constantly had to protect against unjust insults and accusations.[20] This she was able to do, so that at a very early age she felt the power of her personality and her ability to impose her will on those with whom she came into contact. Her mother increasingly allowed her to have her own way.

From her youngest years, Huda resented the way girls in the harem were effaced like shadows whose presence went unnoticed and whose voice was unheard. Girls were subjected to very strict rules of restraint and obedience, while activity and vitality seemed to be the prerogative of boys. From the start, she sought vigorous women on whom to model herself. She knew that there were exceptions to the rule. Her uncles had told her that in Circassian society the women were not only treated with courtesy and even deference but could also emulate the men. For example, Huria, Sharaluqa's cousin, had ridden horses and fought against the Russian invaders like a man, side by side with her brothers. She was not the only woman who commanded Huda's respect. Her aunt, Sultan Pasha's sister Amna, the widow of Hasan Shaarawi, was another woman whose example she wanted to follow. Though a widow, she managed her own estates and rode horses like a man. She was also a strong and capable mother who had taught Huda's guardian, Ali Shaarawi, all he knew about how to manage property and land.

Huda often thought of these two women, whom she could not help comparing with the shy and retiring Iqbal and Hasiba and with her quiet, self-effacing elder half-sisters Luza and Nissim. She felt the urge for space, freedom and activity. Living side by side with her younger brother Umar, Huda pined for his privileges, not least because she felt physically stronger than he was. Her insistent demand was to be educated in the same way as her brother, but much to her dismay it seemed to be Said Agha's duty to impede it, whether at his own initiative or as instructed by her guardian. She desperately wanted to read and write in Arabic as the boys were taught to do, and to ride a pony in the garden like her brother. As a child, she already felt a strong urge to disregard conventional rules of conduct. She failed to understand why being a lady of accomplishment could not be reconciled with vigour and the love of life.

Within the family, her brother Umar was in fact her most loyal friend. He protected her and kept her secrets. When the children were tiny, it was she who told him the news of their father's death, which had been kept from him. The result was that he was so overcome by grief that he fainted and was unwell for two days, but he never disclosed the source of his information, so as to spare her punishment. But she, as a robust little girl, still resented the fact that her sickly brother was automatically granted privileges that she was denied. Envy often led her to feel angry with him. Nevertheless, over the years, Umar would always support her in her struggle to obtain what he, with his honesty, recognised as her legitimate rights. He helped her to gain access to culture and knowledge of the world of politics. Since he had grown up in the intellectual atmosphere bequeathed by his father, he was aware that there were educated and knowledgeable women who were able to entertain and to converse as equals with the most sophisticated men. Umar accustomed Huda to what would become her lifelong habit of turning to men she loved and trusted for their help in the social and political struggles in which she participated later.

When she was still only a girl of 12, Huda had a startling experience, when an event occurred that would probably have led most families in Egypt at the time to rejoice rather than the reverse. Iqbal heard gossip that the Khedive himself was talking of choosing Huda to become the wife of one of his protégés. It is to be assumed that the size of the late Sultan Pasha's fortune was such as not to be ignored in khedivial circles, and Huda's status as an heiress of part of that inheritance made her a desirable bride. Iqbal was not pleased with this, however, seeing it as a threat to the family and its possessions. Huda, who happened to be ill, resting in bed, overheard Iqbal discussing the question with Jazb Ashiq. Iqbal suggested that one way to avoid this match would be to promise Huda's hand to her cousin Ali Shaarawi, who was also her guardian. Thus she could tell the Khedive that the girl was already engaged to her cousin, which was a perfect excuse.

Iqbal was apparently well aware that Ali Shaarawi had already had in mind the possibility of such a marriage long before Khedive Tawfiq's unexpected whim precipitated the issue. His motivation was the desire to consolidate the family's estates. This appealed to Iqbal, who was well aware that it was thanks to Ali's integrity and hard work that the family's lands and estates had been preserved so far. For Huda's share of the Sultan estates in Minya to fall under the ownership of her late husband's nephew, keeping the land in the family, seemed to Iqbal a desirable outcome. This was what the family decided was to happen. The drawback was that Ali Shaarawi already had a wife, but Iqbal insisted that he should agree to divorce her so that Huda would be his sole spouse. This he promised to do. During his visits as the children's guardian, he had always struck Huda as imposing and stern, and would ignore her and spend his time talking to Umar. This had understandably meant that she did not enjoy his company. Now he had a new incentive to see Huda, however, Ali's visits to Jami Sharkas Street became increasingly frequent. This was, incidentally, also much to the delight of Umar, who yearned for someone to look up to as a father.

One day, Iqbal called Huda to her room and showed her a chest full of jewels from which to choose. Huda picked a beautiful diamond necklace, together with two bracelets, and immediately ran to share her joy with Hasiba, without even suspecting that this was a wedding gift from her future husband.[21] The older woman greeted her with her usual affectionate warmth and admired the jewels, to which she added a ring of her own. This ring later became, in Huda's mind, a symbolic legacy from one who had devised for herself an elegant and detached way of inhabiting this world and departing from it. Having settled Huda's future, Iqbal then rented a little house for the season at Helwan-les-Bains, the finest and most salubrious suburb of Cairo, where Khedive Tawfiq and the entire upper class had taken to spending the winter months. Life seemed simpler and less restricted in Helwan than in Cairo. Huda enjoyed going to the entertainments that were held there, such as Sheikh Salama Hijazi's history plays presented at the casino, as well as taking long walks with her young friends.[22]

The wedding took place in 1892, when Huda was 13. The official proposal was made through Ali Fahmi Pasha, the husband of Munira Sabri, the sister of Yusuf Sabri Pasha, who was Iqbal's uncle. Ali Fahmi Pasha was a renowned architect, originally from Maghagha, in the vicinity of Minya. His reputation rested on his contribution to the construction of the Cairo Opera House, built for the inauguration of the Suez Canal. The proposal was formally accepted on Huda's behalf by Fuad Saad al-Din Bey, the husband of Jazb Ashiq. The marriage was therefore arranged as a family affair, and formal procedures were rigidly followed, despite the absence of both fathers.[23]

The bridegroom was 26 years older than his bride. As her guardian and her cousin, he had always diligently worked to protect her interests, and he was a courageous patriot. Despite his virtues, however, the difference in their ages meant that the marriage was not destined immediately to become a match. The bride was, after all, a 13-year-old child who still played games, as children do, whose ruling passion was for her beloved piano. As Islamic law forbids the marriage of girls against their will, Huda was persuaded to agree to it. Said Agha whispered in her ear that if she refused it would kill her mother. She decided to dry her tears, curb her own will and submit, to save her mother's life. Whatever the consequences, she told herself, she would allow the family to dispose of her as they pleased.[24]

She felt distanced from all that was taking place around her, as if it was happening to somebody else. Childishly, she enjoyed the preparations. She was, after all, to live in her own glamorously decorated apartment in the house in Jami Sharkas Street, and she had been given diamonds and jewels of her own as well as heaps of elegant garments. All the fine accoutrements of upper-class weddings were hers. Even the wedding party, which she went through in a sort of daze, did not bring her any closer to reality. She was enchanted by her lace dress and its silver and gold embroideries. Her head and neck were weighed down by a diamond tiara and necklace which, together with the assiduous attention paid to her by the guests, made her feel she was the star in a magnificent performance. Those invited laid flowers and valuable gifts at her feet as she sat on the bridal throne. During the three days of the wedding ceremony, she enjoyed herself with her young friends and contrived to forget the ultimate conclusion of the revelry. At last, however, the singers surrounded her and she walked, with the help of her young friends through banks of shining candles and fresh flowers along the corridor that led to the great hall where the bridegroom was to join her. Ali's arrival was loudly proclaimed by one of the eunuchs, and he walked towards her, lifted the veil from her face, gently kissed her brow and invited her to sit down. The two cups of red syrup were then presented to him. He offered one of them to his bride and took the other one for himself.[25]

Eugénie Lebrun, the French wife of Husain Rushdi Pasha, attended the wedding and wrote about it in her book *Harems et Musulmanes d'Égypte*. She described a beautiful young bride who met her destiny in a glamorous dress and royal settings, like the victim of a ritual waiting to be sacrificed on the altar. Diamonds flowed down her neck, constellated her hair, and enclosed her waist, wrists and fingers. Two long ribbons of gold streamed from her temples and fell dazzlingly to the floor. In this attire, knees slightly bent by the weight of her jewellery, she appeared to Lebrun like a pagan deity, or as she put it, 'a Cathedral's divinity, a Byzantine Icon, or a Spanish virgin'.[26]

After the wedding, during the first night spent with her husband, Huda's childish tears moved Ali's heart and he, for the first time but not for the last, manifested his genuine affection for her by letting her be. Having known her as a child, and well aware that she was still a child, despite her bridal finery and nascent adolescent beauty, he behaved with restraint and compassion, acting with an almost parental solicitude. He had rescued her from an unwanted marriage that might have threatened the family's domains and her own integrity. However, living with a child-wife was neither easy nor amusing for a man in his late thirties, and her heartfelt tears when she found out that many of the trees she loved in the garden at Jami Sharkas Street had been uprooted to make space for the wedding tent, challenged his patience.[27] It was clear that the garden, where she spent most of her time, still mattered more to her than the role she was expected to play as a responsible married woman. It was difficult for him to communicate with her, as she romped about the house, ran up in her muddy clothes from the garden, or focused her attention on long hours of practice at the piano. It was as if she was trying to be oblivious of herself and the change in her life, and to disregard her changed situation. Meanwhile, Ali felt increasingly lonely, and went often to Minya to occupy himself with the family estates.

A virtually unbridgeable gulf opened between them in spite of the sacred bonds of marriage, or perhaps because of them. The age difference between the marriage partners was not untypical for its day, but neither the behaviour of the husband nor of the wife was typical. Ali continued to have compassion for his child-wife, and made no attempt to exercise his marital rights. He was an uncommunicative, hard-working, sentimental, generous and reasonable man who could feel tenderness but had little charm. Unthinking, he had assumed Huda would grow up overnight into a woman, but soon realised that such was not to be the case. She continued to play games with Umar

19

in the garden, or sat with the gardener laughing at his stories, and often sat at her piano, her long hair flowing freely on her shoulders, passionately caught up in the intricacies of the classical pieces she loved to play. If her husband unexpectedly appeared at the house, as he had every right to do, she sometimes ran from him in dismay, paralysed by her own shyness and his. They were the prisoners of convention that said it was normal for a man of his age to marry a girl of hers, and his reaction to the resulting situation, which was eventually to show increasing irritation, was in the end to be the key to her liberation.

Busy as Huda was with play, music and study, she had been hardly aware of his growing aloofness. She had enjoyed his affection during the first days, but then his attitude towards her changed. He virtually imprisoned her in the house, interrogating her about her conversations if she entertained her friends, scolding her when she played the piano, and sternly staring at her whenever he crossed her path. Huda wept a great deal, and moved from room to room carrying the books to whose influence Ali attributed her tears.[28] She was too young, however, to understand what had brought about his change of mood. In the end, in desperation Ali broke the promise he had made to Iqbal that Huda would be unchallenged as his sole spouse, and returned to his first wife, who uncomplainingly welcomed him back and finally bore him a son.[29]

Huda's mother broke this news to her, and she realised at once that it could permit her to regain her freedom. She felt a sudden relief. When Ali next came to the house, Huda greeted him with a formal welcome, congratulated him on his wise decision to return to his first wife and on his recent paternity, and suggested he return without more ado to the mother of Hasan, his newborn son. Huda had been disappointed by his evident belief that she should adopt adult manners and by his failure to make any attempt to meet her half way. He never understood how to be playful. Now, since she neither had a husband nor had not, since there was to be no divorce, she was able to remain in her mother's home with her dearest brother Umar and the rest of her family and friends. She was able to simply revert to her former way of life. Huda could see that in the unique situation of being a married woman unencumbered by a husband, she could at last set about acquiring a proper education. This had always been her dearest wish and her greatest desire.

In this way, the household continued on an even keel. In 1899, 15 years after Sultan Pasha's death, Iqbal was still head of the household in Jami Sharkas Street, with Umar living close to her in the same apartment within the house. Huda had her own quarters, though she made her rooms available to other members of the household according to need. Jazb Ashiq also spent some years living in the house with her husband, together with their son Ali, who was born in 1889. The children enjoyed the matriarchal way of life, the coming and going of guests and family members, all within the tranquil serenity of the great house with its separate wings and spacious garden. When Umar became an adult, he had built for himself his own *salamlik*, a separate villa on the edge of the garden, in the oriental style he liked so much, designed for him by the renowned Italian architect Antonio Lasciac. There, he kept his office and received his own guests.[30] The various members of the household paid more or less formal visits to each other in the mansion's different wings and apartments.

During the seven years that followed her separation from Ali, and as she grew from a child into a young woman, Huda began to socialise with women friends. As she grew older, she also took up the ways of smart society and began to smoke cigarettes. Two women played an important role in Huda's social life at this point. One of these was Adila al-Nabarawi, a sensitive and refined woman who had cultural interests in common with Huda and often accompanied her to the theatre.

Adila was a refined and beautiful woman, somewhat older than Huda. She was the daughter of Yusuf al-Nabarawi Pasha and had grown up in France, where her father was a diplomat at the Egyptian legation. She spoke perfect French and was well versed in French plays and literature. Adila was married to her cousin, Subhi al-Nabarawi, who had profligate habits and gambled rashly. He travelled widely, taking Adila with him everywhere. She was a graceful figure with a slim silhouette, a fragile, porcelain-white complexion, long brown hair that she often pulled back, and a soft, warm smile. She was, most importantly, genuine and loving in her friendship. She would call Huda 'Ma chérie', or 'Ma jolie', hugging her as one would a child. They went regularly together to the Opera, where Adila had a box reserved for most performances, but they also enjoyed going together to other theatres. It was Adila who selected and organised these outings. In 1886, they shared a subscription at the Opera House at 30 Egyptian pounds for the box and four additional pounds for extras such as the muslin curtains behind which the women were obliged to hide, though they were in any case veiled. The cost was duly divided between them until 1895, when Subhi al-Nabarawi's finances became very strained following a bad cotton crop and Adila could no longer afford to pay her share.[31] From then on, Huda willingly paid the entire cost, since she valued both her theatre visits and Adila's company. As Huda's thirst for knowledge and culture developed, it became the most important factor in her selection of friends. At the Opera House, she became increasingly familiar with both Eastern and Western classical music and singing, and with theatrical performances, such as the plays of Najib al-Rihani, or the songs of Abdu al-Hamuli and his wife Almaz.

There was a regular exchange of correspondence between the two women.[32] 'There will be Abdu and Abu Khalil at the Casino of Helwan, I shall be going there this evening and would be delighted if you came with me, we would leave by train at seven fifteen and would be in Helwan within twenty minutes, and we could return by train at midnight or at one a.m.,' wrote Adila. Again, following a summer holiday in Alexandria, Adila wrote, 'I cannot tell you how unhappy I was to leave you; living near you really grows on one as a sweet habit.' It was still hot in Cairo, she pointed out, but the weather usually improved in September. The letters usually began with 'Ma chérie' and ended with 'Deux bons baisers'. In a letter sent while Huda was in Istanbul with Iqbal, spending the summer as she often did at the Princes' Islands in the Sea of Marmara, a fashionable resort close to the city, Adila told her of recent births and marriages, including that of Huda's elder half-sister Luza, in Minya.

In these last years of the nineteenth century, the two women, once Huda had returned from Turkey, would meet in Alexandria, or sometimes stayed in Cairo if the summer heat was endurable. Adila, who could not have children of her own, had adopted a three-year-old child called Zainab Murad, born in 1896, who was the daughter of a cousin who had many children and whose death, much later, was mentioned in *L'Égyptienne*.[33] Adila called her Saiza, spelled in the French fashion Céza, and was devoted to her, often taking her on journeys she made with her husband. In 1900, Subhi al-Nabarawi was sent by the Government to Paris to organise the Egyptian pavilion for the Universal Fair. From July to mid-September 1900, Adila was in Paris. She was always happy to take the child with her on her journeys because the days spent in hotels were lonely.

Adila always stayed in touch with Huda, and in her letters she would express her sadness at being separated from her and also her constant worry about Huda's health. She blamed Huda's fragile constitution on cigarettes and melancholy, and often gently scolded her:

> It is also because you are not reasonable, my darling, you are a bit responsible for your own suffering. You never want to take care of yourself. You need a lot of exercise, of recreation, rather than giving in to melancholy. I know your life is monotonous, but what can we do; we must find a remedy to this. I am saying all this as an older sister, Huda, because I am indeed older than you are, and I must be able to chide you a little. Do have the courage to take good care of yourself, to regularly take the medicines prescribed for you, and if you were gentle and wise, you would demonstrate your strength by renouncing the nasty cigarettes that have made you ill again!

Adila also pointed out another trait of Huda's character in a letter written on 11 April 1901, in which she said, 'I know that when you are angered you do not easily forget.' She would pay Huda a visit, she added, were she not wary of a cold welcome and would, at all events, remain her ever devoted friend. The reason for this coldness is now forever lost, but whatever the cause the two women put their differences aside, so that little Céza continued to grow up in the vicinity of her dear 'Tante Hoda', to whom she also began to write her own missives, into which she slipped dried flowers and warm kisses.

As time passed, however, Adila's financial circumstances deteriorated, due to her husband's profligacy. She breathlessly followed her husband, whose gambling had become incorrigible, from one European city to the other, and was obliged to leave Céza in a convent school in Marseilles. Always a meticulous woman, she seemed to become disorganised and often failed to date the letters she obviously felt a deep need to write. Huda, in order to make her laugh, sent her pictures of her pet dog and her housekeeper, Léontine, but Adila's last years were marred by exhaustion and desperation. When her husband finally lost his entire fortune in an ill-advised stock-exchange venture, this beautiful, proud, wise, serene, sophisticated and most feminine of women, disregarding Huda's offer to send her money, finally took her own life in 1903.

Huda's other main friend was a Circassian woman, Attia al-Saqqaf. Attia was married to Umar al-Saqqaf, a wealthy merchant of Yemeni origin born in Singapore, and had led an impressively adventurous life. She was almost in her thirties when Huda first met her after she came to live at Iqbal's invitation in the house in Jami Sharkas Street, where she spent some years. Both Huda and Attia were at the time separated from their husbands, and Attia, some years older than Huda, was already the mother of two children, Muhammad and Huda. Attia's life had been complicated and hard, so that she was wary of her own fate and distrusted society. She was greedy for affection and overly possessive, so that Huda often felt stifled by her proximity. She had been unhappy in love as an adolescent, and her mother and stepfather had in desperation married her off to Umar al-Saqqaf, at the time based in Medina, one of Arabia's holy cities. The Saqqaf family claimed the status of sharifs, descendants of the Prophet Muhammad, and had made an immense fortune trading in south-east Asia. Unfortunately Umar was a womaniser. Attia felt hurt by his unfaithfulness and, as a Circassian, she also deprecated his dark complexion. She nevertheless stayed with him for a long time. He returned in 1906 to Singapore, where he became an important figure, holding many public appointments as well as becoming a pillar of the Arab community and occupying important positions in Arab and Muslim associations.[34]

Huda was amazed by such stoicism, and began to perceive, for the first time in her life, that it was perhaps possible for a woman to subject herself to another person. Attia was aware that she had grown fond of her husband despite her initial repugnance, but was increasingly intolerant of his repeated betrayals. When she eventually ran away from him, taking her two children with her, she attached herself to a caravan across Arabia, intending to travel as far as her mother's home in Turkey, but was abducted by Bedouin tribesmen. She was saved only by her husband's seal, which she had taken with her, testifying to her being the wife of a descendant of the Prophet. This brought her the Bedouins' deference. The vicissitudes she suffered did not, however, diminish her determination to leave her husband. Attia eventually found her way to Cairo, where she met Iqbal, who invited her to share her home. Huda never tired of hearing Attia's thrilling story. Attia spent some years as a guest in the house, together with her two children. In 1914, however, she would rejoin her husband in Singapore.

Another friend Huda acquired during these years of freedom was a young French girl whose father was a Counsellor at the Ministry of Defence in Egypt. This was Louisette, who was a little younger than Huda. Again the two girls had affinities of different kinds. Louisette was spontaneous and affectionate, scribbling hurried notes:

> My dear Huda, father has returned to the ministry, the marquise has just gone out, the gardener went on an errand, I am therefore alone. If it does not inconvenience you, and if you are free, come and see me a few moments, we can stroll about the garden. I'll show you all our lovely flowers and cut the prettiest ones for you but do pick them with me, if you like. Come as you are my darling, do not get dressed, we shall be alone. Throw your 'habara' on, I am expecting you, right? Come quickly, quickly!! quickly!!

Sadly, Louisette also had the misfortune to be unhappy in love. She eloped to France with a young Frenchman who had become her lover but whom her father would not accept. Her lover betrayed her, and she returned to Egypt, where she later died of a fever. Huda was deeply moved. The deaths of Adila and Louisette led Huda to examine the society of her time. They brought home to her the fact that her predicament was not entirely due to the oriental environment of Egypt in which she lived. The plight of women, she saw, was the same all over the world. But this meant that it was susceptible to improvement, in Egypt as elsewhere. She began to think, at first inarticulately, in terms of what would later come to be called a feminist approach to women's problems and rights. There was also a personal lesson to be learned. Huda decided to brace herself against any inclination to romance. She considered romance a weakness and a source of unhappiness that she decided to avoid at all costs.

The starting point of any feminine friendship at the time was the 'salon'. Here, the women threw aside their impersonal coats and the obligations of their lives, expressing themselves freely among women. In social gatherings of this kind, Huda met another woman who was to have a great bearing on her life. This was Eugénie Lebrun, who had written about her wedding, long before the two knew each other personally. Eugénie was the French wife of Husain Rushdi Pasha, then a prominent Egyptian official, who would in the future be Egypt's Prime Minister. He had married her in 1892 in France, where he had gone to complete his studies. When he brought his wife with him to Egypt, she set about describing the Muslim world and Egyptian Muslim society and customs to her French readers. Her books were much appreciated in the West, and were seen as an introduction to a world that was considered mysterious and impenetrable. *Harems et Musulmanes d'Égypte*, on the manners and morals of Egyptian women, and *Les Répudiées*, on the thorny issue of divorce in Egypt, were precious social testimonials written by a woman who had a privileged insight. When Huda's brother Umar met Eugénie socially, he decided to introduce her to Huda on board the glamorous Nile houseboat he kept to entertain his friends.

When Eugénie met Huda again, she saw she was no longer a child but a young woman with great intellectual potential. She was moved by Huda's thirst for knowledge, her eagerness to learn, and her interest in differing cultures. She was able to introduce Huda properly to modern French literature and culture, and suggested many books for her library. Eugénie was also determined to offer support to those Egyptians who struggled against the domination of their country by Britain. A circle comprising both foreigners and Egyptians came into existence, centred on Umar's Nile boat. It included Rushdi Pasha and Eugénie, Mustapha Kamil, Juliette Adam, Pierre Loti and many others. Huda was also always welcome at Eugénie's Saturday salon, where foreign and Egyptian women met and talked over tea and pastries.

Umar also opened Huda's eyes in a different way. During the journey he made to France in the summer of 1904, he wrote his sister long

Huda in her youth.

letters. Soon after his departure on 22 June, he sent her a letter which she repeatedly re-read. His enthusiasm made her feel she must travel to Europe and come to know it for herself:

> You probably think that a whole day on a train must be really exhausting. You are mistaken, my dear Huda, one does not have enough time to apprehend the measure of time, caught as one is in the contemplation of the landscape unfolding before one's eyes. It's like sitting in front of a magic lantern, there is so much beauty to admire. I was dazzled, this is the right word, and I felt sorry the train was so speedy and did not leave me enough time to witness and praise the beauty of nature. It is so different from our flat and uniform land, with its unchanging colours, and what a contrast! Nothing is ever the same here. From the golden wheat fields mingled with the green vineyards, to the blue plum trees, the black plums, the red, the yellow the white and what have you. Then darkness falls while traversing a tunnel and all of a sudden on the left hand side there is the blue sea, and on the right a mountain that looks like an English park with a forest of trees on its peak. Then there is a village, or two or three at a distance, surrounded by gardens, with red roofs, then a stream shaded by trees, then a river and who knows what else. One never tires of looking and admiring. I might be able to make you understand all the emotions I felt when contemplating all this, when we sit together.

At the age of 24, Umar's youthful verve and love of life were irrepressible, as was his eagerness for new destinations. His enormous fortune already placed him at the centre of attention, but he was truly distinguished for his self-assurance, combined with an uncomplicated belief in the virtue of benevolence for its own sake. In one respect his influence on Huda was highly significant. Despite the elevated circles in which he now moved, he never lost the affection and admiration that he had felt since he was a boy for Ali Shaarawi, and his earnest wish was that Huda should return to her husband's side.

2

First steps in social work

In 1901, Huda was 22 and had been separated from her husband for more than seven years, since soon after their marriage in 1892, which had never in truth existed. Ali Shaarawi, meanwhile, was anxious to make the marriage a reality. Huda's brother Umar was by now 20 and had already been engaged for two years to the wife Iqbal had chosen for her son, a lively Egyptian girl named Inayat al-Daramalli, the daughter of Abbas al-Daramalli Pasha. Umar, however, had made it clear to his mother that he would marry only if Huda returned to her husband, on the grounds that he would be reluctant to leave Huda to languish alone in the empty family house with only her mother for company. Umar's fiancée was irritated by what she saw as his obsessive concern for his sister, which she regarded as abnormal. He hoped, however, that his obduracy might bring Huda to listen with a more willing ear to Ali's pleas to resume their marriage, which were becoming ever more insistent.

Ali sought the assistance of family friends and of people in Huda's circle. He went to Eugénie Lebrun, to whom he knew Huda listened, as well as to other persons whom Huda cared for, to plead his cause and beseech their intercession, approaching all whom he thought might have some influence over his young wife. Sultan Pasha's old friend Zubair Pasha came to the house to chide Huda for not returning to her husband, and told her that rumour and gossip were beginning to circulate. He even coarsely insinuated that he was himself beginning to wonder whether her affections might be engaged elsewhere. This enraged Huda, who angrily retorted that had her father been alive, nobody would have dared talk to her as he just had, storming out of the public salon at Jami Sharkas Street to take refuge in her own sitting room. Shaikh Ali al-Laithi, of whom she was very fond, also tried to change her mind, although he retracted at once when he realised that she was genuinely distressed by the subject.[1]

The general chorus of insistence that it was time to resume her marriage, together with Ali's constant reproaches, began to make her feel depressed. She declared herself ill and malingered for two whole months in the summer of 1901, when Iqbal rented a summer house in the smart seaside district of Ramleh, in Alexandria, where Huda could shun friends and pretend to be convalescent. It was during this stay in Alexandria, incidentally, that Huda first began to shop for herself, rather than rely on servants to buy clothes for her, in a small blow for feminine freedom. She dressed formally, with her veil, and went out with Lala Said to one of the big shops. His fierce stares terrified the salesgirls, who inquired who this woman was and why she was so well guarded. After this, Huda continued to buy her own clothes until Iqbal accepted that the quality of the products and garments she purchased was better, and the prices lower, when she did her own shopping. After this, mother and daughter went shopping together, which became a regular habit.

Finally, Ilwi Pasha, the family doctor and an old friend, came to see Huda, reminding her that Umar was postponing his marriage for her sake. She felt she was being blackmailed, but airily replied that in that case she would sooner or later have to accept her husband's overtures of reconciliation. Her ploy was to lay down conditions to which she imagined that Ali would never consent, stipulating that Ali must leave his first wife once and for all, as he had in the first instance promised to do. In a sense, this gesture against polygamy was probably the first political standpoint she adopted, without her being conscious at the time of its political character. She would not hear of being any man's second wife, and it was this that led her to make the first in what would become a long series of political demands throughout her life.[2]

If Huda thought that Ali would never give up the mother of his only son, however, she was mistaken. This was precisely what he did. He had apparently become disenchanted with his ageing, albeit obedient, spouse and her complacent acceptance of all his whims. He admired Huda's increasing sophistication and her straightforward manners, and found himself pining for her company. To her surprise, he accepted all Huda's conditions, giving in to all her requests. Perhaps to his own surprise, he had fallen desperately in love with her, and admired her dignified and blunt rejection of whatever went against her beliefs. At the same time, he was well aware that if she agreed to return to him it would be because he had come to play an important role in the political arena and she would be able to use him to implement her own ideas for reform. From the first, Huda was pragmatic. She was, however, also conscious of family issues, and he was able to convince her that staying together would preserve the family estates and thus endow them both with enhanced social and political power. In 1901, Ali and Huda resumed their life together. Umar's influence in the reconciliation had been decisive.

During the seven years of separation, Huda had developed into a beautiful, accomplished and personable young woman, well versed in both oriental culture and Western academic subjects. She had studied the Qur'an and religious sciences, as well as reading widely in French and Arabic history and literature; and, in the cultural realm, she had developed her knowledge of music and had become an accomplished pianist. In general, she had developed a clear vision of life and an independent mind. She had resolved to live the rest of her life soberly, not to fall prey to impulse and emotion, and to make good use of all the time she was to be granted. She knew, however, that in her married life she would need to compromise with her husband, who was powerful and himself a determined person. They were not likely to clash, as Ali appreciated Huda's principled concern for the future of her country and for Egyptian society. The one disagreement they were to have, which came much later, was because she felt he had fallen below his own high standards. As for Huda, her own political and social activity had already begun, even before the marriage. As early as 1895, she had joined a committee for assistance to Turkey set up by Riad Pasha's wife during the Greco–Turkish war. This had been Huda's first experience in public life, and she had learned a lot from it, despite her young age.[3]

Once Huda had made her decision, Umar's marriage could proceed. When Umar was planning the wedding, he came to Huda's apartment one day to discuss the form it should take. His plan was to hold a simple ceremony and to distribute to the poor the money that would have been spent on an elaborate wedding. There was an army of the disabled and the destitute in Minya that the family had more or less maintained for many years, and Umar felt that money could be spent in more useful ways than in the celebration of a marriage.[4] Huda, however, wanted her brother's wedding day to be memorable, and argued that Umar was wealthy enough to hold a spectacular ceremony and still give charity in other ways. In the event, Umar followed her advice, and his lavish wedding was an unforgettable event. An article by the poet Khalil Mutran, one of Umar's guests, writing in the magazine *Al Majalla al-Misria* testifies to the enchantment of the three full days and nights of celebration.

For the resumption of his married life with Huda, Ali Shaarawi built a magnificent new town house at 2 Qasr al-Nil, at the junction of that street and another of Cairo's principal thoroughfares, Champollion Street, in the heart of Cairo, scarcely a step from the old Sultan family mansion in Jami Sharkas Street. The new house stood opposite the Egyptian Museum built by Mariette Pasha, and faced the Qasr al-Nil Palace, which had become the British military barracks.[5] It was built in the style of the time, Art Nouveau. Ali also spent much time in Minya, and he built another mansion there. His hope was to persuade his new wife to take up residence with him in Minya to help him manage the land, creating a new life for them both in Upper Egypt. The house in Minya was as attractive as he could make it, and was surrounded by an enchanting garden. The stately sitting rooms, with their gigantic crystal chandeliers, tall mirrors with gilt frames, golden furniture and boundless Persian carpets contrasted with the cosy comfort and simplicity of the upper-floor bedrooms and bathrooms. Huda's bathroom was full of light, with coloured cups of glass embedded in the stucco decorations of the ceiling that let in vivacious beams of light and colours that filled the room with an atmosphere that was dreamy but bright. It was an architectural *tour de force*, towering above an isolated village known as Bani Muhammad Shaarawi, in the Mansafis area some 16 kilometres to the south of Minya, where the *fellaheen* lived on the doorstep of the Pasha's mansion.

During the first months following Huda's return to her husband, she did indeed spend some time in Minya. She focused her attention on the plight of the rural poor, and resolved to work to improve their situation. Much could be done to improve their life, she was sure. The rigid customs and social barriers of Upper Egyptian society, however, made it difficult for her to get to grips in detail with the situation of the people. As the lady of the manor, she was impeded by social tenets, and found it hard to approach them. In the end, small-scale charity at close quarters presented excessive difficulties. Huda concluded that the task was hopeless and decided that her field of action had to be Cairo, where reform was feasible. In Cairo, after all, she could enlist the support and goodwill of influential people, including many members of the royal family. In any case, when Huda became pregnant shortly after the resumption of her marital life, the die was cast. She felt it was incumbent on her to return to Cairo to obtain the care she required for herself and her unborn child.

Two children were born to Ali and Huda in the space of three years. Their daughter, whom they called Bassna, was born in 1903, and she was followed in 1906 by a son, Muhammad. The children kept Huda busy for some years, as she was resolved to care for them as far as possible herself, though of course she also employed a nanny. Bassna was sickly, as Huda's brother Umar had been as a child, and Huda became an apprehensive mother who gave all her attention to the children. She soon became entirely absorbed in her new role in life. An alarming accident, when a fire surprised her little family aboard a Nile boat in Cairo, only served to add to her concern. The boat was moored to a dock, so that she and Ali were able to save the children and themselves, but she was conscious of how lucky they had been. During the incident, she was shocked by the indifference of the bystanders to her family's narrow escape.[6]

In the years when her children were small, she often travelled with them, her mother and Jazb Ashiq to Istanbul, where the two women liked to spend their holidays. Iqbal's Circassian brothers, Yusuf and Ahmed Idris, were still resident in the same little seaport town of Bandirma where they had originally settled. Like other Circassians at the turn of the century, they had made themselves at home in Turkey, and by now they spoke Turkish even between themselves. The whole family, the Cairene visitors and the Circassian uncles, went sometimes to the Princes' Islands in the Sea of Marmara, where the Sultan family's friends, the Khulusis, owned a summer house on the island of Kinali.[7]

The occasion for one protracted stay in Istanbul in these early years was Bassna's poor health. The doctors advised Huda to take her out of Egypt in the summer for a change of air and for medical treatment. Though Huda wanted to go to Europe, Ali would not let her take the child further afield than Turkey, though she threatened that should anything happen to Bassna she would blame him for it and would separate from him again, this time forever. She became so emotional about her daughter's welfare that she refused to be parted from her even for the briefest period. When Huda brought Bassna back to Cairo from Turkey, however, there had been no change in the little girl's condition. Fortunately, Eugénie Lebrun called in a French specialist to whom she had described the case, and he diagnosed malaria. The correct treatment was then followed, and the little girl gradually regained her health.[8]

Huda had so far not clearly defined a political role for herself, and such public activity as she became involved in was mainly through her brother and her husband. Both Umar and Ali derived their influence from their positions in society and their immense fortunes, but their credibility was enhanced by the fact that both men were transparently honest, and their plans showed evident common sense. Each was prepared when necessary to reach into his pocket to provide funds for projects conducive to the national good. Each also provided financial support to the politicians who served the causes in which they believed. Umar was an important financial backer of Mustapha Kamil's National Party (al-Hizb al-Watani), originally launched in 1894, and of his Arabic and French newspapers, *Al-Liwa* and *L'Etendard Egyptien* (*Egyptian Standard*), which Kamil set up in 1900. He was intellectually and emotionally involved with the National Party, and vigorously supported Kamil, who had become a national hero. Kamil's overriding goal was to bring about the departure of the British from Egypt, and his interest in social reform, including the early stirrings of feminist ideas, was less strong. Through Umar, who had gained entry to elevated social and intellectual circles in France, Kamil had met the Republican writer and publisher Juliette Adam, in whom he confided, and who came to view him like a son. He wrote her a moving open letter, asking for her support in his struggle against British occupation, which she published in the French press.

For Kamil, the enemy was Lord Cromer, who was in effect the head of the British administration in Egypt. Cromer dealt with the Egyptian opposition by 'giving it a deadly blow',[9] to use his own words. In 1904, Kamil asked how a man whose own country throve on freedom, whose government claimed that it honoured freedom and placed it above all other things, could boast of 'having dealt a deadly blow' to the opposition, meaning freedom itself, in Egypt? Nothing, he declaimed, could bring the Egyptians to renounce their right to education and justice. Cromer's neglect of education was notorious, as was his principle that educating Egyptians was nothing more than the encouragement of troublemakers. Kamil also drew attention to the conscious discouragement of the textile industry in Egypt, following the model developed by the British in India that colonial possessions should serve as a market for British industry. He also deplored Cromer's manifest hostility to Islam and his apparent belief that pan-Islamic movements were a threat to the West. In addition, was Sudan a part of Egypt or was it not? Were Britain to permit Egypt to be free and prosperous, would it not extend its freedom and prosperity to the upper reaches of the Nile? Huda soon began to agree with Kamil that Cromer, who appeared to have a personal grudge against Egypt, exemplified the imperialist will to dominate others. He had even put obstacles in the way of the Egyptian University project in 1890.[10]

In 1904, Umar hosted Kamil, Juliette Adam and Prince Haidar Fazil on a journey to Upper Egypt on his Nile boat, during which she promised to do what she could to help him and his friends to liberate Egypt. Prince Haidar's wife, Zainab Fahmi, who was also the eldest daughter of Ali

Umar Sultan (left) and Mustapha Kamil (right).

Fahmi Pasha and Munira Sabri, travelled with the party to Upper Egypt, where Umar arranged for them all to be sumptuously entertained wherever they went. Umar became the treasurer of the National Party when it was formally constituted as a political party in 1907. Apparently Kamil took the step of forming an official political party partly in reaction to the formation of the supposedly more moderate Umma Party (Hizb al-Umma), with which Ali Shaarawi was associated.[11]

Ali Shaarawi and his friends were less revolutionary than were Kamil's adherents, favouring a gradual approach to change through legal means. Ali's approach was best exemplified by the campaign he began in 1907 to obtain the enactment of a constitution. In response to Cromer's final report, a pamphlet was written by Ismail Abaza and co-signed by Ali, Ahmad Yehia Pasha, who was a wealthy philanthropist from Alexandria, and others, emphasising the need for a constitution and the gradual decentralisation of power, as well as what they called a 'healthy transformation' of government in Egypt. As members of the Legislative Council, they did not quarrel directly with the British. Instead, they sought to negotiate their way to self-rule. In their view, the transfer of power from British to Egyptian hands could only be gradual, and would require hard work. They were aware that, given the circumstances of the military occupation, beggars could not be choosers. The trick of victory would be patience alone, and would lie in judging the correct moment for action. In Sir Eldon Gorst, the British High Commissioner who succeeded Cromer, they found an open-minded interlocutor, and succeeded in laying down a basis for cooperation between the Egyptian Government and the British. The importance of the personal influence of individual officials was brought home to them, however, when Gorst died in July 1911 and was replaced by Lord Kitchener. Kitchener's arrival once more put an end to reconciliation and dialogue.

Meanwhile, until his premature death, Kamil went from strength to strength in Egyptian political life and in the anti-British movement. He lost no opportunity to capitalise on what became known as the Dinshwai trial in 1906, when a British officer died in an altercation between Egyptian *fellaheen* and a party of British officers who carelessly killed a peasant woman while shooting pigeons on the farmers' land. The result was the public hanging of four of the Egyptians allegedly involved and the flogging of many others. The uproar caused by this collective punishment contributed to Cromer's decision to resign in 1907.[12] Sadly, Kamil died in 1908 at the age of 34 of tuberculosis. He had become a real force in Egyptian politics, and was by this time President of the National Party and the editor of four newspapers, three of them dailies, spending his life incessantly campaigning, writing and speaking against the British occupation. The toll of his enormous workload compromised his health, and the loss of his beloved mother in 1907 demoralised him. Kamil's death provoked a wave of grief throughout the country, and his funeral was spectacular. His death was a great loss to all who knew him, and was felt also by Huda, not least because of the pain Umar suffered from the loss of his great friend. Mustapha Kamil had become the spokesman of nationalism in Egypt, with the support of not only the political class but also of the public at large. When he died, his aspirations and doubts became the legacy of others, including in their different ways both Umar Sultan and Ali Shaarawi.

Umar remained attached to Kamil's Nationalist Party all his life, while Ali maintained his association with the Umma Party, though he also revered Kamil's memory. The involvement of Huda herself in nationalist politics was therefore virtually inevitable. Ali was keenly aware of Huda's abilities, and was ahead of his time in believing women could play a role on the political scene. After Kamil's death in 1908, Ali lent his name as a member of the Legislative Council to a further appeal for greater participation by Egyptians in their country's government, calling for the implementation of a constitution on the model of what was being proposed by the Young Turks in Istanbul.

The press supported his campaign, and a delegation chaired by Ismail Abaza Pasha went to Britain to negotiate with the British Foreign Office about the implementation of constitutional rule in Egypt. Khedive Abbas Hilmi asked Eldon Gorst, known as a man of reconciliation, to give his blessing to this delegation. Gorst extracted a promise from Abaza before he left for London, however, that the talks would be limited to a request that the Legislative Council be allowed to play a greater role in the Egyptian Government, without mentioning the crucial issue of British withdrawal. Ali wanted further concessions from the British, and therefore withdrew his support from the delegation before their departure. Fearing further political agitation, Gorst demanded the revival of the 1881 law which allowed press censorship. In response, Saad Zaghlul then threatened to give up his post as Speaker of the Legislative Council, and the 1881 law was amended before being re-enacted. Nevertheless, there were serious demonstrations, and at the Legislative Council's session on 13 April, Ali proposed the law's repeal and revision. Ali's proposals were disregarded, with the result that demonstrations began in earnest against the British and the Khedive. The political situation was delicate.[13]

A serious blow for Huda at this time was the death of her close friend Eugénie, in 1908. Eugénie had stoically borne an illness that inexorably led to her death, despite a fruitless surgical intervention in Paris. She nevertheless found the strength to send word to Huda, through Ali, who was at the time visiting France, that she should not succumb to despair as she had done after the deaths of other friends.[14] However, Huda was for a long time unable to overcome her grief at the loss of Eugénie. She lost her appetite, smoked more heavily than ever, and became obsessed by her children, their health, their moods, their education and their safety. Despite Eugénie's exhortation, Huda became depressed, as she had in the past. This recalled the advice she used to receive from Adila, who would counsel her against giving in to melancholy. Huda missed Adila, whom she felt that she had neglected in her lifetime, and whenever she was not distracted by practical matters she began to brood over her life and what she felt she had failed to do.

Another death which affected Huda at this time was that of Qasim Amin, who died in 1908 at the early age of 47.[15] Amin, a lawyer who rose to be a judge, had been an early and vocal advocate of women's rights in Egypt, and had shocked the establishment with his outspokenness on the issue. He was a disciple of the late Muhammad Abduh, and a staunch supporter of the Umma Party. He had been one of those responsible for the launch of Cairo University. In his book *The Liberation of Women* (*Tahrir al-Mar'a*), published in 1899, he vigorously defended the rights of women, a position which gained him many enemies. In the book, he made the surprising suggestion that the lowly status of women in Egypt was a contributory factor in the perpetuation of Egypt's subjection to British domination. Amin's books were much criticised in the press, and he was the victim of hostility and social ostracism by his conservative critics. His depression at the violent reaction that met his book seems to have been a contributory factor in his death, but he never retracted his views.

In these years, against the background of Egypt's political turbulence, Huda's opinions were often sought by both Umar and Ali. They increasingly sought her out to discuss their political aspirations, their hopes for the future of Egypt and their views on the events of the day. The effect on her was significant. She was learning an important lesson, namely that the most important asset for the weaker party in any political conflict was patience and determination. Ali's calm but firm interventions in Parliament led her to understand that battles could only be won on the basis of constitutional victories. Crude and violent opposition would only result in the crushing of the weaker party. She believed that the poorly organised Urabi revolt had paved the way for the British occupation.

As time went on, while Ali closely followed the administrative and constitutional debate, Umar began to take another direction, following the lead of his father Sultan Pasha, who had hoped to live to see the establishment of indigenous banking institutions in Egypt. Umar increasingly devoted his efforts to the development of an Agricultural Union, based on the development of cooperatives. He was always concerned over the lot of the common people, and his goal was to improve their existence as much as possible. Later, in 1915, his plans were to come to fruition when he was involved in the successful establishment of the first Egyptian agricultural cooperative. Such agricultural cooperatives became the *fellah's* primary source of credit.[16] Umar also strove to raise Egyptian capital to fund the Banque Misr, as he decided to call it in order to differentiate it from the National Bank, which had been founded by the British. His goal was to recruit investors to establish an Egyptian bank in order to enable the development of indigenous Egyptian industry, on the basis of Egyptian capital. The inflow of foreign capital into Egypt had steadily increased since foreign intervention began in 1882, and it was inevitable that the Western banks provided facilities preferentially to foreign investors. This made it difficult for Egyptian merchants to compete with the Europeans. The great Egyptian landowners involved in the cotton trade, with whom Umar was identified, had good reasons to want the foundation of an Egyptian bank. Acting on the basis of the original plan that his father and Umar Lutfi Pasha had developed, Umar canvassed his fellow landlords in Minya, though the bank did not come into existence until later, after Umar's premature death.

In general, on the political and social front, the atmosphere in Egypt in these pre-war years was ripe for reform. Members of the khedivial family were themselves seeking to promote education. They were out of sympathy with the Government and its British links, and there was much they could do to improve the lot of the Egyptian people. Khedive Ismail's wife, Princess Sheshmi Effet, had set up the Sania Secondary School for Girls as long before as 1876. Her son, Prince Fuad, later to be Khedive, founded the Egyptian University in Cairo with the help of his sister, Princess Fatma Ismail, who donated her land and jewels. Lord Cromer opposed the move but permitted it to go ahead. Huda took careful note of the developments at the university.[17] Meanwhile, in 1908, Prince Yusuf Kamal set up a School of Fine Art, a move which attracted less support but was highly important in its own way.

For Egyptian women, the most accessible field of activity under the British occupation was the establishment of charitable organisations.

There were British charitable associations to which Egyptian women were invited as visiting members, but they were not allowed to speak or vote, which was frustrating. They were invited to contribute funds and help in subordinate roles, but the direction of such charities remained in the hands of the English women. Huda had actually refused an invitation to attend a tea party given by the second Lady Cromer to thank the Egyptian women who had financed a dispensary built with Egyptian contributions in honour of the late first Lady Cromer. She felt that this was an incongruous way of celebrating an Egyptian project financed by Egyptian money.

However, Huda was determined to make an effort of her own. She was on excellent terms with Princess Ain al-Hayat Ahmed, despite the wide age gap between them. The Princess always encouraged Huda, whom she saw as a convinced social reformer, and regarded Huda as a young friend on whom she could rely. In 1908, Huda proposed the foundation of a charitable association to establish a clinic which would be funded and run by Egyptian women under the Princess's sponsorship, and she swiftly obtained the Princess's support. The first meeting to discuss the project took place in the Princess's palace in al-Dawawin Street, where a founding committee was set up, with Princess Nazli Halim as its President and Princess Ain al-Hayat as its Treasurer. A French woman, Mme Fouquet, placed her administrative and practical experience at the group's service. Each of the women who attended the meeting offered an annual contribution amounting to 50 Egyptian pounds, while Princess Amina, Khedive Tawfiq's widow and the mother of Khedive Abbas Hilmi, promised 120. Khedive Abbas Hilmi and his wife also supported the project.[18]

The Muhammad Ali Dispensary (Mabarrat Muhammad Ali) came into being a year later, in 1909. A small building in Sharia al-Baramuni was converted to be the dispensary's headquarters. Various committee members contributed furniture, but Huda and Umar covered all the other expenses. Princess Amina attended the inauguration and Princess Nazli Halim delivered an inaugural address and proposed a vote of thanks.

Later, Huda agreed to become the Chair of the executive committee of the dispensary. The director, Mrs Hetty Crowther, an Irishwoman, worked with a number of European physicians, Dr Roeder, Dr Forcart and Dr Thomsen, who had volunteered to give their services at the clinic, while the committee provided support and raised funds through charitable events. Paradoxically, dazzling social occasions provided lavish funding and led to an increase in well being for some of Cairo's poorest. But the positive direction of the efforts of the Egyptian elite at that time should not be underestimated. They certainly felt closer to their people than they ever had in the past.

Other new encounters at this time helped pull Huda out of the depression that Eugénie Lebrun's death had caused. She spent a great deal of time in the company of Eugénie's sister, Francine Daurat, who became Iqbal's carer in Heliopolis, Jami Sharkas Street or Ramleh, depending on the season. Huda herself had already begun to suffer from poor blood circulation and varicose veins, and whenever Francine returned to France she came back with medicines and medical support stockings for Huda's legs. She also brought her silk stockings, 'so soft, one hardly feels them on one's legs'.[19] Huda had also been introduced to another French woman, Marguerite Clément, a professional lecturer on women's issues. Ali saw that the organisation of events for women could be the key to his wife's recovery from depression, and encouraged her to organise public lectures for an audience of women to be given by Clément and others at the newly founded University of Cairo under the auspices of the Umma Party. Ali also offered the headquarters of the recently founded newspaper Al-Jarida, the organ of the Umma Party, as an alternative venue for some of the proposed lectures. Ali had many friends who sat on the new university's board of governors. One of these, Ilwi Pasha, the same family friend who had previously intervened with Huda on Ali's behalf, enthusiastically gave his support to the women's initiative.

Huda's work at the Muhammad Ali Dispensary, and in connection with the lectures, in addition to her visits to the West, which had by now taken on more the character of fact-finding visits than holidays, certainly helped to mitigate her depression. These outlets served as an effective means of recovery from her mourning for Eugénie. For the rest of her life, activity was Huda's way to banish melancholy. In addition to her work, she was still kept busy by her children and by her ailing mother. She also began to worry about Umar, as she heard he had begun to lead an irresponsible life, especially during his repeated and frequent trips to Europe. Without the company of Mustapha Kamil, he found it hard to devote his life to the party, and often disapproved of the behaviour of some of its members. Huda thought he had become too rich at too young an age. In 1910, Huda, Ali and their children went on holiday to Europe with Iqbal, Umar, Inayat and their family. Huda increasingly felt that her sister-in-law was very possessive of her husband, especially when Huda was present. She was still jealous of Huda because of the closeness of the relationship between Umar and Huda since their childhood in Jami Sharkas Street. Yet this was an enjoyable trip. Huda had heard many stories about Naples, and yearned to see it. In the event, she adored the welcome given in the harbour to the passenger ship on which her party arrived from Egypt. Boats full of musicians and singers greeted the steamer under blue skies, and the exploits of diving children were exciting. In Marseilles, by contrast, the skies were grey, but there were other diversions, such as visits to galleries and museums and fine French restaurants. In Paris, she and Umar splashed out, booking a whole floor at the Princess Hotel on the Avenue des Champs Élysées. This was a treat, and the family felt really at home in the privacy they enjoyed at the hotel. A visit to Paris with Umar was a wonderful experience for Huda, because he knew the city so well. She recovered her former closeness to her brother as they chatted about everything they saw. Huda's reason for visiting France was medical treatment, but at the beginning of the holiday they put this to the backs of their minds. They spent a month in Paris before going on to the spa at St-Laurent-les-Bains before returning to Cairo. It was during this trip that she first contacted Marguerite Clément to plan her series of lectures in Cairo.[20]

Jazb Ashiq, who had long suffered from a cardiac condition, died suddenly in 1911 after a massive heart attack. Iqbal had selflessly cared for her and was physically and emotionally stricken by her death. Iqbal was a kind soul whose philosophy of life was to bear good and bad fortune as it came, submitting to fate. The understanding and compassion she showed attracted kindness in return, and fate had been kind to her in many ways. After Jazb Ashiq's death, however, Iqbal's own health began to decline. Her lungs became more delicate, and her heart was apparently being strained. Huda asked Louise du Brucq, a Belgian painter who had become a family friend, to find a house for Iqbal in Heliopolis, the new district on the outskirts of Cairo that was being developed by Nubar Pasha and the Belgian entrepreneur Baron Empain, where the dry desert air was unpolluted and invigorating.

Marguerite Clément's lectures, sponsored by Princess Ain al-Hayat, were held in 1911, taking place in the event alternately at Huda's house and at the University. They were warmly received in Egyptian circles sympathetic to women's rights. Clément was an experienced educationist, and spoke in very practical terms about the condition of women at the time. After the enthusiastic reception her lectures received, Huda invited her to give another series which would on this occasion be printed and distributed to the audience. Prince Ahmad Fuad and his wife Princess Shivekar also supported this initiative. For the second series, Khayri Pasha's mansion, which was later to be the principal building of the American University in Cairo, was chosen as the meeting place.

A further lecturer in the series was Malak Hifni Nasif, a pioneer of Egyptian feminism and an acquaintance of Huda. She was a disciple of Muhammad Abduh, and Huda admired her intellect and determination. Malak had taken the pseudonym 'Bahitha al-Badia' ('the Seeker in the Desert') to use for her writing and political activities. She was married to Abd al-Sattar al-Basil Pasha, the brother of a prominent politician, Hamad al-Basil Pasha. Al-Basil, who lived in the Fayum oasis, where he managed his family's estates, was no intellectual. When he sought Malak's hand in marriage, the proposal came as a surprise to her family and to herself. She was a clever and sympathetic woman, as well as a talented poet, but she was neither a beauty nor an heiress. It was assumed that al-Basil wanted to marry her because he wished to be associated with her family. Malak was observant of tradition, and had no desire for radical action such as would have been implied by removing her veil, but she was a passionate advocate of education for girls and women. Nevertheless, she consented to the match, only to discover that she had been taken as a second wife. He was already married to a cousin, of whom he was very fond and by whom he had a daughter. He had apparently married Malak in the hope that she would educate his beloved daughter, since there were no schools for girls in the Fayum and he wanted her to have the best of teachers.

A broken heart was not enough, however, to make the sturdy Bahitha quit her husband or leave her new home. She decided to dedicate herself to the welfare of the community of Fayum, and to help the inhabitants as much as she could to cope with the hardships of their primitive existence. She saw herself as an explorer of local manners and morals, and dressed like the rural women among whom she lived. She demanded the right for women to pray in mosques like men, as they had in the early days of Islam, as well as asking that they receive at least a primary level of education, and that their safety should be guaranteed if they ventured outside their homes. She drew attention to the need for hospitals and vocational schools. In addition, she argued that polygamy should be strictly controlled, and that divorce should not be recognised without mutual agreement between husband and wife. In due course, she began to tackle the issue of social reform at the national level.

Malak continued to wear the veil because she believed in doing so, perhaps to fit in with her new environment, but also perhaps because of her own plain looks. Her economic and social concerns went beyond gender issues. She saw no virtue in social life for its own sake, and never felt the need to communicate with a greater range of people than the ones she normally mingled with. At the same time, her exceptional knowledge of the Arabic language made it enjoyable for her to write in her mother tongue, and this occupied a great deal of her time. She wrote essays, poems and many letters, and her lectures were the first advocating the rights of women and the need for social change by an Egyptian woman. She contributed many articles to newspapers advocating women's rights and arguing specifically against polygamy, which reflected her personal experience.[21]

In 1911, the Bahitha submitted ten recommendations to the Muslim National Congress held in Heliopolis, chaired by the former Prime Minister Mustafa Riad Pasha, a comprehensive gathering of some two thousand nationalist and religious figures. In her petition, which was circulated to the participants, she demanded education and emancipation for women. She was not allowed to address the gathering in person, and her ten recommendations were not taken up by the men, but it was significant that she was permitted to make her views known. Her specific proposals were seen as important, and were later adopted by a range of organisations which promoted the interests of women. They included demands for more and better education for women, and specifically in the professional fields of law, medicine and education. She also asked for religious equality for women, and for greater protection in terms of the law relating to marriage and divorce.

Another of Huda's lecturers was Mayy Ziadé, whom Huda had met at one of the Bahitha's talks. Mayy, who was Lebanese, was a gifted writer and a well-known journalist. Huda found her stunning.[22] Those who knew her said she had the vitality and joy of a bird, though it seemed she saw herself as a bird in a cage. She was single, adulated by a number of famous men, and lived with her parents, to whom she was strongly attached. She led an independent social life, and as a Christian, she was free to mingle with men in salons, and her wit and vivacious mind, together with her great ability as a writer in both Arabic and French, made her a legend.

Inspired by the encouraging experience of the lectures and the success of the Muhammad Ali dispensary, Huda at that point decided that there was an urgent need for an intellectual association that would bring together like-minded Egyptian women. She once more sought the help of the Princesses, and obtained it. Those in Ali's Umma Party circles who were involved in political and educational matters, having witnessed the success of Huda's cultural initiatives, supported the plan to set up a women's association. Abd al-Aziz Fahmi Pasha, a lawyer by profession and a fervent patriot, sent Huda an official letter inviting her to elaborate on her project and suggest what the rules of procedure of such an association might be.[23] The Intellectual Association of Egyptian Women (al-Ittihad al-Nisa'i al-Tahdhibi) came into being in April 1914 in the course of a meeting at Huda's house in Qasr al-Nil Street chaired by Princess Amina Halim. Mayy Ziadé and Labiba Hashim, who had founded a magazine, *Fatat al-Sharq* (*The Eastern Maiden*), were among the first members. A spin-off society, the Ladies Literary Improvement Society, was instituted to promote more lectures, and Marguerite Clément was once more invited to deliver a series of talks. The women's movement in Egypt could be said to have begun to take shape.

Huda was obliged to travel to Europe again with Ali and Umar in the summer of 1914, due to a combination of circumstances. This, as it later proved, was not the best time for such a visit, and the trip involuntarily turned into a rather unwelcome adventure. One reason for the visit was Umar's frame of mind. His little daughter, named Huda after her aunt, was worshipped by her father and also by Huda's own small son, Muhammad. Little Huda contracted an unexpected illness which was diagnosed as meningitis, and she sadly died, leaving the whole family shattered. Huda's son Muhammad was extremely upset. His health seemed to suffer, and his doctors recommended a change, preferably a holiday in a mountain resort. Umar was also advised to take a holiday away from the place where his beloved daughter had passed away. He always recalled her last words, when she declared that she was playing a game called 'going to Heaven'. She confidently said she heard birds chirping in the garden, 'a beautiful garden, just like the garden of Eden,' she muttered, as her innocent spirit left her little body.[24]

Huda braced herself to be strong and to help her son and her brother shake off their depression. As Ali had separately been advised to travel to Vittel for treatment, there was a collective decision that the whole family would go to Europe for the summer, leaving Iqbal in the care of Attia al-Saqqaf in Cairo. Ali's son from his first marriage, Hasan, was at school in England, and was to join them in Paris, where Umar now owned a flat. While Ali was in Vittel, Huda spent her time at the flat in Paris, with her own children and with Hasan.[25] Huda was anxious, and would go for long walks in the streets of Paris, brooding about her own mother's condition. She felt defeated.

The war in Europe was imminent, and Huda was invited to attend a meeting of women held in Paris to advocate peace and women's suffrage. The meeting took place at the offices of a newspaper, and the speakers, in addition to Clément, who had sent Huda the invitation, were Mme de Sévigné and Mme Avril de St Croix. After the meeting, Huda became engaged in a discussion about whether peace in Europe could be preserved. The question by now had become whether any hope still remained for peace despite the unmistakable signs of war on the horizon.[26] Paris was grey and sad during the last months before the war, and there was a general air of disintegration. General military mobilisation had begun, with effects on civilian life that included an unpredictability in train timetables which was disturbing for those who had to travel home across Europe.

Consequently, the Shaarawi and Sultan family's journey home, through Basel, Zurich and Milan was disorganised and exhausting. Huda was unsettled, and now that her brother Umar and her son Muhammad were in better health, she allowed herself to worry about her mother's welfare. She began to be concerned about Iqbal, feeling that the future boded ill, and was eager to reach Egypt, despite the reassuring tone of her mother's letters. From 1911 to 1914, Huda had kept close watch on her mother, asking Francine Daurat to be her companion so that she had someone with her at all times. Nevertheless, she had long been aware that Iqbal's health was worsening, and suddenly began to fear she might be in mortal danger. The family spent one night at the Princess Hotel in Paris, but Huda could not bear to remain there because she had stayed there before with Iqbal. Ali booked a suite for her in the Continental Hotel, where he left her and the children while he spent a few days taking Hasan to a boarding school in London, where he was to enrol. Bassna's eleventh birthday was on 18 June, and Huda was at least able to give thanks for her daughter's good health.[27]

Ali then returned from England, and the family moved on from Paris to Vittel. Once there, however, Huda's concern over Iqbal became more acute and her misery deepened.[28] She went to Paris with her housekeeper Marguerite to shop and to collect Hasan, who they had decided should for the best return with them to Egypt, given the deteriorating political situation in Europe. In Paris, the streets were becoming deserted. In the meantime, the children remained with Ali in Vittel, where the atmosphere was also full of apprehension. The whole party left Vittel three days later on a train whose destination was unclear, but which was at least running. They reached the Swiss city of Basel in the middle of the night, and with difficulty found a hotel room. Food was already in short supply. They travelled on to Zurich, where they were lucky enough to spend a few wonderful days, as they planned their onward journey, in a comfortable hotel on the shore of the lake, with clean air, verdant woods and people who greeted them with courtesy.

Then they went on to Milan, in those days a rather poor city, where they found rooms at a small hotel adjacent to the cathedral. The nights spent in Zurich quickly felt like memories of another life. During the night they spent in Milan, they could hear the voices of newspaper sellers shouting out 'News of the war!' They sounded like owls screeching in the quietness of the night, Huda thought.[29] They met several Egyptian friends there, some of whom were stranded without the means to pay for what had become a complicated journey home. Ali never refused to help, so that he and his family in the end had less money for themselves. The people were sullen and hostile. War was imminent, and it affected everyone. The noisy crowd on the piazza in front of the cathedral bred an uneasy atmosphere night and day.

As soon as they could, they travelled on to Genoa, whence on 10 August 1914 they were at last able to board an Italian ship sailing to Egypt, the SS *Oriente*. The cabins were dirty and smelly, and they paid exorbitant sums to the ships' officers to rent the officers' cabins. Even there, they were pestered by cockroaches, and ended up on deck, where they slept on their chairs in the open. They later had a tent set up for them on deck during the night.[30] A stop at the port of Catania allowed Huda to see the traces of Arab culture in southern Italy, an experience that even in the midst of such tribulation prompted her to think about the way in which cultures interacted. Ever the intellectual, even in the midst of difficulties, she absorbed experiences.

On 19 August 1914, they landed at last in Alexandria.[31] Nobody was there to greet them save their accountant and a young woman who was Bassna's Arabic language teacher. At their home in Ramleh, a fateful telegram awaited them with the news that Iqbal had passed away just before their arrival. Huda felt drained. All her terrible premonitions had been fulfilled. Her feelings towards her mother were both filial and motherly, but it was too late now even to say goodbye. The only solace was that Attia had been constantly by her side during her last month. Iqbal had been desperate for the safe return of her family from war-stricken Europe, and to comfort her Attia had arranged before the ship actually reached Egypt for a telegram to be sent prematurely from Alexandria with news of their arrival there.[32] Iqbal had therefore died in the expectation of seeing her family soon, reassured by Attia that they were safely home. Ali and Huda went at once to Cairo so that Huda could spend the night near her mother's body, and they buried her the next day in Minya, in Sultan Pasha's tomb. Once more, Umar helped Huda to bear the grief they shared.

Meanwhile the war had profound consequences for the future of Egypt. In 1914, the British Government, at war with Germany, in order to secure its strategic interests in the Middle East, felt justified in declaring a formal protectorate over Egypt to replace its unofficial domination. Turkey entered the war on Germany's side, and Khedive Abbas Hilmi was in Turkey when the war broke out. The British demanded that he be deposed, allegedly for reasons of security, but also because of his outspoken criticism of the protectorate. Britain also wanted to break the bond between Egypt and the Ottoman Empire. Abbas Hilmi's uncle, Prince Husain Kamal al-Din, a son of the Khedive Ismail, who was the acting President of the Legislative Council, was declared the new ruler of Egypt, with the title of Sultan rather than Khedive, thus emphasising the fact that Egypt was no longer Turkey's vassal state. Prince Husain Kamal al-Din had previously said he would remain loyal to Khedive Abbas Hilmi, and vowed not to accept the British proposal. When the offer of the throne was put to him, however, he accepted, allegedly because they had threatened to give the throne to a foreign Muslim ruler, the Agha Khan.[33] The country was in despair. Abbas Hilmi's former court poet, Ahmad Shawqi, wrote a poem excoriating Sultan Husain for accepting the throne. This spread like wildfire through the country, and led to Shawqi's exile to Spain.[34]

Umar and Huda became ever closer after Iqbal's death, despite Inayat's jealousy. Each morning and evening Umar would come to reminisce about the past, talk over family matters, and discuss the political situation of Egypt and the fighting in Europe. Umar's fear was that the post-war intentions of the allies would be no better for Egypt than the plans of the Germans and allies. Echoing the philosophy of his old friend Mustapha Kamil, he blamed imperialism for the war. Like Kamil, he believed that the impending destruction of the Ottoman Empire would have dire consequences for the Arab lands and Egypt.

Death struck again at Huda's circle while war raged in Europe. First, Munira Sabri, the sister of Yusuf Sabri Pasha, passed away in 1916. Munira's children, Zainab, Fatma, Aziza, Aisha and Ali were Huda's cousins. Munira's eldest daughter Zainab was the wife of Prince Haidar Fazil. Huda consoled the Fahmi family for the loss of their mother. This meant that on Iqbal's side of Huda's family only Yusuf and Ahmed Idris's family now remained. Though they continued to live in Turkey, she swore she would never again lose touch with them.

The war moved towards its close, but tragedy in Huda's life had not yet run its course. In February 1918, she suffered the cruellest loss imaginable with the sudden death of her beloved and precious brother Umar from an aneurism at the young age of 37. At the beginning of 1918, she had already begun to worry about Umar's health, and had been plagued by bad dreams that seemed to portend that something bad would befall him. Umar himself seemed to have forebodings. When he left Cairo for the last time to go to Minya, he made Huda promise that she would visit him there in the near future.[35] Soon afterwards, Ali was informed confidentially of Umar's death by messengers from Minya despatched to Cairo with the news. He could not think how Huda could be told, as he knew and feared the effect the news would have on her. At first, he clumsily hid the truth from her, unwilling to cause her distress. Instead, he told her that she needed to go to Minya because her half-sister Luza, who was much older than herself, had passed away.

She agreed to go to her half-sister's funeral, and set off, accompanied by Ali and by Said Agha, who looked after her on the train in the women's accommodation. On their arrival in Minya, a carriage was waiting to take her and Said Agha from the station to Umar's house. Her enquiries about how her half-sister had died were answered vaguely, and questions about Umar were met with silence. Ominously, a silent, sad crowd filled the streets. This was customary for the death of important men, and Huda began to feel that there was something she was not being told. When the party reached the house, the truth came out. Inayat was there to greet her, and blurted out at once, 'It's Umar; a tragedy for all of us!' For Huda, the hurt was all but unbearable. When the funeral was over she sank into a long period of depression.

Umar was buried next to his father Sultan Pasha in the family tomb at the cemetery on the eastern bank of the Nile at Minya, at the foot of the hills. After crossing the Nile, the drive to the cemetery was long, and the carriage was surrounded by a horde of poor people. The funeral itself was carried out with full pomp and ceremony. Police officers and soldiers marched to the cemetery with the coffin, behind a band. The British army sent a contingent of troops to accompany the cortège. Ali and other men of the family led the procession of mourners on foot, with the women following behind in carriages.[36] The poor formed a rabble that followed the funeral all the way to the tomb. Many had crossed the Nile in fragile rowing boats, then walked miles on their bare feet to the cemetery. Some seemed almost too weak to walk, and others were gaunt, haggard, and obviously ill-fed. Umar had supported many of these people out of his personal generosity, but could not sustain all. The crowd pressed forward to try to touch the coffin, as they did at the burials of holy men. When the coachman raised his whip to keep the mob at bay, Huda forbade him. Instead, she seized a bag of silver coins intended for distribution at the cemetery, and threw them out among the people with all her might. Handfuls of silver coins glittered in the air above the people, who ran to collect them. She continued to do the same all the way to the cemetery, determined, as she put it, that nobody should be whipped at Umar's funeral.

She later read and re-read his letters. They were a constant reminder to her of the depth of his affection and his generosity of spirit. For example, in one letter written while he was away on a journey in 1904, when he was aged just 24, he showed his love for his family: 'I beg you to comfort our adored mother, who was very sad and depressed when I left her, and tell her that I shall be in your arms in two months' time to tell both of you that I love you more than anything else in the world.'[37]

Umar and Huda had always enjoyed their laughter together, and his boisterous enthusiasm was contagious. He enjoyed life so much. This had been the cause of his worst quarrels with Inayat, when he angrily refused her attempts to restrict his freedom. After Mustapha Kamil's death, he had become increasingly dissatisfied with political life.

Huda's sense of loss was unassuageable. Umar had been Huda's best friend in adulthood as well as her precious little brother. The two had grown up side by side, and he had consoled her for every injustice that she had suffered as a girl. It was he who had introduced her to Eugénie Lebrun, as well as to Juliette Adam, and he had been a source of encouragement and support in Huda's determination to read and to acquire a solid education. He had always supported her initiatives, such as the dispensary and the Intellectual Association. He had persuaded Ali to trust her judgment and convinced him that his best plan was to help his wife with her projects. He had developed and sharpened Huda's interest in politics, which was why Ali came to trust her judgment even in fields usually restricted to men. In short, Umar had believed in her.

After the prescribed 40 days of mourning had passed, Huda remained in a state of depression. The doctors said that she was badly in need of calm and rest. She sought this in the company of her children, taking them to Minya, where they could spend time with Umar's children, Muhammad and Naila. She grew ever closer to the children. She read to them and discussed every aspect of life with them endlessly. Her heartbreak, however, did not diminish. She had felt Umar's death as a cruel injustice, and her awareness of his absence weighed on her like a burden she could not shrug off. In this way, five months in Minya with the children passed by. At least she knew that Umar was remembered in Egypt.

Ali was moved by her distress. The house in Minya, which he had built especially for her, was meant to have brought her happiness. As she looked out of the windows, she could see the emerald fields and the palm trees swinging slowly by the banks of the Nile. Ali hoped the idyllic nature of her life there would eventually help her to recover her optimism. He also felt sure from his knowledge of her character that she would not long endure inactivity in Minya, and that her passionate concern over public issues would take precedence once more. He constantly exhorted her to go back to Cairo and to play once more her part in Egypt's political and cultural life. 'You are not just any woman,' he said to her, 'you have much to give to our people and so you must. This is what Umar would have wanted you to do.'

She returned to Cairo, but before she could resume her activities, however, she was obliged to face yet another unwelcome shock. On 17 October 1918, one of her former servants, weeping and dressed in mourning apparel, came to her door at Qasr al-Nil Street to bring bad news. This was that the Bahitha was dead. 'Malak Hifni Nasif has passed away,' the woman sobbed. The funeral was to take place that same day. Huda ran to find the procession, and met the coffin on her way. There were many mourners, with women in the streets alongside the men. A throng of notables and intellectuals were there, together with many of the high-school students for whom the Bahitha was a heroine. The Palace had sent an envoy to offer condolences to the family, though by convention the Palace did not walk in women's funerals. However, the Prime Minister and other members of the Government and high officials were there. Representatives from missions, other foreigners and correspondents of the local and foreign press also joined the cortège. As the procession passed, women stood on their balconies, in tears.[38] Huda followed the cortège to the cemetery. As she put it in her diary, 'they buried this vigorous body and closed the tombstone on whatever was left of this burning flame of intelligence.'[39]

Both women and men expressed their reverence for Malak Hifni Nasif, whose modesty and dignity had complemented her intelligence and insight. The word 'authentic', 'asila' in Arabic, seemed to have been coined especially for her. Huda felt the need to offer her own appreciation of her loyal friend, who had been an inspiration to her, as a powerful writer and a noble human being. The women's ceremony of remembrance was held at the University of Cairo, in the hall where Malak had spoken so many times. The women present invited Huda to chair the ceremony, and she gave her first public speech on this sad occasion. She felt the loss of the Bahitha for the rest of her life, especially during the hard days of the revolution of 1919, when, in Huda's own words, she 'called out to her within myself, because her voice was no longer heard, except by my own consciousness'.[40]

Huda drew her own conclusions from these foreshortened lives. Umar beckoned from the world of shadows to remind her of his unfulfilled plans. The only way to liberate the country, he had always said, was through the development of a free indigenous economy. Egypt was a rich country and its soil was pure gold. Meanwhile, Malak Hifni Nasif had revealed to Huda that reform was a wiser principle to follow than revolution. To be a feminist meant above all to be a woman with feminine attributes. There would be no emulation of men's ways. Feminine, not feministic, ways were to be enshrined in the laws. Before removing the veil, women had to be educated, since ignorant women would not be able to understand the social implications. Any misuse of freedom would expose women to shame and to a consequent loss of rights, and would be a barrier to positive change. Huda decided that for the time being there was not much she could do to further Malak's work. She would therefore throw her weight behind Umar's ambitions for the foundation of an Egyptian bank, whose realisation was more urgent.

She discussed the idea with Inayat. Talaat Harb was well known to them both, since earlier in his career, until Umar's death, he had managed the Minya estates Umar had inherited from Sultan Pasha, and was well acquainted with Umar's ideas. Harb expressed some reservations, believing that it would be difficult to persuade investors to contribute to the bank's capital, due to their mistrust of the ability of Egyptians to manage such an enterprise. Nevertheless, he agreed to lend his name to a revival of the scheme to set up a national bank on the basis of subscription by wealthy Egyptians, including Muslims, Christians and Jews. Huda pledged to use her influence and contacts to help him find the necessary funds. Huda asked Harb to find suitable premises for the bank while she recruited her half-sister Luza's son, Fuad Khalifa Marzuq, to assist her in a campaign to raise the necessary capital.

The bank was established in 1920, and in due course amassed sufficient funds to begin its operations. Huda's efforts bore fruit, and she was able to persuade many members of her family and her social circle to participate. A list of shares purchased by 11 January 1921 included 250 shares purchased by herself, while many substantial holdings were taken by wealthy women of her acquaintance. These contributions served to prime the pump. In 1924, the bank opened its doors, with Talaat Harb as Chairman of the board of directors.[41] Fuad Sultan became Secretary of the board and at the first board meeting he and Hafiz Afifi moved that Huda should become an honorary life member of the board, and that she would be invited to attend the meeting at the beginning of each financial year that approved the bank's budget.[42] The bank was part of the plan to free Egypt from British domination, and immediately identified itself as an institution opposed to imperialism.

Looking ahead to 1924, the bank was to have an impact on wider Arab politics. In that year, a group of Palestinian notables, who were under pressure to sell their lands to the Zionists, sent letters to Harb, asking him to open a branch in their country, so that they could obtain loans to continue with their affairs and save their fortunes and lands rather than sell to the incoming settlers.[43] This was the first Huda had heard of what was taking place in Palestine. At first, she found it hard to believe that the Jewish settlers, whom she had been told were honest and hardworking, were being unfair to the local population. However, she had also made herself aware of the conclusions of the King–Crane report of 1919, commissioned by the United States, which questioned whether the Palestinian population would acquiesce to steadily escalating Zionist settlements, suggesting they were unlikely to welcome the rising tide of immigration of European Jews into their country. Of course, she did not know at this point that Charles Crane was destined later to become a friend.

3

International feminism and the EFU

As 1918 drew towards its close, the world war seemed destined to end soon and all thoughts in Egypt were focused on one objective, to secure true independence for the country after the conclusion of the world conflict. Huda's ideas began to turn back more towards politics than to the social and charitable activity that had recently occupied her. Without a political resolution of Egypt's strained relationship with Britain, it appeared that no meaningful social progress could be secured. The national question must take priority. Egypt's ruler, Sultan Husain Kamal al-Din, had died in the autumn of 1917 after a short illness. His son, Prince Kamal al-Din Husain, had refused the succession, reputedly because of the British protectorate declared at the onset of the Great War in 1914. Husain Kamal's brother, Prince Ahmad Fuad, ascended the throne on 9 October 1917, becoming Sultan, then years later King Fuad. He had participated in the foundation of the University of Cairo, in the face of British opposition, and was well known to Egypt's nationalists.

In 1918, Egypt was under martial law, and political activity was strictly forbidden. In the autumn of 1918, Huda was told in confidence by Ali that a secret meeting was to be held at the country estate of the nationalist leader Saad Zaghlul at Masjid Wasif. Zaghlul was already a distinguished man of politics, born in 1859 to a prosperous family in the rural areas. His birthplace was the village of Ibiana, in the Delta, where his father was a well-to-do local notable, and he was a true son of Egypt. He studied at al-Azhar, and followed a legal career, rising to be a judge. He was appointed Egypt's Minister of Education in 1906, the year when he married his wife Safia, the daughter of the Prime Minister, Mustafa Fahmi Pasha. This helped his career, but it was his own immense charisma and ability that eventually carried him to the top. By 1912, he had swung over to the nationalist cause and argued for it vociferously in Egypt's Legislative Assembly, which, however, had limited powers. In 1913, he lent his weight to the campaign for greater constitutional rights for the Legislative Assembly. In 1920, he was appointed Minister of Justice. The meeting at Masjid Wasif was to be attended by all those who had supported Zaghlul since then. As well as Ali Shaarawi, those present would include Abd al-Aziz Fahmi, Ahmad Lutfi al-Sayid, Abd al-Latif al-Makabbati, Muhammad Ali Alluba, Hamad al-Basil and Sinnot Hanna. It may be conjectured that Ali would have liked to ask his wife to accompany him to the meeting, had this been possible, but women conventionally did not yet participate in such meetings. Huda therefore waited impatiently at home for him to return and report on what had transpired.

The meeting went farther than the group of Egyptian nationalist leaders who attended had expected. It was decided that an Egyptian delegation, which later became known as the 'Wafd', the Arabic word for 'Delegation', would go to see Sir Reginald Wingate, the British High Commissioner, as soon as possible after the signature of the armistice had brought the Great War to an end. In the light of President Woodrow Wilson's 14 points and the French Declaration of 1918, it seemed that the intention of the Allies was to free the peoples whom the Ottoman Empire had oppressed.[1] The nationalists hoped that Egypt might benefit from this new dispensation. Zaghlul, Ali and Abd al-Aziz Fahmi were chosen as the three members of the delegation, that would seek the

British High Commissioner's permission to go to London to plead their country's cause. The Wafdists, as they soon became known, believed that Egypt was ready for independence and that, when they put their case, the British would have no alternative but at long last to withdraw their military forces.

The Armistice was signed on 11 November 1918, and the Wafd went to see Wingate, as planned, on 13 November to demand the end of the protectorate and full independence for Egypt. Ali recounted to Huda what took place, and she pondered deeply on what had occurred. She thought often about what Ali had said to Sir Reginald: 'We long to enjoy the friendship of one free man for another, rather than the kind of friendship that binds a slave to a master!' Ali also reported Wingate's question: 'Egypt was Turkey's slave; would she be in a lower position as the slave of England?' Ali's answer resounded in her mind: 'Were I the slave of a man from the Ja'iliyin (an Arab tribe), or were I the slave of Lord Wingate, I would be equally unhappy in both cases, since I detest slavery, and can not agree to live under its humiliation. As I have already said, we want to be England's friends as free men and not as slaves.'[2]

Wingate, for his part, was impressed by the three men, though he decided to treat the meeting as an informal approach on the part of a group of Egyptians without official status. He advised the British Government to take the Wafd leaders seriously, but in vain. There was no change of policy on Britain's part, and, as was to be expected, the Egyptian people intensified their protests and agitation against the British occupation. Husain Rushdi Pasha, who was still Prime Minister, gave his full support to the Wafd. His position was that since Egypt had helped the British throughout the war, the time had come for the British to reciprocate the courtesy.

The tension heightened. The British would not agree to allow any kind of Egyptian delegation to travel to Europe to put their case, and refused to consider the termination of the British protectorate, insisting that Egypt was not yet ready for political freedom. Rushdi Pasha pointed out to Sir William Brunyate, who was the British-imposed legal and financial adviser to the Egyptian Government, that disregard for Egypt's rights would lead only to more serious trouble and that a conflagration might break out. The only answer he received was the notorious but possibly apocryphal response by Brunyate: 'Then I shall tame the fire with a spit.'[3]

On 3 March 1919, faced with Britain's persistent rejection of all overtures from the Egyptian nationalists, Rushdi Pasha resigned as Prime Minister. Unrest began to spread as a nationwide campaign for freedom from British rule got under way. On 8 March, General Watson, the Commander-in-Chief of the occupying forces, arrested four leading figures connected with the Wafd who were accused of provoking the disturbances. They were Zaghlul, Ismail Sidqi Pasha, Muhammad Mahmud Pasha and Hamad al-Basil Pasha. The four were taken first to the British barracks at Qasr al-Nil, across the square from the Shaarawis' Cairo house, where Huda and Ali fumed impotently, able to see the place of their colleagues' and friends' incarceration but not to help them.

The next day, 9 March 1919, Zaghlul and his three colleagues were unceremoniously deported to Malta. The people reacted to the four Wafd leaders' exile with mounting anger and an escalation of violence. A wave of unrest ran through the country. With Zaghlul in exile, Ali replaced him at the head of the Wafd. As the troubles continued, the Wafd began to develop into a fully fledged political party. Ali kept Huda informed of every development, apprehensive that he himself might be arrested at any time, as his fellow Wafdists had been before him. The British press embarked on a violent campaign against Egypt, and Lord Curzon delivered a vitriolic speech criticising the Egyptian people in the British House of Commons. As acting leader of the Wafd, Ali's name stood at the head of a list of signatories to a number of letters of protest against Britain's position. He played his part with dignity, and pledged both his personal prestige and his vast fortune to the cause of Egypt's liberation. His principle was that any victory achieved through legal and constitutional manoeuvres was more secure and permanent than anything that might appear to be gained by violent means.

A report, drafted by Ali, was sent to the High Commissioner, expressing the hopes of the members of the Wafd that moral support would be forthcoming from Egypt's new ruler who, as the Wafdists said, sat 'on the throne of Muhammad Ali the Great'. 'This movement was born,' wrote Ali, 'not because we harbour any hatred towards the British but because the right to freedom is the natural prerogative of all nations'.[4] Ali also added in his report that the Wafd now desired to be allowed to go to Paris to submit their petition for independence to the Peace Conference. A telegram was also sent to the British Prime Minister, David Lloyd George to protest against the exile of their fellow Wafd members.[5]

During the troubles, Huda was surprised one afternoon to receive an unexpected visit from one of her French acquaintances, Jeanne Marquès, who was almost fainting when she reached Qasr el-Nil. She fell sobbing on the floor, telling Huda that she had just come as fast as her legs would carry her from her house in Rod al-Farag because she had heard a rumour that Ali Shaarawi Pasha was about to be shot by British soldiers and that a British gun emplacement had been set up outside his home.[6] Ali had certainly attracted the unfavourable attention of the British, having endorsed the proposal made by Zaghlul's wife Safia to declare Saad's Cairo house the headquarters of the Wafd. Zaghlul's house quickly became known as the House of the Nation (Bait al-Umma). Ali had attended an official Wafdist dinner there with other members of the party, in defiance of a British edict.[7] He also made no secret of having been involved with the publication of revolutionary brochures.

By now, a general strike was paralysing the country. The strikers were supported by the whole population, including wealthy women who waited for striking employees outside their offices and places of work to donate their jewels to the strikers, thus compensating them for their financial losses and encouraging them to maintain the strike.[8] Riots sometimes degenerated into bloody battles, and both men and women were shot in the streets by British soldiers. In one unpleasant incident, a woman who held a national flag from her carriage window was badly beaten by British soldiers, who unsuccessfully tried to wrench the flag from her while some observing foreigners made fun of them.[9]

At that point, Huda decided to throw her own weight into the balance. Her plan was to mount a protest march, to be organised by her circle of upper-class women. If women marched alone, she thought,

Ali Shaarawi.

nobody would dare to shoot them. Were any to be killed, she reasoned, international public opinion would not overlook such a massacre. This could offer an opportunity to bring pressure to bear on the British, because of the impact that the women's demonstration would have on world opinion. Ali could only approve of his wife's spirited response.

Huda decided first of all to write to Lady Brunyate, Sir William's American wife, who at the end of the war, had paid Huda a visit at her house in Ramleh. In the course of that meeting, she insisted that Britain had entered the war for the sole purpose of coming to the assistance of poorer and more helpless countries, and not with any colonialist goal in view. She also averred that Egypt had played a positive role on the British side during the war, and should therefore be recompensed for it. So far, however, Huda saw that what had taken place in Egypt did not at all bear out these statements. In her letter, she therefore reminded Lady Brunyate of what she had said, and deplored the injustice of the exile of the Wafd leaders. She also drew attention to the brutality of the British soldiers during the riots, and stressed the injustice of the curfew that had been imposed on the country to curb the revolution, which was having the effect of keeping the Egyptian people paralysed and isolated in their homes. This letter was the first in what would become a long series of letters of protest written by Huda.[10]

Huda had been in a highly emotional state when she wrote the letter to Lady Brunyate, and the passion of its uncompromising language was such that Ali decided to show it to the legal counsel of the party, to be certain it violated no laws. In the event, the letter filled his Wafd colleagues with admiration, and they kept a copy of it with the party's archives. It was also important enough for Huda to be placed on a list, compiled by British officials, of those who might present a danger to the British administration. As to Lady Brunyate, she apparently showed the letter dismissively to her circle, saying that it made no sense to her. Her attitude greatly upset Huda. In the event, ironically, Sir William and his wife were obliged to make an unpublicised departure from Cairo for fear of retaliation by the angry mob.

On 16 March 1919, Huda's planned demonstration took place some three hundred or more upper-class Egyptian women marching through Cairo to bear witness to the solidarity and determination of the Egyptian people. Safia Zaghlul, Huda, Sherifa Riad, Wajida Khulusi and Dr Habib Khayat's wife Regina were among those who marched in the front ranks. This march symbolised in many ways the spirit of Egypt. Women of all classes took part, Muslims, Christians and Jews. Some held high the flag of Egyptian unity they had devised, on which the three stars embraced by the crescent on its green background had been replaced by crosses. Within the women's movement, rich women and poor marched side by side, in what later came to be seen as a significant event in modern Egyptian history. These were the same wealthy women as those who had offered their support to Egypt's poorer citizens during the riots and the general strike that paralysed the country. The Wafdist women initially consisted of the Wafdist men's wives, sisters or daughters, and they enjoyed their men's support. Like other factions seeking to liberate their country from the British protectorate they regarded as so odious, Egypt's Coptic and Muslim women would sit side by side in the Committee and march shoulder to shoulder against the occupation, under the whole world's eyes.

Naturally, the British sought to halt the women's march, as they had suppressed other demonstrations. Russell Pasha, the chief of police, feared it might lead to student riots and to disturbances of a more serious nature. The British adamantly opposed the principle of any demonstration in which the students might join with the women, thus being able to use them, in Russell's words, 'as a shield against the police and troops'.[11] The women were therefore refused permission to hold their peaceful demonstration, and their plan to march was frustrated by the presence of police cordons and British troops. Nevertheless, by arriving separately in their carriages and then descending to form up into a phalanx, the women succeeded in staging their march.

Russell Pasha took great pleasure in setting the stage for a situation that he thought would ridicule the demonstrators. In his memoirs, he recalled the day:

At a given signal, I closed the cordon and the ladies found their way opposed by a formidable line of Egyptian conscript police, who had been previously warned that they were to use no violence but to stand still and, if necessary, let their faces be scratched by irate finger-nails. The idea of being attacked by what they considered to be extremely immodest females amused my men enormously and considerable license was given them by their officers to practice their ready peasant wit on the smart ladies who confronted them.[12]

The idea was to keep what Russell Pasha referred to as 'the poor dears' standing under the midday sun 'without fulfilling their requests'.

An Egyptian contemporary observer saw the events quite differently, however:

The spouses from the finest families marched through the various quarters of Cairo, shouting 'Long live freedom and liberty,' as the crowds thronged the pavements to applaud and cheer them on and women leaned out from windows and balconies, ululating in jubilant support. It was a fantastic scene that stirred every heart![13]

The women were disgusted by the misogynist attitude of the police and the troops. Huda tried to break through the police cordon in order to lead the demonstration onward, but a British soldier pointed his bayonet at her chest. She screamed out 'Oh yes! Go ahead and kill me! Come on! Make another Miss Cavell out of me!' However, Regina Khayat, who was right behind her, took advantage of the young man's bemused hesitation to catch Huda's shoulders and pull her out of his reach. She told Huda that this was madness, and that if Huda got herself killed there would be a massacre, since the unarmed students who were present would certainly throw themselves against the armed soldiers. Regina's words brought Huda back to her senses.[14] In the meantime, parties of students had gone to alert the embassies of America, Italy and France and to seek help. The American Ambassador came in person to see what was taking place, and took photographs of the women facing the British soldiers outside Zaghlul's house. Russell Pasha then came to speak personally to Huda, leaving her no choice but to halt the demonstration.

Crowds had been waiting for the women near the embassies, and many foreigners were present. Onlookers had brought flowers to strew on the ground as the women marched past. A few pictures remain to testify that the march took place. Veiled women carrying a flag on which the crescent and the cross symbolised religious harmony had marched unarmed, and they had been stopped by armed soldiers. The news spread around the world, and the feminists of the International Woman Suffrage Alliance heard of it, leading them to take an interest in this daring act of participation by Egyptian women in the political struggle of their country.

The situation in Egypt was becoming increasingly uncontrollable. The demonstrations, which had so far been broadly peaceful apart from isolated outbreaks, turned into widespread disorder and a heavy-handed clampdown by the British. Government employees, workers, students, lawyers and other professionals went on general strike. Riots broke out, shops were assailed and looted, railways and tramways were suspended, communication was interrupted, strikes were called, and incidents of arson were reported from all over the country. The situation became hard for the British to control, and the soldiers retaliated with force of arms in various incidents across the country, shooting to kill at any group of Egyptians they perceived as a threat. The country was paralysed, and decisive action was indicated.[15] Lord Allenby was sent to Cairo as an extraordinary High Commissioner. He reached Cairo on 25 March with a mandate to restore law and order in the country, with an iron fist if necessary. He arrived by train from Alexandria accompanied by a small personal staff, and was met at Cairo Station by representatives of the civil and military authorities, including Sultan Fuad's representative, the President of the Legislative Assembly, the Governor of Cairo and others. It was clear there was a desire for reconciliation on the part of the local authorities. On 31 March, Allenby issued a proclamation calling on responsible Egyptians to restore tranquillity.

On 7 April 1919, after representations from many sides in Egypt including King Fuad himself, General Allenby announced that Zaghlul and his companions in exile would be freed. The four exiled Wafdists were duly set at liberty and were granted permission to travel where they wished. They therefore set off to the Peace Conference in Paris to present their case. A party of more than a dozen Wafd representatives, including Ali, voyaged from Alexandria to meet the four heroes in Malta and, after discussions there, sailed on with them to France. The hope of the Wafd was to open a fruitful dialogue with the world leaders attending the Peace Conference. Meanwhile, in Cairo, sporadic disturbances continued amidst a general air of triumph that the British had apparently backed down.

In Paris, however, the Egyptian delegation was simply disregarded by the European powers. They received no official welcome in the French capital, nor were they made unwelcome. They were simply ignored. In the meantime, Muhammad Said became Egypt's new Prime Minister. The Wafd members languished in their hotel in Paris, awaiting a positive signal from the European representatives at the Conference of Versailles, but the few appointments granted to them were inconclusive. Zaghlul did succeed several times in meeting the French Prime Minister Georges Clémenceau, but these encounters were on a purely personal basis. Muhammad Mahmud was sent to the United States to present Egypt's cause there, but President Woodrow Wilson also turned a deaf ear, despite his earlier rhetoric about the rights of small nations. The Wafd concluded that the United States was about to recognise the British protectorate in Egypt, an outcome that had already been implicit in the talks held by Britain and the United States at the margins of the Conference of Versailles.

From afar, Huda followed earnestly the Wafd's travails in France. These men represented the hopes of the whole country, and their failure would provoke havoc in Egypt. She had been proud of Ali's decision to contribute the huge sum of three thousand pounds to the Wafd's expenses, a large amount for one person. He had already done what he could to lend moral support to the Wafd in Egypt while its members were in exile. In her eyes, Ali had done his utmost to free Egypt of the British occupation. In November 1919, however, Ali was among the first Wafd members to return to Egypt, following an unpleasant difference of opinion between him and Zaghlul, who had insulted him.

Huda found it hard to believe that at such a historic moment, members of the delegation in which all in Egypt had invested such hopes had allowed themselves to quarrel with each other.

Ali felt he had lost a dear friend when he fell out with Zaghlul, but there were in fact good reasons for his return. The Egyptian delegation had spent six months in Paris without obtaining any concessions for the Wafd, and Ali was increasingly convinced that a longer stay was unlikely to be any more productive. He had also begun to suspect that Zaghlul was simply enjoying having large funds at his disposal, and wished to stay longer in Paris for that reason. The sticking point was that not only had Zaghlul refused to account for his expenses to Ali, who was the delegation's treasurer, but he had also demanded more money. The three thousand pounds Ali had already donated and the personal contributions of one hundred pounds made by each of the other members were apparently insufficient. In the course of the harsh words that were spoken between them, Zaghlul had said hurtful things. 'You are rich, Pasha, but wealth is not everything and we are also well endowed to a certain extent. But we let you join the Wafd because of your fortune...'[16]

Ali was humiliated and resentful. He had, after all, been present at the birth of the Wafd. He had played a full part in the original meeting with Sir Reginald Wingate. He had also willingly served as the acting leader of the Wafd during Zaghlul's exile. To be told now that he had been permitted to become a member of the delegation only because of his money was deeply unpleasant, precisely because he had been so generous, placing his person, his money and his time at the Wafd's disposal. Although it was as a result of this row with Zaghlul that Ali decided to leave Paris early, his view was shared by others, including Husain Wasif, Georges Khayat and Wisa Wasif, who also decided that a longer stay in Paris would be fruitless. Ali placed the remaining funds he held on the Wafd's behalf at the disposal of those other members of the delegation who wished to remain, and went home in silence.[17]

Meanwhile, as these events were taking place in Paris, Huda and the women who had marched with her against the British had been considering how to give practical expression to their desire for change. The result was that later in 1919 a society they called the New Woman Association was brought into being, with premises in a poorer area of Cairo, in order to educate girls from underprivileged backgrounds and improve their lives. Again, all the wealthy women in Huda's circle contributed from their ample resources. Huda was elected president. In 1919, she was 40 years old.

When Ali returned early to Cairo, Huda was stunned, and disapproved of his decision. She refused to hear any explanations. Distance and lack of empathy reminiscent of the early days of their marriage began once more to pervade their life together, and he suffered tremendously from it. Her reaction saddened him. The political struggle had taken a bad turn, but Huda's affection meant even more to him than politics. She was resentful and distant. He took refuge in Minya, where he occupied his days with the family estate. The care and attention he invested in the land gave him satisfaction, but still he felt bereft. He wrote to Huda,

> My dear, I am waiting for the time when your coldness turns into acceptance, when reconciliation takes the place of resentment in your heart, for I have a great hope for this. My concern for your safety has grown only greater, as has my attachment to your person, and I believe that, despite everything, you are well-intentioned and generous. Your lineage is noble, courageous and generous and if you are ever misled, your better disposition always brings you back to your senses...Let me tell you now that I need you and that I wish to end this disagreement. My need for harmony steadily increases with time. I love you and am deeply attached to you, and I am ready to do everything in my power to be on good terms with you, to please you and to fulfil all your desires in every possible way. We would be so fortunate if this were to happen! I shall wait for your answer, hoping that this misunderstanding will soon be relegated to the past forever.[18]

In the absence of any encouragement from Huda, however, Ali lapsed into silence. He was deeply depressed by Huda's furious reaction to the clash with Zaghlul, and was unable either to defend himself against her criticism or to shrug it off. He ceased to plead for reconciliation, and lapsed into silence. At the same time, his disappointment with his fellow politicians persisted, although some, such as Ahmad Lutfi al-Sayid,

Muhammad Mahmud and Ali Alluba, supported him. Something seemed gradually to die within him. He continued to be wounded by Zaghlul's unjust attitude, and even more by Huda's. He was hurt that she seemed to side with Zaghlul against him. He felt that she had not even tried to give him a hearing. He was also bitter at the way Egypt had been disregarded by the world community at the peace conference. The French writer Victor Margueritte, who commented on the affront to the dignity of the Egyptian people, said that they had been like 'voices in the desert'.[19]

However, as Ali saw it, the situation was continuing to grow worse day by day due to Zaghlul's insistence on remaining in Paris in what had become an uncomfortable and undignified situation. In addition, there was a widening split at home between the various Egyptian political factions, which was becoming detrimental to the national movement. There had for a moment been consensus behind the Wafd that had seemed to offer real hope. Now that was dissipating. The gradual disintegration of unity in Egypt's political life began to affect Ali's peace of mind, making him feel his life's efforts had been wasted.

Huda continued to find it hard to be sympathetic, and could not dismiss her hostile reaction to what she saw as his premature and unjustified return. In contrast to Ali, she believed that Zaghlul was right to remain in Paris and stand his ground. In her view, something had to be done to obtain independence from the British, and only patience and time would gain Egypt an audience. Meanwhile the disagreements that had broken out between the Wafd leaders worsened the country's predicament. Violent incidents, which had seemed the last resort of the Egyptian people under the British occupation but had died down since the departure of the Wafd, once more became prevalent. The British had turned a deaf ear to the delegation in Europe, and the protectorate remained as unacceptable as ever to Egyptian minds. There was apparently no middle ground, and a vicious circle of misunderstanding and mutual antagonism began to become entrenched.

In the end, the troubling situation in Egypt could no longer be ignored by the world. The British Government realised that unmitigated repression was no longer the answer to Egypt's popular unrest, which was increasingly deep-rooted, and decided that Egypt's political future demanded serious attention. A Commission of Inquiry headed by Alfred Milner arrived in Egypt on 7 December 1919 to investigate the causes of dissatisfaction in the country and to make proposals for a permanent agreement. Lord Milner was to submit a report that would take into consideration the demands of the Egyptian people and seek to reconcile them with the interests of Britain and other powers. The presence of Milner's mission, however, which seemed to be trying to go over the head of the Wafd, gave rise to yet more popular disturbances, and Muhammad Said Pasha stepped down as Prime Minister when he was unable to persuade the British to postpone Lord Milner's investigation to a more propitious moment. Milner, meanwhile, found his efforts frustrated. With Zaghlul, still regarded as the authentic representative of the nationalists and, still in Paris, Milner was unanimously boycotted in Egypt. Even the Egyptian Government chose not to speak to him, only addressing themselves to the existing representatives of the protectorate. When Milner attempted to ask the *fellaheen* directly what they thought, he received the blunt response, 'Ask Saad.'[20]

On 12 January 1920, the Egyptian women of the Wafdist group again held a protest meeting, this time at the Coptic Cathedral of St Mark in Cairo. At this meeting the Wafdist Women's Central Committee was formed. Despite Ali's defection from the Wafd in Paris, Huda was sticking to her Wafdist guns. Though Huda was not present at the meeting, she was chosen as president of the Committee. She had just returned from a visit to Luxor when Ester Fahmi Wissa wrote to inform her that the women had already elected a Committee and Huda, in absentia, had gained the highest vote, 136. The Committee was to have 15 members including Ester herself, who was a prime mover, Huda's sister-in-law Inayat, and Sherifa Riad.[21] The Committee's activities were of course to be open to Muslim, Christian and Jewish women alike, following the same policy as the Wafdist men. Interest was growing on the part of international women's associations in what the women were doing in Egypt, and it became clear that the participation of women in the Egyptian freedom movement was acquiring real significance.

The creation of the Wafdist Women's Central Committee gave a formal status to the women's political impetus that had begun to express itself with the women's demonstration of March 1919. The women's movement was a development of a new kind in Egypt, stretching as it did across classes and religions. The mainstream Wafd had at its outset, in common with many initiatives in Egypt at the time, been dominated by a restricted clique. The time was ripe for reform, however. In Egypt, Muhammad Ali had long before laid down the basis of a system of scholarships which allowed indigenous elites to develop. A class of intellectuals, writers, philosophers, economists, medical doctors and others had long since emerged, ready to take political responsibility for the affairs of their own country and to take its government into their own hands. It was from these groups that much of the membership of the Wafdist movement had begun to be drawn. The women's group consciously set out to be if anything even more comprehensive.

However, though her commitment to the idea of the Wafd remained unshaken, even Huda began eventually to experience a degree of disillusionment with Zaghlul. The problem was that his quarrels had begun to be not merely with the British but also with the Egyptian Government as well as with more of his erstwhile colleagues. In the light of this, Huda began to reconsider her hostile reaction to Ali's decision to split with the Wafd and step down as treasurer. She began to look at past events in the light of more recent developments, which led her to conclude that Zaghlul had perhaps changed, and was no longer the figure she had for so long admired. She had always believed that Zaghlul had much to offer Egypt, but she came to feel that personal ambition might now have started to play a more prominent part in his life. He had gained the people's support, and still enjoyed it, but had begun to exploit popular emotions and manipulate them, apparently heedless that the constant riots he inspired were gradually becoming a permanent state of anarchy, and were therefore no longer an effective weapon in the struggle against the British occupation. Despite her admiration for Zaghlul, Huda began to think he had made errors. She began increasingly to see that she could have been too harsh in her judgment of Ali when he left the Wafd in Paris.

Wishing to find out more about what had happened in Paris, she sought out other members of the Wafd who had been close to Ali. One of them, Muhammad Ali Alluba Pasha, in private life a famous lawyer who enjoyed the respect and admiration of all those who knew him, told her how hurt Ali had been when Zaghlul insulted him, and how he had said repeatedly, 'What need is there for these words, Saad Pasha?'[22] Alluba also spoke of her husband's final days in Paris, when Ali distanced himself from the members of the delegation and simply sat alone in his room waiting for the time to come for him to take the ship back to Egypt. He also recounted an anecdote relating to the delegation's visit to London in 1920, after Ali's departure, which seemed to demonstrate that Zaghlul's personal ambitions had begun to be unreasonable. A group of them had gone to Maidenhead together for a lunch on the Thames. The car broke down on the way back, and they began to discuss politics as they waited in the midst of the English countryside. It was then that Zaghlul had suddenly told them about his idea of making concessions in the talks with Milner while proposing to the British Government as a quid pro quo that they should compel the present King of Egypt to abdicate. He was clearly seeking the approval of the others, who looked askance at him, wondering what his motivation was. Apparently, his idea was that Farouk, the newborn heir to the crown would become King, and Zaghlul would be regent, thus effectively becoming Egypt's sovereign himself until Farouk's majority.[23]

Lord Milner left Egypt in March 1920, and during the summer of that year he met Zaghlul in London. On 8 August, Milner presented a memorandum to Zaghlul outlining his proposals, which amounted to the end of the British protectorate but contained what were described as safeguards for Britain. These negotiations were unofficial, and Zaghlul said he would be unable to agree to anything on Egypt's behalf without consultation at home. Some members of the Wafd returned to Cairo. On 9 November, Zaghlul had a final meeting with Milner, and made additional proposals which led Milner to break off the negotiations. Milner's report to the British Government, which he presented at the end of 1920, was made public in February 1921. The British Government had by now come to accept that there was no future for the protectorate in its present form, but the question remained under what circumstances it would be abrogated. The British invited Egypt to send an official delegation to London to discuss terms.

In April 1921, Zaghlul finally returned to Egypt, only to fall immediately into conflict with Adly Yakan Pasha, Egypt's Prime Minister since March, over who was to represent Egypt in these further negotiations. Egypt's political establishment was divided into two camps. However, other Wafd members believed it was more important to keep the negotiations going than to quarrel over who would head the Egyptian side. A joint delegation including both Yakan and Zaghlul, and representing both the Government and the Wafd seemed to be the way ahead, rather than carrying on the personal feuds that had begun to characterise Egyptian political life. The British, for their part, were adamant that they would talk only to a single official delegation. Demonstrations in support of Zaghlul were seen by the British as anarchy, and the personal attacks he made on Yakan that were widely publicised in the press were seen as irresponsible. The conflict between them was apparently irreconcilable, however. The British concluded that the political following enjoyed by Yakan, who was at that time attempting to inaugurate a new liberal and constitutional political party, meant he was their only realistic interlocutor. On the other hand, he was constantly undermined by what a British observer later called the 'popular veneration' in which Zaghlul was held.[24]

Yakan's talks in London were a failure because Zaghlul systematically sabotaged them, apparently to satisfy his vanity and his own personal interests. Yakan resigned on 8 December 1921, but the outcome was worse for Zaghlul, who was once more exiled, this time to the Seychelles. Zaghlul, meanwhile, who had begun as a pillar of the constitutionalist Umma Party, now seemed to have begun to see himself as the political heir of Colonel Urabi. The plan Zaghlul had hatched in Britain, to compel the abdication of the King and rule as regent, on behalf of Farouk, had now become the subject of common gossip.[25]

Huda now questioned in earnest her own hostility toward Ali. She had left her reconsideration too late, however, to achieve a reconciliation. For the first time in their life together, Ali seemed irrevocably to have shut her out. He also withdrew from society, becoming introverted and distant. There seemed to be no way to heal his suffering and draw him back from the refuge he had found deep within himself. After his return to Cairo, Ali had wanted nothing further to do with the Wafd, refusing to deputise, as he had always done in the past, for other Wafd members such as Mahmud Suliman Pasha when the latter was arrested. His disappointment with political life seemed complete, and as he had no personal political ambition he had in due course decided to withdraw from politics. Ali's principle had always been that any political programme that was not inspired by a utopian vision was worthless. In April 1921, his disillusionment with the Wafd led him eventually to quit the movement entirely. During Zaghlul's second exile, Ali showed no interest in how the Wafd might be kept going.

By now, Ali appeared to those around him to have in some way withdrawn from the world. His vitality dwindled and his health visibly declined. Finally, in February 1922, exhausted and increasingly apathetic, he decided to move out from central Cairo to rest at the Mena House Hotel, near the Pyramids, where the pure desert air might heal him, saying he did not wish to be disturbed. Huda fretted about him, however, and decided a few days later that she had to visit him. She went out to the Mena House with the children and Gabrielle (Gaby) Rousseau, then the children's tutor. They went on the night of a full moon, when, as she later remembered it, the moon spread like a golden ball against the sky, eerily illuminating the desert and the pyramids. Huda and the children went up to find the Pasha in his room, but to their shock found only his body there, looking, as she at first thought, peacefully asleep in the moonlight. She would always remember the full moon, the stillness of Ali's room, and Ali's body in the bed. The man had departed. The pure desert air had failed to revive him. Ali had died alone of sudden heart failure at the age of 68.[26]

4

Against the occupation

By early 1922, despite the frustrations endured by the Wafd in Paris and London, Egypt was moving ever more swiftly towards a semblance of independence. The British had apparently come to recognise, despite themselves, that the continued subjugation of an unwilling nation was not a viable plan. It fell ultimately to Yakan's successor as Prime Minister, Abd al-Khaliq Tharwat Pasha, to reach an accommodation with the British and bring about the much-desired goal. Talks between Tharwat and Viscount Allenby eventually reached the conclusion which the two sides had been moving towards since the Milner mission. On 28 February 1922, the British unilaterally proclaimed the abolition of the protectorate in a statement in the British House of Commons, and Egypt became independent once more. The decision was formally published in the official gazette of 16 March 1922.[1] The problem, as it would emerge, lay in the areas in which the British wished to reserve power for themselves. Nevertheless, had Ali lived, he would have been so happy to see the achievement of the goal for which he had always worked. After his death, Huda was remorseful that she had been unjust to Ali, as she could no longer set things right with him. Though she had in the past admired Zaghlul almost without reservation, she had by now become yet more disillusioned with him.

Ali's death was a turning point for Huda, a moment of profound sadness and regret, and she began to mull over her future. Her marriage had begun strangely, with the lavish wedding of a child bride, followed by seven years of separation in which she had been allowed time to grow from a girl into a woman. But after her married life had begun again in earnest, Ali and she had grown together and had become close. She admired his serious approach to life, and his sense of responsibility, but he also admired his young wife for her intellect, her passionate beliefs and her determination. As the new era of her life without Ali began, Huda mentally revisited the faces of all the dear ones she had lost, who had struggled for a better life in Egypt or waited for the day of independence to dawn. The list included her father, her mother, Hasiba, Jazb-Ashiq, Eugénie, Adila, even Louisette, but especially the Bahitha, Malak Hifni Nasif, and most of all her brother Umar and Ali himself.

On the other hand, each of these individuals had left someone behind with whom Huda had maintained a relationship. Each of her late friends had left behind children or dear friends of their own, all of whom now surrounded Huda. She had taken under her wing Adila's adopted little girl, Céza, and Jazb Ashiq's son Ali Saad al-Din, who was the bosom friend of Attia's son, al-Sayyid Muhammad al-Saqqaf. These two young men were very close to Huda, especially Ali Saad al-Din, who regularly communicated with her and wrote her long, affectionate letters from Liverpool, where he was studying engineering. Others who were close to her were the circles of friends left by her brother Umar and the late nationalist hero Mustapha Kamil, including Juliette Adam. With Ali's death she was also now solely responsible for her own children, her beloved Bassna and Muhammad. She felt as though a chapter of her life had come to an end, and a new one had begun. The challenge now lay in making another life for herself and for the people who were left around her.

Huda had taken on some responsibility for Malak's brother and sister, Magd al-Din and Kawkab Hifni Nasif. Huda paid for their studies abroad. Magd al-Din was in Paris, where he had become the president of the Egyptian Students' Association, while Kawkab was a medical student in England. In addition, from the incomparable Bahitha's ashes, Mayy Ziadé had arisen, a young woman whom Huda admired and loved, who had participated in the lectures for women Huda had been instrumental in organising at the University of Cairo. She was a writer, a poetess, a journalist, and most of all an unusually free-minded woman whose presence in Cairo was appreciated by all who met her.

Other friends were attracted to her side. In her circle in 1922 was Jeanne Marquès, who had grown up on the French island of Guadeloupe. It was she who had run to tell Huda at the height of the nationalist fervour that there was a rumour that her husband Ali was being targeted by the police. Jeanne told her many stories about the wonderful tropical island of her birth, with its turquoise waters. She spoke in a very individual low, grave whisper. She was of pure French descent, she said, and 'the blood throbbing in her veins was that of her buccaneer ancestors.' She was an intrepid woman who seemed never to have known fear in her life, but was haunted by the memory of the kisses and farewell hugs of her nanny, who had taught her Creole as her first language. Huda soon found out that Jeanne, who was a linguist by default, was also a gifted writer, like her famous sister, Marcelle Capy, who lived in France. While in Europe, Huda had also often met Francine Lebrun, Eugénie's sister, whose husband was Franck Daurat. They kept in touch with Huda by correspondence, and were like a second family to her in France. Francine Daurat had come to Cairo to be with Huda. Odile Rodin, who was the niece of Huda's own former teacher Mme Richard, had also joined her set.

Eugénie had long before introduced Huda to the lively and strikingly witty French woman Gabrielle Rousseau, director of the 'Petit Lycée', the primary school for girls at the Lycée Français in Bab al-Luq, in the heart of Cairo. Gaby had swiftly agreed to become the children's private tutor at home, and introduced them to the joys of reading French. In due course, Gaby began to spend her summer holidays with the children in

Ramleh, where she also enjoyed the luxurious house, the sea, the long walks along the seashore and the fresh air coming from the north, which made her dream of France, across the Mediterranean. She was close to the family, and became yet closer to Huda after being at her side when she discovered Ali dead at the Mena House, one of the worst moments of her life. Gaby was a tiny, thin woman whose poise concealed her great mental and physical energy. She was naturally boisterous, and found stimulation in the environment of Huda's household, where she was able to meet and make friends with such people as the sculptor Mahmud Mukhtar and other artists and thinkers.

Mukhtar became a great friend of Gaby's and therefore of Huda's. He was an enormously talented sculptor, originally from a humble family in a village near Mehalla al-Kubra. His talent and good fortune took him to the School of Fine Arts in Cairo and then to Paris, where he soon made a reputation. Gaby admired his work, and was amazed by his wild wit, which she was able to share with him because she herself had such a sense of humour. He told her all about his conversations with the poet Hafiz Ibrahim at the Café Riche every day, his escapades at al-Liwa bar and the activities of La Chimère, the group of artists of which he was president, and which he had set up with other artists such as Ragheb Ayad, Muhammad Hasan and others. They enjoyed the patronage of Prince Yusuf Kamal, who had founded an art school on his estate in Darb al-Gamamiz, and were supported by Guillaume Laplagne, the French artist who was the school's director.[2]

Another venue where Huda's friendships had developed was the Société des Amis de l'Art, where wealthy Egyptians mingled with artists from Egypt and abroad. Art and politics were linked, and the artists were passionately committed to the nationalist movement. In 1920, the Association of Egyptian Students in France had arranged a meeting between Mukhtar and the Wafd delegation which had arrived in Paris in 1919, and the outcome was that the young sculptor would be commissioned immediately to start work on a project to be called *Egypt's Awakening* (*Nahdat Misr*) intended to symbolise Egypt's renaissance. It was agreed that the Wafd, with its rich sponsors, of whom Ali was one, would cover his expenses. Mukhtar began work on the project at once, and returned to Cairo in 1922 to begin the actual construction.

In the event, the cost was enormous, and after Zaghlul's death in 1927 Government funds were necessary to see the project through. The sculpture took the form of a gigantic monument in which a sphinx, symbolising eternal Egypt, sits poised next to a graceful female figure lifting her veil from her face and head, symbolising the future of Egypt freed from its ancestral constraints. Finally unveiled by the King on 20 May 1928, the statue stood in Bab al-Hadid Square, next to Cairo's principal railway station, where it remained until 1955, when it was replaced by the ancient statue of Ramses II brought from Upper Egypt to be put there in its place. Mukhtar's statue now stands at the gates of Cairo University.

The link between art and politics was made much of at the time and many articles were written promoting Mukhtar as the Egyptian artist *par excellence*. Magd al-Din Hifni Nasif wrote an article in *Al-Akhbar* newspaper entitled 'Mukhtar and the artistic Renaissance of Egypt'. Huda had given Mukhtar and his Cairo project her enthusiastic support, and she continued to support him after Ali's death. Huda's belief was that art played a key role in civilisation, and that her support for cultural activities would assist in her promotion of intellectual societies for women. She built up her own collection, and used her purchasing power to support Egyptian artists.

Weekly salons were a well-established custom in cultivated circles in Egypt, and many were held by people in Huda's circle at their various houses. After Ali's death, Huda continued with her own weekly salon. Her day was always Tuesday, as her father's had been in the past. Salons teemed with writers, poets, thinkers, painters, sculptors, singers and politicians, and the elites of both East and West. Under Huda's aegis, women participated in this world. Many people tried their hand at writing in prose and verse, others chose to paint or to sculpt, and most engaged in conversations conveying their wit, their wide ranging education and their will to be creative and to take their destiny into their own hands. Literary salons were also held in the houses of writers such as Abbas Mahmud al-Aqqad and Mayy Ziadé, as in the houses of politicians, royal-family members and other wealthy men and women belonging to the high society of Egypt. An Egyptian social life, the roots of which went back to the days of Ismail and even Muhammad Ali, ran parallel to and often overlapped with the social life of the British rulers and of the foreign community established in the country.

Egypt was blessed with many able men in its political parties, its professions and its social institutions. It was Huda's insight that the potential of Egypt's women also needed to be realised. The new feminist movement could be of service, at the international level, to make known the capacities of Egyptian women and to bring about a change in the world's attitude towards Egypt. The Egyptian elite as a whole was highly articulate. In addition to Arabic and sometimes Turkish, many possessed at least one European language, and all were conversant with both Western and oriental culture. By bringing such people together, Huda hoped to widen horizons even further.

In sharp contrast to her successful social and public life, however, Huda's home situation changed enormously, and potentially for the worse after Ali's death. The effect of his departure was profound on all those who surrounded him. He had been the sole master of the family fortune. Now, all within the family were their own masters, and each held his or her own share of the enormous but fragmented estate, with the potential for dissent that this implied. This meant that Huda's children were to be not merely independent but rich in their own right. However, in accordance with Islamic law, the home was part of the widow's inheritance, and Huda became the owner of the vast family mansion. All felt in their hearts that Huda had become the head of her household. Her prime concern, in her private life, was the welfare of the circle of young people for whom she felt responsible.

Huda's immediate family had also already been enlarged by the constant presence of her younger friends and cousins. When Huda's uncle Ahmed Idris, Iqbal's brother, had died in a riding accident, her two young Circassian cousins, Hawa and Huria, had been sent first to live with their uncle Yusuf, who still lived in Bandirma. Huda had asked Yusuf to bring them from Turkey to live with her and her children. Her other protégés, Ali Saad al-Din, Jazb-Ashiq's son, and Muhammad al-Saqqaf, Attia's son, caused her some concern. They had been attached to the family for a long time, having once lived as children in Jami Sharkas Street, where the old Sultan family house had been and where their mothers, Jazb-Ashiq and Attia, had for a long time been welcome guests. The two young men had gone to England, where they both studied engineering in Liverpool. Ali Saad al-Din sent long letters to his cousin, faithfully describing what he saw and did. However, the news he sent from Liverpool about Muhammad was alarming. According to these reports, the young Saqqaf was too fond of amusement, and squandered his money. Huda came to believe he should have gone to live in Singapore with his father, who had returned there to be a wealthy and influential merchant. Rather than quietly absorbing the strength that his powerful father might have passed on to him, the young man had apparently chosen to lead a profligate student life in Liverpool.

In Cairo, there had been something in the air between Muhammad al-Saqqaf and Céza Nabarawi, Adila's adopted daughter. Both were attached to the Shaarawi household, though without being from within it, and they had played together as children. Céza went to a French convent boarding school in Alexandria and then lived with her grandparents. Thus, they had drifted apart. In England, Muhammad, amply supplied with funds by his father, had now seemingly justified Huda's concern by behaving irresponsibly. Céza still seemed to be thinking of Muhammad as a romantic prospect, but Huda took it upon herself to warn Céza against considering an alliance with a young man she was informed was unreliable, whatever his wealth. Much later, Huda came to regret this, and felt she might have misjudged the young man.

Céza grew into a tall, slender and self-possessed young woman. She wore her hair long, and gracefully tied it behind her head. She and Bassna had become close friends over the years, despite their differing personalities. They were two girls of an age, and were perhaps brought closer by their shared passion for French culture and devotion to the French language. Céza was a great lover of everything French, and she spoke and wrote the language impeccably. She was also a very determined young woman, who was sober, intelligent and never succumbed to whimsicality. She did not allow difficulties to ruffle her imperturbability, and she was intellectually insatiable. Her steady temperament belied the Irish blood that ran in her veins, inherited from her grandfather, Abdalla Bey al-Ingilizi, an Irishman who had re-invented himself as a Muslim Egyptian. She was no beauty, however, in contrast to her late mother, and her attractiveness lay more in her mind and expression than in her features, which were plain though pleasant.

Both Bassna and Muhammad were adolescents when Ali died, but were already attracted to the political and intellectual ideals that made up Huda's world, and which Ali had so effectively supported. Bassna and Muhammad both read widely and were inclined to philosophising. They were attracted more by abstract thinking than mundane aspirations. Huda's daughter Bassna in particular was devastated by the loss of her father, and would mourn him for the rest of her life. She spoke good French and was passionate about French culture, and devoted to Gabrielle Rousseau, her tutor who had become her friend. In addition, like Huda in her younger years, she was predisposed to melancholy. Her deep upset at her father's death led her to seek at a very young age the reassurance of an older man's affection. She very soon became engaged to a rising politician named Mahmud Sami Pasha, to whom she was married a few months later. Sami's career had been brilliant. He had risen to be Minister of Communications, and had just been posted to lead the new Egyptian Embassy in Washington as Egypt's Ambassador to the United States. He was a big man, large in girth, but had presence and charisma. He had a reassuring manner, and emanated an air of great competence. He was kind and charming to all he met, and very attentive to Bassna, who clearly adored him. The only possible problem between them was the age difference.

As Bassna saw it, however, this was a minor difficulty. The age difference between her own parents had been 26 years, but she felt that her mother had been lucky to be married to her father. Her instinct was that she had no time to lose. She was proud, at the age of 19, to be marrying a man who was a Pasha and a brilliant diplomat. She was awed by Huda's achievements, and was determined to live up to her standards, feeling that Huda might have good cause to be proud of her one day. For the moment, however, she sought refuge in her husband's strong personality and kindly temperament. Asked if she was too young for the marriage, she would reply, 'I shall be the youngest ambassador's wife in the world!' Huda had some misgivings, but bowed to Bassna's will, and the marriage went ahead. Once married, Bassna went to England with her new husband in the summer of 1923. Their plan was to spend some time together in England, and then to go to Washington, where their first task would be to purchase suitable premises for the new Egyptian Embassy in Washington and to set about the vital task of conquering the hearts of the American people for Egypt.

Huda's son Muhammad also grieved for his father, but for him there were other consequences. At the age of just 17, notwithstanding the intellectual inclinations he had shown, he seemed to grasp with both hands the sudden freedom resulting from his father's death. So far, he had spent most of his time with his books and teachers, but now he suddenly enjoyed a new freedom to do as he pleased and to spend his money as he wished. His sudden release from his father's watchful eye led to alarming signs of vulnerability at an early age. He was a frail, dark, attractive boy, with Eastern looks, who had been a passionate reader and almost a recluse. He had a side that was not merely intellectual but even scholarly. For example, he had carefully read Rousseau's *Social Contract* in French, although it had recently been translated into Arabic by Muhammad Husain Haikal Pasha. Haikal's translation was widely read in Egypt at the time. Having read the book in both languages, young

Muhammad was able to compare the two versions, so that he came to know the book almost by heart. Nevertheless, he had gained until now little knowledge of the world. His friendships had been limited to members of his own family and their close circle, and he felt most at ease with women. With his cousin Muhammad Sultan, Umar Sultan's son, and Muhammad Sultan's sister Naila, together with Céza, Bassna, Hawa, Huria and other young people of their age, he played endless games and acted out fantasies. His romantic leanings were reinforced by the lack of responsibilities and by his penchant for the imagination and towards such romantic writers as Goethe. The difficulty for Huda was to keep immediate family matters under control while continuing to lead her own increasingly intense social and intellectual life. The day would inevitably come when her own children would cause her grief, leading her to rue the time she had spent on her public commitments and to regret her outside enthusiasms.

For now, however, it was time for Huda to embark on new ventures. In 1922, after Ali's death, Huda realised that in his lifetime, though he had in some ways circumscribed her freedom, the support and advice he had given her had been invaluable. This was all the more surprising in view of the fact that he had not been a young man, and in the light of the prevalent conservative mentality of the age. At first, Huda continued to attempt to play a part on the political scene. Soon after Ali's death, she addressed a meeting of the Central Committee of Wafdist Women, assuring them that she would not desert their cause:

> Neither illness, grief, nor fear of censure can prevent me from shouldering my duty with you in the continuing fight for our national rights. I have vowed to you and to myself to struggle until the end of my life to rescue our beloved country from occupation and oppression. I shall always honour the trust you have placed in me. Let it never be said that there was a woman in Egypt who failed, for personal reasons, to perform her duty to the nation. I would rather die than bring shame upon myself and my sisters. I will remain by your side and at your head through good and bad times, with hope in the future while we defend the rights of our beloved country. Repeated hardships…will not deter me from fighting for the full independence of my country.[3]

~ Against the occupation ~

Coincidentally, in the month before Ali's death, Huda had also received encouragement to continue her political struggle in the shape of a letter from Juliette Adam, Umar's and Mustapha Kamil's old friend and mentor in France, who addressed her as 'My dear Huda':

> My son Ali Kamil, the brother of my much loved Mustafa, the intimate friend of our dear Umar, has told me that you have been struggling during the past three years for the martyred homeland, and that you have been the leader of all those noble Egyptian women and girls who have defended their beloved country against the foreign incursion. I congratulate you for choosing this courageous mission, which is worthy of you and of your family. I wish you and your heroic Party a well deserved success in these efforts. We love Egypt as a painfully oppressed sister and in France we shall continue to defend her. For us, she is personified by the valiant freedom fighter, the late Mustapha Kamil, the former head of Egypt's National Party. My affectionate wishes, Juliette Adam.[4]

For Huda, there was a kind of magic to this letter. As with other moments that were significant for her, it brought with it a vivid recollection of the past. Both her brother Umar Sultan and Mustapha Kamil seemed instantly to be once more in her presence. Huda had shown Ali the letter, which he too appeared to appreciate, as he also felt keenly the absence of Umar Sultan and Mustapha Kamil, and wished they were still by his side. The letter was to become Huda's credo. The time had come, she argued, for the women of Egypt to demonstrate that, even in contemporary times, they were not inferior to their men. She memorised its words until she learned them by heart.

On 27 January 1922, Huda sent a response to Juliette's letter, picking up her pen to write this spontaneous reply:

> Madam, I find it difficult to say how much I have been moved by this affectionate remembrance. It has furnished me with moral comfort at a moment when, in the passion of the struggle, we need all the more to feel supported and encouraged. We are proud and honoured by your expression of sympathy. Permit me, on behalf of all my Egyptian sisters, to thank you, Madam, for the interest you take in our unfortunate country. Because we firmly believe in our rights and are confident in the future, we are determined to struggle to the end and to achieve our freedom at all costs. We wish to remain worthy of those who have sacrificed everything for their homeland and work with us even in exile. Please accept, Madam, our best regards and our profound gratitude.[5]

This letter crossed with a postcard, sent the previous day by Juliette from her summer residence in France at the Abbaye de Gif, at Gif-sur-Yvette, overlooking the Yvette river in the Chevreuse valley not far to the south-west of Paris. Umar, who had often visited the Abbaye, had described to Huda the romantic scene, where an ancient abbey stood in a garden with fountains near a folly in the shape of a Greek temple built by Juliette's father. Juliette wrote in pressing terms:

> Dear Madam, I am a very old woman – 85 years old – but I want to save Egypt before dying. I wish to see it free: I wish to found a newspaper. I shall need money, a great deal of money. You have certainly read my article in le Figaro. I want to write a hundred more articles in a newspaper of my own, edited by myself, Madam, in the name of my friend Umar. Two women must liberate Egypt – you and I. I have an admirable reputation and you must look out for the Egyptian patriots.[6]

Friendship and common interests would later lead Huda to the Abbaye de Gif, as Juliette became fragile in her old age and found it difficult to undertake long journeys. On the basis of the memory of their loved ones and a natural inclination to serve the same ideals, the two women developed a friendship that death alone would interrupt.

From 1919 until Ali's death in 1922, Huda had tended to involve herself more in politics than in feminism or social work. After Ali's death, Huda was kept abreast of the inside story of political developments in Egypt by Ali's closest friends, including Ali Alluba, Muhammad Husain Haikal, Abd al-Rahman Fahmi and Muhammad Mahmud. In the weeks after Ali's death, events moved rapidly. The clash between Zaghlul and Yakan over how to negotiate with the British had resulted in a split in the ranks of the Wafd party. One faction continued to support Zaghlul, while other Wafd members followed Yakan into the new Liberal Constitutionalist Party he formed when Tharwat took over and he went into opposition. The primary concern of this latter group was to draft a constitution for Egypt and to militate for constitutional government. Ali's friends now for the most part became members of Yakan's new party. Soon a bitter struggle was to begin, in which these more cautious former nationalist politicians opposed Zaghlul, whose popular support in Egypt continued to be vast and enthusiastic. Huda was torn between the two positions. She made a further intervention in politics from her position as chair of the Central Committee of Wafdist Women, publishing a letter in the press that was deeply critical of aspects of the British declaration of 28 February 1922 negotiated by Tharwat, effectively ending the protectorate. In particular, her wrath was aroused by the reservations expressed by Britain, which included the clear intention to retain in British hands responsibility for defence and to continue to protect as they saw fit foreign interests in Egypt, as well as to administer the Sudan. In the course of a lengthy and impassioned letter to the press, she wrote,

> We have heard that a government will be formed. It is astonishing that an Egyptian patriot might agree to take upon himself the position of prime minister at this most difficult moment for our defeated country; if indeed it is true that there exists a man in Egypt who would agree to be a tool in the hands of the British for the execution of this death sentence pronounced against the country where he was born and fed, and where he drank the waters of the Nile.[7]

She also sent Tharwat a letter, on behalf of the Wafdist Women's Central Committee, attacking his Government's repression of popular protest against Britain's intentions. On behalf of the women's movement, she threatened that she would herself be willing to stand at the forefront of riots against his administration: 'The prisons are now full of Egypt's innocent sons, the land is soaked in the blood of its martyrs, their mothers' eyes are sore and their widows and orphans are broken hearted. Do you still believe that you are acting to fulfil the nation's hopes, or is some force driving you to act contrary to truth and justice?'[8]

Despite the temptation to continue her struggle in the political arena after Ali's death, however, Huda soon judged it more expedient to return to her former field of action in social activity. Rather than attempting to take part in the political development of the new Liberal Constitutionalist movement, she turned her attention elsewhere.

Nevertheless, she was still able to count on the support of her husband's influential friends for her initiatives on social issues.

The year 1922 marked an important turning point for Huda. This was when it could be said that she began in earnest to promote the feminist cause. As long before as 1920, Huda had been contacted by the London-based International Woman Suffrage Alliance (IWSA), founded in 1904 by an American woman, Carrie Chapman Catt. With Ali's approval, she had accepted an invitation to the organisation's congress in Geneva that unfortunately she had not in the end been able to attend. Other women she had asked to come with her had failed to persuade their husbands to allow them to travel alone. In addition, the Wafd was still in Paris, though Ali had already returned to Cairo, and Huda, still a passionate Wafdist, did not want to leave Egypt while there still might be dramatic developments. She was very interested in the world women's organisation, however, and began to think more widely about Egypt's possible involvement in such a project.

The remit of the IWSA was to advocate the extension of the right to vote to women, and to extend its scrutiny over gender issues on a global scale, and the women who ran it wanted an Egyptian organisation to be affiliated to their global network. Chapman Catt had met Egyptian women campaigners during a pre-war visit to Cairo, and her hope was that Huda would have the potential to bring such an organisation into being. At the time, however, Huda had not previously given consideration to anything of this kind, and there was no precedent in Egypt. Despite her personal commitment to political issues, charity had hitherto been the focus of the upper- and middle-class women's groups with which she had been associated. In the wake of the First World War, however, national organisations advocating women's rights were being founded in all the countries of the Western world. Women had taken much responsibility in Western countries in the absence of the men during the war, and now began to demand recognition of their skills and civil rights. There was also a general call for masculine solidarity with the women's aspirations.

Huda had much experience of setting up women's organisations of a charitable and social type. In 1914, she had played her part in setting up the intellectual society for women sponsored by Princess Amina Halim. This association, with a strictly female membership, held lectures on art, science, literature, history and archaeology, among other subjects, and sponsored musical evenings. During the war, however, the society had fallen into abeyance. The founder of the *Egyptian Woman's Magazine* (*Majallat al-Mar'a al-Misria*), Balsam Abd al-Malik, suggested to Huda that a new society could be formed under the umbrella of the New Woman Association (Jami'at al-Mar'a al-Jadida) that had been set up in 1919. In February 1920, Huda held a bazaar to collect funds for the project. The new association thus raised almost four thousand pounds. Of this, members of the royal family contributed almost a thousand pounds, while other major donations amounted to some 910 pounds. Huda discussed the project with Ali, despite their estrangement, and he added a personal donation of 1000 pounds.

On 22 April 1920, Huda held a gathering of those interested at her house. The first task was to find premises for the new association, where the intention was that there would also be a cultural club for Egyptian women where various activities could be undertaken, together with a library available to women. Huda became honorary president, while Amina Sidqi and Jamila Attia took charge of the day-to-day administration. Balsam Abd al-Malik published the accounts of the new association in her magazine. The association retained the name al-Mar'a al-Jadida (the New Woman). Its programme of activities got under way at once, and it flourished.[9]

The subsequent creation of the Egyptian Feminist Union (EFU) in 1923 was a milestone in Huda's life and in Egyptian history. The spur was a further invitation from the IWSA in February 1923 to attend the international organisation's Ninth Congress, held on this occasion in Rome. The initial letter of invitation was sent on 7 February 1923 by Chrystal Macmillan, the Scottish vice-president. The congress was to be held between 12 and 19 May 1923, and the affiliation of the Egyptian movement would be top of the agenda. On 14 February, Huda wrote to the Prime Minister, Muhammad Tawfiq Nessim Pasha, who had taken office in November 1922, formally requesting permission for a delegation of women to attend as Egyptian representatives. His response was that once an organisation was set up he would give his blessing.

On 16 March 1923, Huda invited her colleagues from the Wafdist Women's Central Committee, from the Muhammad Ali dispensary (the Mabarra) and from the New Woman group to a meeting in the great reception room at 2 Qasr al-Nil Street to set up the Permanent Committee of Egyptian Women, which would be charged with framing a constitution for a women's organisation to be known as the Egyptian Feminist Union. Huda was elected chair, with Sherifa Riad as her deputy, Attia Fuad as treasurer, and Ihsan Ahmad as secretary. Other women elected to serve on the committee included Céza Nabarawi and Nabawiya Musa, a

The EFU board (Céza, Huda, Mary Kahil, Regina Khayat, Inayat Sultan, Sherifa Riad).

prominent intellectual and noted feminist activist. All were old friends of Huda who had participated in the women's activities during and after the 1919 riots. Premises were found for the EFU, and formal permission was sought from the Egyptian Government for the women to represent Egypt at the congress in Rome once the members making up the delegation were selected and appointed.

The new Prime Minister, Yehia Ibrahim Pasha, who had come to power on 15 March, immediately gave his permission, and it was agreed that Huda would go to Rome accompanied by Céza Nabarawi and Nabawiya Musa, her two most articulate colleagues. Both were unmarried, and therefore needed no personal permission to travel. Céza had grown into a gifted writer with a strong personality, qualified by her Western education to engage in dialogue with Western women, while Nabawiya was a powerful intellect, an assiduous scholar, and accomplished in Arabic. Huda was fascinated by the international character of the IWSA. The organisation's offices were in London, but Carrie Chapman Catt was based in New York. The four vice presidents were French, Scottish, German and Swedish. Huda sensed at once that this would be a useful and influential platform from which to promote Egypt's interests.

On 6 May, the three women arrived in Brindisi on board the SS *Helwan* from Alexandria. A group of Italian students were there to welcome them and take them to Rome. On 7 May, Chrystal Macmillan met them in Rome, and they gave the IWSA executive committee their draft project for the establishment of an affiliated Egyptian organisation. When they discovered there was no Egyptian flag among the flags flown in the conference hall, they asked Yusuf Kamil, a young Egyptian painter for whose studies in Rome Huda was paying, to recreate for the occasion a flag like the one carried by the women in their 1919 demonstration. The three of them stitched the flag with their own hands, and it was flown at the opening session, with its white crescent and crosses against a green background, replacing the stars of the national flag. As a special ecumenical and feminist flag devised by the women's groups, it caused a quiver of concern to the conference organisers until they were sure there would be no formal Egyptian objection. As the congress got under way, the three newcomers from Egypt saw that, for them, it would serve as a workshop where they could learn about the international women's movement and acquire useful information. On Saturday 12 May, for example, the proceedings were split into four committees that were to discuss equality in wages and employment, the married woman's nationality, unity, and the legal situation of women, all issues of crucial concern in Egypt.[10]

Some two thousand women participated in the congress. Benito Mussolini, then Prime Minister of Italy, came to the opening ceremony with three of his ministers. Mussolini was welcomed to the hall by the Italian delegates, Margherita Ancona from Milan and Alice Schiavoni-Bosio, a well-known Italian feminist and president of the Roman Comitato Centrale della Federazione Nazionale Pro-Suffragio Femminile. He was greeted with enthusiastic applause by the assembled delegates. Mussolini said in his speech that the Italian Government intended to give careful study to the issue of women's suffrage. However, he went on to make remarks less welcome to his audience in relation to what he described as women's duties and activities in the household and the primary importance of such activities in the life of women and in society.[11]

Chapman Catt placed Huda at her right hand on the platform, and in her presidential address she introduced her to the other delegations. It gave her great pleasure, she said, to introduce a newcomer, the leader of the delegation of Egypt, a country known for its ancient civilisation and glorious history. The three Egyptian delegates were given a warm welcome. They were asked many questions about their specially designed flag with the white crescent and crosses. They explained the symbolism of the cross and the crescent, and that the Coptic and Muslim communities stood side by side in the struggle to free Egypt from British occupation. The hearing they received was sympathetic. Huda and Céza made many important contacts, including Romania's Princess Alexandrina Cantacuzino, the Romanian delegate and later one of the prime movers of the International Council of Women, with whom Huda was to stay in touch for the rest of her life.

The streets of Rome were thronged with the women delegates, who had flocked in from all parts of the world, many clad in their traditional native clothes. The exotic Asian and African women, with their saris and flowing robes, were at the centre of attention.[12] The Italian press was ecstatic. It was a surprise to the Italians to discover that these Japanese, Chinese, Indian and Egyptian women, who came from distant lands and different cultures, were for the most part journalists, lawyers, politicians and university graduates. Huda and Céza wore Western clothes and spoke perfect French. They conceded in interviews that Egyptian women did not yet have the right to vote, but pointed out that neither did the women of such an advanced country as France. When political rights were restored in Egypt, they wished them to be extended to women as well as to men. Questioned about polygamy, they explained that it was not yet forbidden, but had ceased to be the custom. Ester Lombardo, an Italian journalist who wrote for the daily *Giornale di Roma*, exclaimed that for her to have the opportunity to meet sisters from distant continents was sufficient justification in itself for holding the congress, as 'no amount of travel and no new discovery in the world could equal the voyage of the soul.'[13]

The decision by Huda and Céza to remove their veils when they returned to Cairo sprang naturally from their experience in Rome. During the proceedings at the congress, the three women had uncovered their faces, having discovered that a veiled face was an obstacle to communication and therefore diminished the effectiveness of their work. Nabawiya Musa set off for Egypt first, in order to prepare a reception for the other two, while Huda and Céza travelled home together. During the homeward journey, when the issue of the veil arose, Céza insisted that she would henceforth remain unveiled. Huda had promised in the past that she would remove the veil when the time was ripe. This seemed the appropriate moment. They had appeared with uncovered faces before everyone at the congress, and it followed that they should go home proudly with their faces equally uncovered. Not to do so, they said to each other, would be hypocritical. The argument sounded convincing and logical. Huda, however, still felt she had to reassure herself that she would not jeopardise her daughter's social life or her marriage by taking such a revolutionary step.

The ship arrived in Alexandria on 28 May 1923. Mahmud Sami, Huda's son-in-law, had come to Alexandria to welcome her home, and when he came on board she discussed with him her plan to unveil, in order to reassure herself that he would not be scandalised. She was delighted to find that he approved of her plan. He told her that his view was that the time had come for such a gesture to be made in Egypt. Huda's flawless reputation, he said, would lend legitimacy to her gesture. Nabawiya Musa had organised coverage of the two women's return in order to make it a media event and gain the maximum publicity. A correspondent from *Al-Ahram* newspaper met them in Alexandria and accompanied them on the train to Cairo. At Cairo Station they descended from the train with their faces uncovered. They were met by a moment of stunned silence, following which all the women of their circle who were waiting to welcome them also removed their veils. The scene was magnificent, and was always recounted with enthusiasm in later days by those who had attended it.

Once Huda and her associates were back in Cairo, the next task was to put the newly formed Egyptian Feminist Union on a firm financial footing. An inaugural charity ball to raise funds for the EFU and the Al-Mar'a al-Jadida had already been held in their absence at the Ezbekieh Garden on 16 May 1923. The garden, with its stately white marble fountain, wooden gazebos and lush vegetation, was a beautiful setting for any kind of social event, and the pleasant May weather in Cairo that year contributed to attracting a large and fashionable crowd. Such charity events were a highly effective way of raising funds for organisations from the Egyptian moneyed classes. Feminism had evidently become such a cause. Its moment had come. This initial event paved the way for what would in due course become systematic fundraising in Egyptian high society.

As Huda's professional plans blossomed, she was upset by a personal upheaval. Disaster struck her Fahmi cousins when Ali Kamil Fahmi was murdered in London on 1 July 1923. Munira Sabri, his mother, had passed away in 1916, predeceased by his father Ali, who left a vast fortune. At the age of 20, Ali Kamil had inherited much of his father's money. He was not unmindful of his family duties, and built a hospital and a school in Maghagha, near Minya, where the family estates were, in addition to funding scholarships for students from his father's home village. However, he was fundamentally irresponsible in his attitude to his wealth. He was easily led, and fell victim to unsuitable companions who encouraged him to lead a life that was enormously extravagant. His generosity and his lavish lifestyle led him to be known as 'Prince' Ali Fahmi. His vanity led him to do little to discourage the impression in European countries that he truly held the title of prince, and that was how Western newspapers usually referred to him.

He was still only 22 years old in 1922, when he fell in love with a French adventuress of dubious reputation, whom he had met in Cairo. This was Marguerite Laurent Meller, the daughter of a Paris taxi driver, who was some ten years Ali's senior. The couple had married on 27 December 1922. She was already twice a widow, and was reputed to have stabbed to death her second husband, the father of her daughter, in the course of a quarrel. Ali was besotted, and she had in any case concealed her past from him. He had showered her with jewels, which she sold. The marriage degenerated into a series of degrading quarrels. The young man attempted to control his wife, then, having failed, he planned to take back his gifts and repudiate her. For the time being, however, he did nothing, which proved a mistake.[14]

Six months later, staying at the Savoy Hotel in London, Meller shot Ali with a pistol they illegally kept in their room, firing three shots into his head from behind as his attention was distracted by a pet dog. When the case came to court, she was defended by the celebrated British barrister Sir Edward Marshall Hall. He cast terrible aspersions on Ali, and reviled the institution of marriage as practiced in Egypt, denigrating Egyptian customs and manners in general, and presenting Meller as an innocent European victim of what he defined as oriental maltreatment. Balsam Abd al-Malik reported the case in her magazine,[15] and Huda, on behalf of the Wafdist Women's Central Committee, sent a telegram of protest to the British Government:

> The Central Committee of Wafdist women deplores, on behalf of all the women of Egypt, the odious and false accusations directed by Mrs Marguerite Fahmi's lawyers and by most of the English newspapers, against all Easterners and against Egyptian men in particular. The women of Egypt believe that this is nothing but a premeditated attack on Egypt and a new kind of propaganda which, by defaming the Egyptian people, can justify the policies enforced by the British occupation. Seeing that such accusations represent the lowest kind of aggression, it is regrettable that the arguments of the defence should have been directed against a whole nation, especially in a Court of Justice, which ought to rise above hatred and refrain from making any aberrant accusations, thus violating the law.

As the Ali Fahmi trial took its course in London, Huda received reports from Bassna, who was attending the hearings with Mahmud Sami. As an Egyptian diplomat resident in London, he had been delegated to follow the case. Bassna was reticent in her account, however, as she found it hard to talk about such unpleasant events. She did, however, tell Huda about the intervention of a young lawyer, Odette Simon, who had volunteered as a French interpreter to the court. Bassna sought out Odette and befriended her, admiring her courage in choosing law as her profession at a time when there were relatively few women lawyers. As the distasteful proceedings continued, Huda could see that Bassna missed her mother's presence, despite the support she drew from her husband. Bassna's affection for her mother came through clearly in her letters, never failing to address her with such special family endearments as 'Ma petite maman chérie'.

In Egypt, meanwhile, major political developments were under way. Nessim Pasha resigned as Prime Minister on 5 February 1923 after British pressure on him not to insist on Egypt's rights in Sudan. Lord Allenby, the British High Commissioner, arrested many Wafdists and sealed Zaghlul's house, the Bait al-Umma, preventing it from being used as the Wafd's headquarters by Zaghlul's supporters. All this suddenly went into reverse, however, when Yehia Pasha was appointed Prime Minister on 15 March. Yehia obtained Zaghlul's release from exile in the Seychelles, and the British also allowed other political prisoners to be freed. The new constitution was proclaimed on 19 April 1923, and an electoral law providing for manhood suffrage was passed on 30 April. Zaghlul would eventually return to the country in September, when he judged the time was ripe to begin his own campaign to seek election as prime minister.

Other surprises and disappointments were in store in Huda's personal life. In the summer of 1923, putting the bad memories of the Fahmi case behind her, Huda and her son Muhammad visited Paris together. Each was planning an onward journey. Huda intended to go to the Abbaye de Gif to see Juliette Adam, who was mourning the death of Pierre Loti. She had taken up the habit of visiting her ageing friend at the Abbaye, with which by this time she was well acquainted. After this particular visit, in a letter dated 17 October 1923, Juliette wrote,

> I can still see you on my terrace, talking about our dear Egypt. I recall the summer days when I talked about this same Egypt with Mustapha and Umar. They were the leaders of the future, just as you are fighting for this future. Remember, Egyptian women, your great Queens whose reigns were not inferior to those of your Kings, but such equality must not be masculine. Go on being wives, go on being mothers, aspire to the great role of advisors and, at this point in time, when the great future of ancient Egypt is perhaps at stake, be a source of inspiration for legitimate national demands. Go to the people, enlighten them if they do not know about themselves, and cause them to know their right to freedom and their national responsibility. You are the valiant one, conscious of the power of courage, the value of action. My wishes are carried to you by the Egyptian swallows, which have just left us and will bring back next year to the Abbey, where they are more numerous than elsewhere, the news of an Egypt liberated from its foreign yoke.

Muhammad's plan, meanwhile, was to go from Paris to London to see his sister and then travel elsewhere in Europe on his own. Huda's trip was going swimmingly. Magd al-Din Hifni Nasif, the Bahitha's young brother, who was finishing his studies in Paris, had planned a comprehensive programme for her stay. To attract the attention of the French press to her visit, he arranged for her to visit the Tomb of the Unknown Soldier, on which she laid a wreath. Then he organised a tea party in her honour for the young Egyptian students who were studying in France and Britain thanks to the scholarships she had granted them, which also served to celebrate Magd al-Din's imminent return to Egypt, as he had just completed his degree in economics and political science. This gathering gave her an opportunity to speak to the students about events in Egypt and the situation of Egyptian women. She also wanted to talk about Islam, where she felt there needed to be more understanding between East and West in view of the appalling things that had been said at the trial of Ali Fahmi's wife. Her intention was to explain that Islam was not responsible for the backwardness of Egyptian women. The veil was an Ottoman innovation and was imposed on the women of the upper classes of Egypt under the Ottoman Empire. It was absurd, she also wished to say, that women should be deprived of a higher education, as educated women would educate their own children, thus raising the level of the whole country.

Huda found the time she spent in Paris with Magd al-Din and Muhammad in the summer of 1923 extremely pleasant. Muhammad appeared to enjoy Paris, where he felt at home, and to be refreshed by Magd al-Din's wit and sense of humour. He gave the appearance of being relaxed and happy. When he left her, intending first to visit his sister Bassna in England, Huda was quite lighthearted and confident that her own journey would lead her, as usual, towards interesting people and places.

In September 1923, as she returned to Egypt, Huda had the great surprise of bumping into Saad and Safia Zaghlul aboard the ship, as he at last made his own journey back to Egypt. He had been transferred from his place of exile in the Seychelles to Gibraltar, and though free since March had remained abroad, directing the Wafd from outside the country. At first, Huda, Saad and Safia spent much time together on deck, in the salons and in the dining room, exchanging ideas. Saad expressed his admiration for her decision earlier in the year to remove the veil. He said his opinion was that his wife should do the same. He asked Huda to show Safia how to readjust the veil in order to bare her face. They both told Huda about their difficult time in the Seychelles, where their life had been made comfortable but where it had also been frustrating to be separated from their friends and their home. Her presence on the ship, they said, made them feel closer to Egypt. She, in turn, told them about her activities with the IWSA, the EFU, the Arts Society about her projects for a pottery factory in Rod al-Farag and a carpet workshop at the EFU. There was indeed a revival in Egypt, she added, which had originated with its cultural awakening.

Saad had heard about Huda's criticism of his Wafdist colleagues. He was aware that Muhammad Tawfiq Nessim Pasha, Tharwat's successor as Prime Minister, had irked Huda when he gave in to the British Government's demand that the Egyptian monarch's constitutional title should now be 'King of Egypt' rather than 'King of Egypt and the Sudan'. Further demonstrations had resulted in the closure of Saad's house, the Bait al-Umma, which had become a focal point for the Wafd, and the arrest of several activists. What the Egyptian street wanted now was Saad Zaghlul in power at any price, irrespective of policies, and Saad seemed to think it was more important that he should take power than that he should stick to his principles, even if he had to accept the concessions that Nessim had made. Saad seemed unduly anxious about what had befallen his house, and also pumped Huda for information about what support he could expect from members of his party. Sensing a return of what she regarded as his egotistical approach, Huda reproached him for what she told him was his excessive concern for his own future. Zaghlul was annoyed by Huda's reproaches, and there began to be a difficult atmosphere between them. He spent the rest of the journey refusing to speak to her, and it was also evident that Safia was angry with her. Huda had misgivings at the time about what Safia's future reaction to this conversation might be, and it certainly led to cooler relations.

When they came within sight of the coast, many people came out in small boats to welcome Saad, calling out his name from below the ship. In his absence, he had become a legend. Ismail Abaza Pasha, who was on his deathbed, sent a telegram out to him, asking him to let bygones be bygones and to continue to serve his country as he had in the past. Saad ran to Safia, brandishing the telegram. Huda began to realise that she was correct to harbour misgivings about what his ambitions might be. She began to wonder how the 'Old Lion', as Zaghlul was known in some circles, had changed during his exile.[16]

After all the conversation there had been between Huda and Safia about the veil, Safia was wearing hers as always when she left the ship on 19 September. When Huda expressed her astonishment at this disregard for her husband's opinion, Safia responded, 'My husband is not working alone, and Wasif Ghali Pasha has told me that changing my headgear might have a negative impact on the crowd that has come to welcome us.'[17] Huda was perplexed by this sudden reversion to the veil, especially since it seemed to be based on the view of a Christian. She was saddened by the couple's coldness towards her as they departed from the ship.

Two months later, on 13 November, Huda would remember the chilly farewell Saad had given her aboard ship when he failed to invite her as chair of the Wafdist Women's Central Committee to the celebration of the Wafd's anniversary at the Casino Cyrus. Strangely, her name was published in the reports in the newspapers as one of the guests, as though she had been there. Adding insult to injury, Saad failed in his speech to mention the important part Ali had played in the Wafd. Huda published a statement making it clear that she had not been invited to the event, and had not attended it.

Later in November 1923, Huda and her colleagues published a statement listing the nine main principles of the EFU. Its goals would be to seek to elevate the intellectual and moral standards of Egyptian women; to enable them to obtain social, political, legal and moral equality with men; and to obtain the right to higher education for girls.

It would also seek a change in matrimonial customs to allow the two individuals directly concerned to meet each other before committing themselves, to alter the law on marriage to prohibit polygamy and divorce without the woman's consent, and to raise the age for marriage to sixteen. It would promote public health and hygiene in Egypt, and discourage immorality. Finally, it would seek to publicise these principles and to win public support. The principles reflected those previously formulated by Malak Hifni Nasif.

Meanwhile, the EFU continued to work towards the establishment for itself of a firm financial base. The committee invited influential and wealthy individuals who were sympathetic to its principles to become members of an honorary board of trustees. Income was to come from grants, individual contributions and members' subscriptions. The EFU's committee invited a large assembly of women to attend a meeting at the Egyptian University Hall to explain the IWSA's programme. The committee formulated two immediate practical proposals, which they asked the Government to incorporate forthwith into Egyptian law. One of these was the prohibition of marriage for girls under sixteen, the other was the institution of gender equality in all branches and at all levels of education.

A small EFU delegation was received by the Prime Minister, Yehia Ibrahim Pasha, who expressed admiration for the women's movement and promised that their demands would be given serious consideration by the Council of Ministers.[18] He was as good as his word, in fact, for five months later the law fixing a minimum marital age for girls was enacted. On 6 December 1923, fearing for the fate of their other demand, the Wafdist Women's Central Committee asked the Government to state explicitly what its legislative programme was to be, since the women feared disappointment. Change on the political front was imminent, however, and forestalled any response there might have been.

5

A Wafdist ministry

O
n 12 January 1924, the Wafd won a sweeping victory in elections held under Egypt's new electoral law, and on 28 January Saad Zaghlul's ambitions finally came to fruition when he became Prime Minister. There was at first some doubt, both within the Wafd and outside it, as to whether it would be appropriate for him to accept the post. It was argued that this would imply that he accepted the British declaration of 28 February 1923, with its reservations, which included restrictions on the freedom of any Egyptian Government and the effective sequestration of the Sudan from Egyptian control. As a nationalist, some contended, he should not place himself in this position. However, it was Zaghlul whom the people wanted, and both logic and emotion in the end dictated that he should lead the nation. He was also determined to take the position for which he had striven for so long. He promised to strive to work unstintingly to achieve the completion of Egypt's independence.

For the EFU, it was regrettable that Yehia Pasha, who had apparently been sympathetic, had stepped down as Prime Minister before implementation of the reforms the women had asked for. On the other hand, it seemed at first sight that reform would continue in any case.[1]

Zaghlul was after all an old friend of Qasim Amin, one of the first proponents of women's causes, and seemed certain to support any moves towards women's emancipation. In addition, his wife Safia was a doughty campaigner for the Wafd, and she and Huda knew each other well. The women were in the event to be sadly disappointed. First of all, Zaghlul issued a snub to the women's movement by failing to invite their representatives to attend the opening of parliament, though Huda and her associates had expected to be asked. The excuse that it would be inappropriate to have women in attendance would not wash, since the wives of ministers, officials and foreign diplomats were invited as a matter of etiquette. Then it also became clear that Zaghlul's inaugural address to the King and parliament would fail to address any of the women's concerns, despite Huda having felt sure that her long acquaintance with Zaghlul would lead him to listen to her representations. The harangue to which Huda had subjected him on the ship from Europe in September might have been unwise. The women were badly disappointed, and their anger began to swell. They had imagined, perhaps naively, that with the Wafd in power they would henceforth be regarded as half of the nation. This was evidently not yet to be so.

At the opening of parliament on 15 March, girls from the EFU's school and workshop, representing both the Wafdist Women's Central Committee and the EFU, protested outside the building with placards. These spelled out their demands, written in Arabic for the general public and in French for the benefit of foreign diplomats and the European press. Of these points, five were of a political nature, relating to Egypt's independence, its constitution and its territorial integrity. Nineteen concerned social affairs, and seven related to feminist issues. The social message focused on the implementation of existing constitutional guarantees, texts relating to the provision of free and compulsory education throughout the country and the legitimate right of every Egyptian to a secondary education. Feminist issues included a call for the prohibition of prostitution and a ban on primitive customs such as the *zar* ceremonies, in which women practised exorcism and healing through dancing, role-playing, animal sacrifice and the induction of trance states. They also asked for the establishment of dispensaries for the poor and the creation of public parks for children in urban areas.

On 31 March 1924, the women tried again to catch the Government's ear. The Wafdist Women's Central Committee met at the headquarters of the *New Woman* magazine and formulated amendments they wanted made to the inaugural address Zaghlul had delivered. These were sober demands, relating to issues of general political relevance rather than to specifically feminist concerns. They concentrated on four specific points which the women saw as crucial if the new Government was not to allow itself to be manipulated by the British. These were, first, that Zaghlul should have called for a clear definition of the frontiers of the Egyptian state and a stipulation that Egypt should never be separated from the Sudan. The second point was that Zaghlul should have given a guarantee of freedom of association to all Egyptians and ought also to have guaranteed the freedom of the press. Third, there should have been an explicit statement of Egypt's right to autonomy and self-rule within its frontiers, including Sudan. And fourth, there should have been a specific commitment to the strengthening of Egypt's armed forces as a guarantee of national security. These points were also spelled out in a message to the Government signed by Huda and her fellow activists. Huda herself seems at this stage to have taken up the cause of Egypt's unity with Sudan as an issue of particular concern.

While Huda was attempting to wrest concessions from Zaghlul through the intervention of the Wafdist Women's Central Committee, she was at the same time, as leader of the EFU, embarking on a programme of social activity of a very practical and down-to-earth-kind. This was centred on a clinic and dispensary that was named the Dar al-Islah, whose rented premises were in Yehia Ibn Zaid Street, in the district known as Sayida Zainab. The director of the clinic was Dr Sami Kamal Bey, and seven doctors volunteered to work there with him. The clinic continued its operations for many years. Many women and children were examined and treated free of charge. Even the medicines prescribed were paid for by the EFU. In addition, the basic principles of hygiene were taught to the poor.

Some time after setting up the clinic, Huda formed a squadron of young girls, as a kind of nimble army of volunteers to take welfare to the doors of the poor. Volunteers from amongst the EFU's younger members, known as the 'Cadettes', were trained in fieldwork and dispatched with soap, detergents and medicines to the more deprived districts of Cairo, where they offered help and advice. The girls would march out in twos carrying baskets filled with soap and cleaning products, as well as first-aid kits. The doctors trained them to give advice on health issues and suggest products that would help the poor to protect their health. The girls included Huda's two young cousins, Hawa and Huria, as well as several of the students Huda had earlier sent to study abroad on scholarships, including Amina and Karima al-Said and Suhair al-Qalamawi, in addition to Sherifa Lutfi, whose grandfather, Umar Lutfi, had been Sultan Pasha's closest friend.

Another of the Cadettes was Munira Asim, the daughter of Fatma Fahmi, who was named for her grandmother Munira Sabri, the cousin and protector of Huda's mother. She was a girl whom Huda had viewed as a possible wife for her son Muhammad, but the plan had not seemed destined to succeed, as the young people appeared not at all interested in each other. However, the two families had drawn closer since Huda had spoken out in support of the character of their murdered brother Ali Kamil Fahmi at the time of his death, for which Fatma and her sisters Aziza and Aisha were grateful. The Fahmi clan were therefore ready to add their very substantial resources to Huda's own by making large financial donations out of their immense family fortune for any projects that Huda deemed necessary for women's welfare and for the nation.

As well as their charitable work, the Cadettes also had fun, taking part in shows that were staged during the charity balls the EFU held to raise funds. The choreographer was generally Gabrielle D'Albret. The girls would appear, often in Pharaonic, Circassian or other attire to represent different ethnicities and civilisations. On one occasion, in a live representation of Mukhtar's *Egypt's Awakening*, Sherifa Lutfi was meant to personify the Egyptian *fellaha*, the peasant girl wearing a long dress and a veil who stands beside the sphinx in the sculpture. According to *L'Égyptienne*, she acted with consummate talent: 'Slowly, painfully,' said the magazine's report, 'she wakes up from her lethargic and centuries-old sleep.'[2] Mingling myth and politics, the tableaux the girls enacted were a plea for worldwide peace and understanding. In the interests of decorum, Huda never considered the possibility of taking part in the shows herself. Nevertheless, she would sometimes jestingly try on the costumes offstage or at home, and was photographed on different occasions as an imaginary Egyptian peasant girl, a Turkish princess, and once as a Dutch woman with two improbably dark-skinned children looking terribly uncomfortable in their Dutch costumes with bonnets and aprons. The same playful spirit possessed the girls. One day, Huria, who was playing the part of a page in a tableau entitled 'Shajarit al-Durr', after the eponymous Ayyubid queen, suddenly seized the costume destined for the queen and posed proudly, a feathered fan held high in her hand, with a great deal of panache, in front of the photographer. The sturdy little battalion of girls that visited poor households throughout the year relished their transformation for the charity balls into glamorous princesses and showgirls bedecked with jewels.

Amusement did not always prevail, however. Political developments meant that trouble was brewing for the Wafdist Women's Central Committee. The confrontation between the Committee and Zaghlul's Government led to a split within the women's ranks. Some found it hard to oppose Zaghlul's policies, as Huda wanted. One of Huda's faithful supporters, Sherifa Riad, had refused to sign the women's declaration critical of the Wafd. On 18 June 1924, Sherifa Riad resigned from the Committee because she found it impossible to cope with the clash between the women's movement under Huda's leadership and Zaghlul's

Wafd. Huda reluctantly accepted her resignation while expressing hope that she would resume her work later on. Sherifa's resignation was a blow to Huda, who nevertheless remained convinced that there was no alternative to what she saw as her constructive criticism of Zaghlul's Government. Many of the other Wafdist women were of Sherifa Riad's persuasion, however, and she set up an alternative group, which she called the Saadist Women's Committee.

Huda was appalled by Zaghlul's obstinate refusal to recognise the women's demands. His position was not untypical of his general attitude, however. At the age of 67, Zaghlul had become a charismatic leader with immense popularity, but also behaved virtually as a dictator. His majority in parliament was so overwhelming that he simply disregarded the opposition. The political situation in Egypt was extremely volatile. Disagreement on major political issues led to open rows between the Wafdists and the Liberal Constitutionalists. Zaghlul would bring law suits against political opponents and even opposition members of parliament, often for trivial reasons such as statements he regarded as libellous or articles in the press criticising his person. Any official who showed less than unbridled enthusiasm for his policies was simply dismissed. He put up with no criticism and accepted no amendment of his legislation.[3]

His weakness, however, was precisely what had been pointed out by those who doubted whether he should become Prime Minister. This was that despite his previous fierce nationalism, he had chosen to accept the highest office in the face of Britain's insistence on retaining the four issues it had specified as its own prerogative in Egypt, namely the privileged status of foreigners, British monopoly of defence control of communications and the status of Sudan. This laid him open to the charge of compromise. Unless he could resolve these issues, his position looked in the longer run likely to be open to challenge. He went to London at the end of September 1924 to hold talks with the British Prime Minister, Ramsay MacDonald, who was known to be sympathetic to Egypt, and whom he met at 10 Downing Street on 25 and 29 September and 3 October. His hope was to find a way of resolving the issue of the four reserved points.[4] When even these talks failed to provide a satisfactory solution, Zaghlul returned to Cairo, where he arrived on 20 October.

In September 1924, Huda was invited to travel to Graz, in Austria, to attend the sixth quinquennial meeting of the International Council of Women. The focus of the conference was to be child protection and the abolition of prostitution. The organiser was Dr Christina Bakker-Van Bosse, whom Huda had already met in Rome. Huda took the occasion to voice her criticisms of the social and legal situation in Egypt relating to marriage. She also took the opportunity to criticise the British occupation of Egypt, and for the first time made a major target of the so-called capitulatory laws. This was the system whereby foreigners resident in Egypt were subject to their own courts rather than to the Egyptian ones. She pointed out that there was a feminist issue involved. In this case, the capitulatory laws prevented the Egyptian Government from taking effective action against brothels, most of which were owned by foreigners. She called upon the conference to ask foreign governments to forgo their capitulatory rights in Egypt.

The capitulatory laws in due course were to become a source of great concern to the Egyptian nationalists, and indeed to all patriots. Originally, they were based on a concept enshrined in treaties signed by the Ottoman Empire with European powers, whereby Western nationals were not subject to local law. Such arrangements were cancelled elsewhere in the former Ottoman territories under the treaty of Lausanne in 1923. Special capitulatory agreements had been made with Egypt in the nineteenth century, due to its administrative autonomy within the Ottoman Empire, and their continuation in Egypt was anomalous. Even though Egypt's independence had been recognised in 1923, the country was still to a great extent under the control of the British Government, which did not intend to abandon the protection enjoyed by its subjects, and consequently by the subjects of other Western nations. The principle that the capitulatory laws should be abolished was not eventually to be recognised until 1937, with the treaty of Montreux, and they lingered in practice through an agreed transition period as late as 1949.

The visit to Graz also stirred deeply buried emotions in Huda's heart. This was of course where her father, Sultan Pasha, had died. At the margins of the conference, she was able to find time to enquire about his last days there. She visited the Elephant Hotel, where he spent his final weeks, and met the hotel's doctor, who still had access to the records from 1884 and was able to provide her with some information. At least she was able to lay to rest a story that had been put into circulation by Qallini Fahmi Pasha, her father's secretary, that he might have been poisoned by agents of the Khedive or by some other enemy. There had in fact been an autopsy, whose results were still on file forty years later, which showed that there were no traces of poison in his body. She was sad, however, to think of her father's lonely death in Graz, and her research put her in a philosophical mood. Had her priorities been correct? Iqbal had also died in her absence, while she was in Europe. Should she not have been with her parents when they were in their last days? Had she failed to observe her duty towards them? These thoughts filled her with sadness, and she was still upset and emotional when she sailed back to Egypt at the end of September 1924.

After her return from Austria, Huda decided that a carefully judged and non-violent reaction was called for in response to the restrictions on Egypt's freedom still imposed by Britain. She was influenced by events in India, where Gandhi had become leader of the Indian National Congress in 1921 and had proceeded to launch a non-violent campaign against the British with the goal of achieving self-rule for India. On 30 October 1924, she invited a group of women to 2 Qasr al-Nil Street to hold a meeting to discuss the idea of forming a committee to organise a boycott of British merchandise, following Gandhi's model. In a follow-up meeting, the committee addressed a message to the entire population of Egypt, appealing to them, as they put it, to 'boycott British banks, insurance companies, means of transportation, and merchandise and to promote Egyptian products'.[5]

They urged the people of Egypt to stop dealing with British shops and British firms. Passive resistance was a technique that had already gained favour around the world, especially with women. Huda's hope was that such a boycott would reinforce Zaghlul's position in his continuing negotiations with Britain. She sent him a telegram in which she urged him to dig in his heels against compromise.

The boycott committee enjoyed a wave of public support.[6] The women did what they could to urge the people to maintain their backing for the scheme:

> Sons of Egypt, you have no arms to fight with, no fleet to cross the seas, no power to stand against their might. But you do have a more efficient weapon in your hands, and one that is more far reaching than guns…abstain from supporting the British in all their economic, commercial and industrial activities. Stop buying their products, do not rent their farming lands, do not rent them your houses, do not invest money in their banks, and be resolute in doing all this, upon your lives and your honour.[7]

On the other hand, the idea of a boycott did not enjoy universal support. On 3 November 1924, a letter was published in *La Bourse Égyptienne* which attacked the boycott and subjected Huda to personal ridicule:

> Mrs Shaarawi Pasha, is appealing to her compatriots' patriotism to stop them purchasing British handkerchiefs, British tablecloths, British underwear, or collars, or ties, or British pyjamas, or indeed anything British at all. One really wonders in what dreamland Mrs Huda Shaarawi lives, as she is obviously unacquainted with Egypt. If she lived amongst us, she would in fact know that her compatriots have no use for knives, glasses, forks, tablecloths or napkins, mattresses, or anything resembling all these objects. For some ten thousand years, perhaps even a hundred thousand, they have done without them. A jug of water, a pot of beans, and the loaf of flat bread that they use as table, plate, tablecloth and napkin as well as food: these are what is needed to satisfy the hunger of twelve million Egyptians. The boycott may in fact lead only to inflation and more poverty in Egypt.

Huda was outraged by this article, which she thought was not only ridiculous but also defamatory. Fortunately, she did not succumb to the litigious urge that had overcome Zaghlul. The women went on with their campaign. On 10 November 1924, an English translation of the committee's resolutions was conveyed to Lord Allenby.

Huda's feelings about Zaghlul were by now deeply ambiguous. Despite her support for the Wafd, she began to feel that the Saad Zaghlul, in whom she had so earnestly believed in the past, despite his disagreements with her husband Ali Shaarawi, seemed to be failing Egypt. He appeared to be weakening in his confrontation against the British but determined to hold on to office. Then events took a hand. On 19 November 1924 Sir Lee Stack, the Military Governor General of the Anglo-Egyptian Sudan, known as the 'Sirdar', was murdered. He was gunned down in his car by a number of assailants as he drove across Cairo. The British immediately laid the blame at Zaghlul's door, despite his immediate expression of horror at the incident. After the shooting, the Sirdar was taken to Allenby's house nearby, where he survived for two whole days before dying from his wounds. This hardened Allenby's personal determination not only to punish the murderers but also to hold the whole country to account. Zaghlul, meanwhile, was by now so self-obsessed that he believed his political career was the real target of this assassination. 'The bullet that took his life was not aimed at his chest,' he deplored, speaking about Sir Lee Stack, 'but rather at mine.'[8] Huda was not the only observer to be shocked by this statement. How could anyone be so egotistical?

On 22 November, Allenby went to the Prime Minister's office, with a heavy military escort, to hand Zaghlul the ultimatum which constituted Britain's response to the incident. The British demanded a formal apology and a commitment to track down the miscreants, as well as an indemnity of half a million pounds and a ban on political demonstrations. However, the British also took the opportunity to press forward other demands unrelated to the murder itself, including the withdrawal of all Egyptian troops from Sudan. Huda, in common with all concerned Egyptians, was passionately concerned.

Zaghlul seemed to have despaired of finding a way out of the crisis. To his fellow parliamentarians, he addressed a rhetorical question to those who had criticised his response to the British as inadequate: 'If you have the ability to impede or the power to obstruct the British, and to oblige them to restore the Sudan to Egypt, please let me know about it.'[9]

His apparent admission that there was no point in struggling against the British belied the brave declarations he had made during his electoral campaign. Huda implored Zaghlul not to despair, and to keep up his pressure against the British, arguing that he alone could keep Egypt afloat. She sent a message to the Cairo press, which was published in the major newspapers, whose text she also sent to many high officials, as well as to organisations and individuals abroad:

> In the name of humanity, Egypt, which is isolated and disarmed, places itself in the hands of the great powers and the League of Nations, the champions of justice, to be protected and defended by them. Let the help we demand come quickly, before the total destruction of our country which was for many centuries the cradle of the world's civilisation and still is the link between the East and the West. By safeguarding Egypt's interests and helping her to live, you will safeguard the interest of the whole world, an interest which includes that of every nation… There can be no greater danger for Egypt than a man who openly admits that he cannot fulfil the promises he made before coming to power.[10]

On 23 November, the Egyptian Minister for Foreign Affairs, Wasif Ghali Pasha, delivered Egypt's response to the British ultimatum. Zaghlul's Government said all efforts would be made to find the murderers, and the indemnity would be paid as a mark of its sorrow and regret. Otherwise, Egypt rejected the British demands. Allenby then took steps to implement the measures Britain had called for by force, occupying the Alexandria customs house and instructing British troops in Sudan to expel the Egyptian forces. Huda concluded this was the end of the line for Zaghlul, and wrote an open letter asking him to step down, which was published in the principal Egyptian newspapers. She was well aware that the strong terms in which she couched this letter were liable to cause Zaghlul offence:

> The country does not want to let you go. It made you its leader in the hope that you would keep your promise of achieving the total independence of both Egypt and the Sudan. However, the longer you stay in power, the greater is the distance between the reality of what is happening in this nation

and what you promised. Your policies have culminated in the separation of Egypt and the Sudan, and the expulsion of the Egyptians from the Sudan, and an even greater level of British interference in Egypt's internal affairs. In the light of your failure as a statesman, I am urging you, not to become an obstacle yourself. Instead, you should rid us of the embarrassment to which we have been subjected by stepping down from your position. There is no other acceptable way at this difficult time.[11]

Many made similar criticisms. Zaghlul knew he was defeated and could not expect to carry on, though his popularity among the Egyptian common people remained undiminished. On 24 November, he offered his resignation to King Fuad, who accepted it. Huda then resigned from the Wafdist Women's Central Committee, of which Sherifa Riad now took the chair. Huda's formal association with the Wafd, which had endured for more than two years after Ali's death, was at an end.

From this point on, Huda dedicated herself wholeheartedly to the EFU, concentrating more on feminist issues and less on Egyptian politics, though she did not lose sight of Egyptian political issues. She decided that it was crucial to publicise the EFU's activities, and initiated a practice that she maintained throughout her life of sending emissaries abroad to wherever their presence might be needed to defend the cause. Her own personal and feminist connections would of course always be useful, but she also used other young Egyptian women to speak on her behalf.

For example, on 1 December 1924, Nadjia Rashid delivered a lecture in Istanbul entitled 'The sources of Egyptian feminism and the struggle for independence and prosperity'. The lecture was well received, and the success of the initiative reinforced the argument that publicity would help to promote the women's ideas at home and in the world at large. Rashid went on to Vienna to deliver her lecture again on 5 December 1924. Later, there were other similar activities abroad that were helpful to her. On 21 February 1925, Magd al-Din Hifni Nasif gave a talk in Paris, under the sponsorship of Maria Verone, and in February 1925, Ihsan Ahmad made a presentation at the American University of Beirut (AUB), where she had gone to attend courses.[12]

Late 1924 saw the arrival of Valentine de Saint-Point, a notorious and somewhat eccentric French woman who introduced herself to Huda. Born in 1875, her name at birth was Anna Jeanne Valentine Marianne Desglans de Cessiat-Vercell. She was the great grand-niece of the poet Alphonse de Lamartine, and the name Saint-Point was that of Lamartine's chateau. Valentine had been a writer and journalist in France, where she was divorced at the age of 49. She had married a rising French politician named Charles Dumont and contrived to meet many politicians, artists and writers who frequented her salon. She was divorced from Dumont in 1904, then became a writer and journalist, and led an adventurous life. Before travelling to Egypt, she had lived with the Italian poet Riciotto Canudo and his wife in a *ménage à trois* and had posed nude for a variety of artists. She had also been a friend of Marinetti and the Italian Futurists, and had helped publicise their ideas in France. Valentine had also been a dancer and had performed Futurist dances during her Marinetti period. After the end of the War in 1918, she had toured Europe with dances intended to convey the failure of Western materialism, as opposed to the rebirth of the East and Eastern spirituality. Her costumes and dance steps were calculated to convey her message.[13] She went to Egypt after Canudo's death, and decided to meet Huda, who was amazed when she found out that she was well versed in Islam and had become a Sufi, having converted to Islam after meeting René Guénon.

Valentine arrived in Egypt with a collaborator, Vivian Postel du-Mas and with Jeanne Canudo, the wife of her former lover, who had died the previous year. Valentine knew of Huda's activities, and was aware of her wealth. She had a proposal to make to her, namely that Huda should finance a French-language magazine that would serve as a link and a messenger of goodwill between the East and the West. For Huda, the attraction was that such a publication could be used to help convince the world that Egypt was ready for independence and needed no foreign protection. Huda said she was interested in Valentine's proposal in principle, though the collaboration was never in the event destined to take place in the way Valentine had hoped.

Zaghlul's fall from power, together with the renewed hard line taken by the British, greatly saddened Huda and her colleagues. Kawkab Hifni Nasif, the Bahitha's sister, who had been sent by Huda on a scholarship to study medicine in England, wrote Huda a letter when she heard the news that expressed well the disappointment felt by most Egyptians. Politicians, she said, were now interested only in saving their own skins. Kawkab had the same scathing sense of humour as her brother Magd al-Din. Despite her very young age, she was capable of seeing politicians for what they were, and she did not hide her disdain for men who were weak. She was regretful that her youth and lack of influence prevented her from helping Huda in her struggle for Egypt as much as she would have wished. She referred to Huda as the head and protector of what she called the family of women. She added that she and her fellow medical students were working very hard at their studies in order to fulfil their country's expectations, but that they should rather have been studying psychiatry so as to treat the mental diseases of Egypt's male politicians. Then, on a personal note, she congratulated Huda on the birth of Bassna's first child, Ali, adding whimsically that she hoped he would not walk too quickly so that he would not have to participate in any riots at his young age.[14]

In these unusual constitutional circumstances, Zaghlul's successor as Prime Minister was Ahmad Ziwar Pasha, a member of the Turco-Circassian elite trusted by the King who had hitherto been the president of the senate. Appointed by King Fuad, in defiance of the democratic constitution brought in the previous year, Ziwar took office the moment Zaghlul's resignation took effect on 24 November 1924. Ziwar's task was quite simply to placate the British by agreeing to the terms of the ultimatum. On 28 November, the women's boycott committee held a further meeting to denounce the British demands, condemning the policies of the British and Egyptian Governments. Meanwhile, the deputy chief of the royal cabinet, Nashat Pasha, was busy recruiting members of Egypt's political class to a new political party to be known as the Ittihad (Union) party, which would represent the King's interests.

Allenby's resignation was announced on 20 May, and he was replaced by a former diplomat and ex-Governor of Bombay, Sir George Lloyd, who was elevated to the British peerage as Lord Lloyd, and took over on 21 October. When Lloyd later wrote his history of the period, he was quite candid, commenting that, 'Ziwar Pasha, alike by his courage and his unswerving loyalty to both King Fuad and the British connexion, had put us under an obligation which I was quite clear must be honoured at all costs.'[15]

On the other hand, an important element of British policy continued to be to placate Egyptian public opinion by restoring the country's democratic political life, and further elections were held on 12 March. Zaghlul's support in the country had not diminished, and once more, therefore, the Wafd won a convincing majority in parliament, despite all efforts to obstruct its electoral victory. Ziwar resigned on 13 March. Despite the renewal of Zaghlul's electoral mandate, however, Ziwar was instructed by the King to form a new Government. The new parliament was installed on 23 March, but to the horror of the authorities, with the Wafd once more having a majority of members of the chamber, Zaghlul was elected speaker of parliament by his colleagues. The King dissolved parliament later that same day, and Ziwar continued to govern without a parliament. Ziwar was now also asked to reform the electoral law to ensure future victory for the newly formed Ittihad party, which the British hoped would get rid of Zaghlul once and for all.

For Zaghlul, however, if Egypt could not be governed by the Wafd, nothing else would do. He knew he had the backing of the people, and his inclination was to withdraw from politics in order to create chaos, since no other government could ever enjoy real popular support. Zaghlul's supporters did not want to see him drop out of politics, however. He was urged on all sides to create a coalition of the three major parties, the Wafd, the Liberal Constitutionalists and the Nationalists, in order to counter the Ittihad. He refused, insisting that the other parties had to submit entirely to his leadership and merge themselves into the Wafd if they wished to enter a coalition. Huda discussed the situation with the

Liberal Constitutionalists she knew, all old friends of Ali, who included Muhammad Haikal, Lutfi al-Sayed, Abd al-Aziz Fahmi and Ali Alluba, whom she found were in general agreement that the time had come for all to work shoulder to shoulder with Zaghlul for the country's sake.

Huda was carried away once more by her patriotic enthusiasm, and she felt under an obligation to do what she could to bring this about. She felt that she could perhaps capitalise on her longstanding acquaintance with Zaghlul despite her recent disagreements with him. If more people tried to convince the leader to cooperate, she thought, a coalition government could perhaps be constructed. She decided to approach Zaghlul herself, to try to persuade him to cooperate with the other nationalist parties in a coalition that might have a chance of saving the situation, sending him a letter asking for a meeting to discuss the idea. At the personal level, she was ready on her side to be reconciled with him, whatever had passed between them. He was, after all, an old friend. She told him she would welcome a visit from him at her home.

Zaghlul did not reject her overture. He was not in good health, however, and indicated he would prefer to meet at his house. On 5 April 1925, the meeting took place, and Huda tells the story of her encounter in her memoirs.[16] She was met at the door of the harem by a European housekeeper. She expressed her surprise not to see Safia, and the housekeeper offered a vague apology. She then explained that the Pasha had not been feeling well and was unable to walk down the staircase. Would the lady mind going upstairs to visit him? Huda silently acquiesced, and followed her upstairs. She found Saad seated in an armchair. He struggled out of it and apologised for the inconvenience. He had suffered from bronchitis during the winter, and his chest had been affected. She suddenly remembered how old he was. Born in 1857, he was as old as Ali had been at his death. Inevitably the thought crossed her mind: was he about to die? She felt a gush of sympathy towards him, and wished him better health.

Then she came straight to the point, asking Saad whether or not he accepted the principle of unity with other parties. Saad insisted that such matters were not as simple as she thought. 'Nobody desires unity more than I do,' he said. 'However, I wish to know with whom this unity is meant to be. What is the basis, the purpose of such unity? Am I to join forces with those who destroyed the Constitution?' Huda continued to insist, telling Saad that he must unite with his erstwhile opponents to save the country. Under pressure, Saad lost his temper and chided her for the embarrassments she had caused him with her campaigns and her letters to the press. If her friends desired Egypt's independence, he wanted to know, why did they not join the Wafd? She told him that the goal of each of the parties was in its own way to achieve Egypt's independence, a policy which was not the monopoly of the Wafd. The conversation continued for three hours. Finally, Huda decided to leave when she could not agree with him; she could not accept the concentration of political power that he wanted to impose. He asked why she would not work with him on his terms, and at the very last, he appeared to utter what almost seemed a threat. 'You'll see what happens to you in the future,' he said. As she left his house for the last time, Huda spoke to him firmly: 'I am not afraid, Saad. The only thing I know for sure is that I am working to serve my country. You cannot reach me. And should you send the Wafd's ruffians to cast stones at my house, or even to kill me, do it – this is the least I could do for my country.'

In the end, Zaghlul was to join forces with the Liberal Constitutionalists and the Nationalists into a coalition of the three major parties, just as Huda had suggested. Their common goal was to obtain independence from British rule by demonstrating the effectiveness of Egyptian self-rule.

6

A lesson in diplomacy

The key development for Huda in 1925 was the foundation of the magazine *L'Égyptienne*, the new French-language magazine of the EFU, which gave her a platform for the publication of her political views on feminist and other subjects. The establishment of workshops and factories was on her mind. Huda had long been aware that a problem for Egypt was the stagnation of small industry. Lord Cromer had actively discouraged industry in Egypt for the same reasons that the British administration had not encouraged local industry in India, that is to say because it would be better for Britain to preserve Egypt as a market for textiles manufactured in Britain than to promote indigenous activity. Local small-scale industry was to a great extent in the hands of foreigners rather than Egyptians, and the enterprise of Egyptians themselves was in no way fostered.[1] Huda believed that small-scale industry desperately needed to be encouraged to take root in Egypt. Similarly, the nationalist Mustapha Kamil had pointed out that under Cromer there was more order and less activity in Egypt. Long ago, he had said in a speech that the British had sought to limit the activity of Egyptians by actually closing down schools.[2] Huda was deeply committed to the encouragement of education.

In 1925, after her foray into politics, Huda was occupied for the most part by the business of the EFU, which was to occupy her for the rest of her life, together with her international feminist activities, as well as keeping a more distant eye on the cultural societies and charitable works she had helped found. With increasing responsibility for administration piling in upon her, Huda began to realise that she had a gift for delegating power to others. Whatever she chose to do, people would seemingly volunteer to support her. Her personal magnetism and charismatic influence ensured she found virtually unlimited assistance. At the same time, her salon continued to enable her to make contact with those who had ideas to express or social or artistic projects to implement. Egypt was being transformed by its foreign and native investors into an affluent society, and Egyptians were at last being trained to replace foreigners at all levels. When Huda set up the new health department of the EFU, she found it possible to substitute Egyptian doctors for the foreign ones and all the distinguished volunteers who made up the medical staff at the Mabarrat, whose help had been invaluable at an earlier stage. Egyptian women were appointed to head the EFU's girls' school and the workshop and handicrafts centre created to teach household management and give courses in embroidery and dressmaking for young girls.

Other plans were afoot. Huda's new scheme for cooperative craft workshops and their linked emporium was consciously modelled on ventures that had been successfully started in India. She invited James Alfred Coulon, a French artist who was a member of the Friends of Art association and would be associated with *L'Égyptienne*, to construct and manage on her behalf a factory for pottery and ceramics which would be her third vocational school, after the workshops for embroidery and carpet weaving that already existed within the EFU. This would be called the al-Huda factory. She conceived the plan partly after having met a gifted Egyptian potter, Ahmad Muhammad Nasir. The plant was to be sited in Rod al-Farag, a new industrial district near Shubra, close to the Nile. On the practical side, its profits would be used to fund new schools and other charities. Coulon designed original pottery that would later be exhibited both in Egypt and abroad. Huda's notion of producing pottery and oriental carpets at the EFU's workshops was part of an overall conception she had of putting back together the pieces of a country that had been cruelly torn apart by colonialism. She conceived of herself as a kind of craftswoman, weaving on her own loom part of the fabric of a liberated society that was preparing for self-rule.

On the personal front, in early 1925 Huda was expecting a visit from her old friend Attia, who still lived in Singapore with her husband, Umar al-Saqqaf. Huda was thrilled to see Attia again. She needed a listening ear, and Attia had always been ready to hear her confidences. Bassna, meanwhile, who now had two children, was at last on the point of leaving England for the United States, where the Egyptian Foreign Ministry was now ready to send Mahmud Sami Pasha to take up his post as Egyptian Ambassador in Washington DC.[3] The couple were to sail on the SS *Majestic* in June 1925. Bassna's letters were as loving and soothing as ever, but Huda pined for her daughter's presence. Bassna, always affectionate to her mother, expressed her love in a letter written on board ship: 'I think of you while eating, while sleeping, everywhere. I cannot get used to the idea of being so far from you my dear.'[4] Mahmud Sami officially became Egypt's Ambassador to the United States on 16 July 1925.

Another project in which Huda became involved in 1925 was the access of women to university education. In 1925, Cairo University, hitherto a private institution whose degrees had not been recognised by the state, was taken under state control and renamed King Fuad I University. However, it also fell under British influence. British teachers were imported, living on princely salaries and underemployed. Courses were no longer taught in Arabic, and free education was suppressed.[5] Nevertheless, Huda believed, reform was not impossible, if undertaken gradually and fearlessly. Ahmad Lutfi al-Sayid, in his newspaper, *Al-Jarida*, had for some time been advocating university education for women. When Lutfi al-Sayid became the rector of Cairo University in

1925, his plan was to begin to admit women as soon as possible. He was seeking suitable students, and approached Huda for her help. Huda gave him a list of names. In the event, women were not to be admitted until 1929, when Suhair al-Qalamawi and several others were admitted by Taha Husain to the faculty of arts, although the head of the faculty of science still refused to accept women. Husain, though he was himself a graduate of the Islamic university of al-Azhar, believed that secular education would benefit the young people of Egypt more than religious education, and that it would be a means to promote a sense of unity in the multi-confessional society that existed in Egypt. After the admission of women to the faculty of arts, it subsequently became easier for them to enrol in the other faculties.

In February 1925, the first issue of *L'Égyptienne* was published. Huda threw herself heart and soul into the project. Valentine de Saint-Point made a bid to become editor, but Huda was not persuaded, even though, ironically, it may have been Valentine's suggestion of a French language magazine that had sowed the seed for Huda's own project. Céza Nabarawi was absolutely determined to take the position herself, which she did. Céza argued forcefully that there was no need for a foreigner to take on the job since she, an Egyptian and Huda's lifelong friend, was fully capable of doing it. She saw no reason why Valentine, whom she saw as an interloper, should be appointed. Valentine abandoned her hope of being editor of *L'Égyptienne* when Céza put her foot down, virtually obliging Huda to appoint her to the post. Céza edited *L'Égyptienne* from the outset, and the magazine's quality and its success were an ample justification of her determination.

Céza was to be the editor of *L'Égyptienne* for the whole 15 years of its publication, and it brought her extremely close to Huda. She went daily to 2 Qasr al-Nil Street, which was always cited as the place of publication of the magazine, and passed her time there close to Huda, from morning till night, until the date of her betrothal and marriage in 1937. The first issue had on its cover a representation of an Egyptian woman in the act of removing a veil strongly reminiscent of the female figure in Mukhtar's famous sculpture. The cover price was five piastres, not cheap but yet not vastly expensive. It was printed at Éditions Paul Barbey, managed by the eponymous publisher-printer, who went on publishing the magazine to the last year of its publication. The magazine was never a source of profit, and Huda effectively subsidised it throughout its run.

Several women's magazines were published in Egypt by 1925, some before L'Égyptienne and others later, although sadly Balsam Abd al-Malik's Al-Mar'a Al-Misria had already closed. A young feminist activist from Alexandria, Munira Thabit, had recently begun to publish magazines in two languages, Al-Amal in Arabic and L'Espoir in French, both names meaning 'hope'. There was also Fatma al-Yusuf's famous magazine Rose al-Yusuf, which first appeared in 1925, as well as Adab Al-Fatat, which was published in Fayum by Victoria Megalli. Finally, later in the year, Valentine de Saint-Point finally began to publish the magazine that she had come to Egypt to create. She called it Le Phénix, and it was intended to increase awareness of the oriental renaissance in the West. This marked the end of Céza's irritation at the mention of Valentine de Saint-Point, since it meant that the latter had given up all claims to L'Égyptienne. Both Valentine and Munira Thabit were in fact offered congratulations in L'Égyptienne for their tireless efforts. Céza even went as far as affirming that Valentine was the best contemporary advocate of oriental values in the West and that Munira, who was a hard worker, was a demonstration that women were capable of thinking clearly and feeling strongly.

The brief of L'Égyptienne was to inform its readers about issues of the present day, as well as presenting a vista of the future for modern Egypt, in addition to reminding them of the glories of the Egyptian past. In the first issue, Huda wrote an article that she entitled 'Yesterday and today', reflecting on the vicissitudes of Egyptian politics. She aimed her attack at

> the blind and exaggerated confidence placed in leaders who have not shouldered their responsibilities – such as the division of the parties, which

was the consequence of the ambition of these leaders. This should not discourage us, however, because although we might disagree between us about the capabilities of our leaders, we are all united against the enemy in our struggle to realise our sacred goal: the integral independence of the Nile Valley.[6]

Against the background of a turbulent Egyptian political scene in 1924 and 1925, in fact since the murder of the Sirdar, Huda, in the tradition of the suffragettes, had become very conscious that the media were a formidable political weapon. Through the medium of *L'Égyptienne* she launched a further appeal to the world against Britain's domination over Egypt, which the British seemed to wish to clamp down with renewed vigour. This appeal very quickly elicited responses from the group abroad who called themselves Friends of Egypt, many of whom were women and members of the IWSA. There was also a feminist movement in France which was conscious of Egypt's situation. Juliette Adam denounced the injustice of the British ultimatum to Egypt and the threat that a British administration of the Sudan would represent for Egypt and for the whole world: 'England in the Sudan, England taking possession of the sources of the Nile, how anguishing for all Egyptians to see the waters of the Nile, of their Nile, traded, measured, perhaps even suppressed by the threatening will...'[7]

Juliette gave her full support to Huda. In 1925, *L'Égyptienne* was able to publish several of her articles in which she lauded Egypt's resistance against the British occupation and condemned the stubborn British insistence on implementing the sanctions contained in the ultimatum. In addition, Juliette passed on to Huda three letters that had been sent to her by three remarkable Englishmen, in which their own Government was heavily criticised for its policies in Egypt.[8] The three letters were from Charles G. Gordon Pasha (24 January 1880), Edward St John Fairman (15 June 1893) and Wilfrid Scawen Blunt (13 October 1906). These three men, who were already notorious for their interventions in the political life of the region, condemned in clear terms the policies of the British Government in Egypt. Gordon, who later lost his life in Sudan, noted in his letter that he had been forbidden by his Ambassador to meet Juliette or to discuss political matters with her. Fairman said that he had returned from Egypt to England because he could not bear to witness what his Government was doing to the country. Blunt, a stubborn supporter of both Egyptian and Irish nationalists against British occupation, spoke eloquently about his belief in the national movement in Egypt. An article by Juliette herself, entitled 'A lesson in diplomacy', which exhorted France not to support the British cause, was reprinted as a pamphlet and widely circulated in and outside Egypt.[9] She insisted that the Suez Canal was an integral part of Egypt's territory, and that it must be kept neutral under Egyptian protection, as stipulated in the treaties signed in the past with the Khedive.[10]

Maria Vérone, meanwhile, the President of the French League for Women's Rights published an article which deplored Britain's virtual annexation of Sudan and paid tribute to the Egyptian women who had, under Huda's leadership, boycotted British goods. Avril de Sainte Croix, the President of the National Council of French Women, and Jehan d'Ivray, a French writer on Egypt, also sent letters condemning British threats and supporting Egyptian and Sudanese independence. The French Human Rights League held a meeting in Paris, arguing the case that either the dispute between Britain and Egypt should go before the International Court at the Hague or it should be raised at the League of Nations.[11] Dr Aletta Jacobs, the President and founder of the Dutch branch of the Women's International League for Peace and Freedom, also proclaimed her support for Egypt. In Britain, the British chapter of the International Feminist Union also voiced a protest against their own Government's decision, and called for negotiations. The British women expressed the view that Britain should have sought a mandate from the League of Nations if they wished to rule the Sudan, and that Egypt should also become a member state of the League. Margery Corbett-Ashby, the new President of the IWSA, who took over after the congress Huda had attended in 1923 in Rome, was quickly seen by Huda as a precious friend whose help could be critical. Huda was gratified by the response to her appeal to world opinion. The encouragement and moral support she received gave her hope that Egypt's political problem might some day find a satisfactory solution.

As to Céza, she was full of energy during her first year as editor of *L'Égyptienne*. She travelled to widen her experience, coincidentally sailing to Turkey on the same boat as the great Egyptian poet Ahmad Shawqi. Shawqi had been court poet to Khedive Abbas II, and still spent the summer at Çubuklu, near Istanbul, where Abbas II had built a summer palace perched on a hill. In a letter home, Céza described Shawqi, the 'Prince of Poets' as he was known, as 'very eccentric'. Wahib Bey Doss, the father of a minister in the Government, was also on the ship. Céza took the opportunity to discuss with him a questionnaire on illegitimacy that she planned to feature in the magazine. Céza throve on journalism, and was becoming a clear-minded woman who knew what she wanted from life. On this trip, she stopped over in Beirut and Damascus, then called on Wajida and Ihap Khulusi in Istanbul, and afterwards visited a Turkish association, La Goutte de Lait, begun by a French charity and now run by Turkish women, whose purpose was to supply milk to the children of a poor quarter. The aim was to look at the possibility of creating a similar association in Egypt, or of integrating such a plan into the programme of the Dar al-Islahi dispensary that the EFU had already set up in Cairo.

In the early summer of 1925, Huda wrote three articles for *L'Égyptienne* that were published in the May, June and July issues, in which she spelt out the issues that were her main concerns at the time. The May article, on the Government's budgetary proposals, was a serious attack on the Ziwar Government, which had been obliged to agree to spend a million pounds of Egypt's money to finance the Sudanese army, despite the fact that Egypt had been made to renounce all its claims to the Sudan. She deplored the Government's acquiescence in what she saw as a shameful measure, spending Egypt's funds on the upkeep of a piece of Egyptian territory that had in effect been stolen from Egypt by the British.[12] In the June article, she denounced the boundary agreement that effectively ceded the Jaghbub oasis to the Italian colonial regime in Libya. 'Ever generous with other people's property,' she wrote, 'England has taken the liberty of granting Italy Egyptian territory it was supposed to protect.'[13] In the July article, she also returned to her demand for the abrogation of the capitulations, that allowed for certain foreign citizens freedom from Egyptian law.

This article clearly shows the influence over her of Muhammad Husain Haikal. He was a man whom she greatly admired, and who was an adviser to the EFU and a family friend. He regularly expressed his own views in his periodical *Al-Siyasa*. Huda had come to believe in a democracy guided by a sophisticated elite of educated citizens, in which culture would be a civilising medium, and where a group of highly informed and expert people, men and women, would direct the country's policy on the basis of constant consultation and discussion. She always strove herself, within her feminine world, to apply these standards in her dealings with her partners and assistants, listening to every person's views. Her privileged financial situation had placed her at the head of the movement, but she allowed each person who worked with her to be responsible for their own activities, as long as they remained on a constructive path. All those who worked with her attended her Tuesday evening salon. Haikal, Lutfi Al-Sayid, Muhammad Alluba, Hafiz Afifi and other Liberal Constitutionalists who advised the EFU also regularly came. Their wives were for the most part already Huda's friends and collaborators. The EFU also relied on many other advisers, such as Shaikh Mustapha Abd al-Raziq, Murad Sid Ahmad, Taha Husain, Antun al-Jamil, Ahmad Fahmi al-Amrusi, Mansur Fahmi, Habib al-Masri, who were all of them high officials in the Egyptian Government at different moments and in different capacities. They served in other functions related to education, journalism and even *waqf*, and taxation. The artists and painters who made up the Friends of Art were also part of the Tuesday circle. As well as her friend Mukhtar, they included the set from La Chimère, an association of artists and intellectuals, Ragheb

Ayad, the Turkish painter Hidayat Dac, Mahmud Said and many others. Foreign artists also came. Journalists and writers sympathetic to her ideas were often there. Finally, there was of course the family, including Muhammad, and Bassna when she was in Cairo, and the rest of the household, especially Hawa, Huria and Céza.

In early 1925, Carrie Chapman Catt invited her to visit the United States. In July 1925, Huda set off on a trip with her son Muhammad which was to take her first to Karlsbad, where they would relax for a while at the spa, thence to Paris, and finally to the United States. Céza was to accompany her as her secretary, for which she received a salary. Once in America, the plan was to make contact with the women's groups in New York and then to visit Huda's daughter Bassna and her husband Mahmud Sami at the Egyptian Embassy in Washington, where Mahmud Sami had by now become highly respected. Bassna always sent very affectionate letters from Washington, and Huda longed to see her again and to give her all the love and support she could, despite the distance that kept them apart. Everything was in order in Egypt as far as Huda could see. James Coulon would take care of the Rod al-Farag factory, while Jeanne Marquès was persuaded to take charge of the magazine, about which she had at first been apprehensive. She promised to shoulder full responsibility for four months, and undertook to write up to three articles every month during Céza's absence.

In France, Huda met many people and travelled widely. She saw all her old friends, including Juliette Adam, the Great Dowager Duchess of Uzès, Maria Vérone, Francine Daurat, Odette Simon and a few others. Magd al-Din Hifni Nasif, as the President of the Association of Egyptian Students in Paris, held a reception in her honour at the Hotel Lutétia on Boulevard Raspail. The Egyptian ambassador, Fakhri Pasha, was on leave of absence but the Chargé, Niazi Bey and the Consul, Dr Abd al-Salam al-Guindi Bey came in his place. Even the Egyptian Embassy's Imam attended the party, which opened in great pomp under a portrait of King Fuad, framed by flags. The Egyptian royal anthem was played, followed by the *Marseillaise*. The French Prime Minister, Paul Painlevé, was among the guests, as well as three former French Prime Ministers, Édouard Herriot, Raymond Poincaré and Aristide Briand. A senior member of the Egyptian royal family, Prince Muhammad Ali, was present, with other Egyptian members of high society as well as lawyers and government officials and representatives of the Egyptian associations of Lyon, Toulouse and Edinburgh, representatives of the France–Egypt Group and the Egyptian Association in France. Magd al-Din delivered the keynote speech. He conveyed the felicitations of all present to the King and Government of Egypt and honoured Huda by expressing the hope that Egypt and its women would be completely liberated during the reign of His Majesty King Fuad. More precisely, he voiced the hope that polygamy would be abolished, divorce controlled, that education would become compulsory for girls and that the right to vote would soon be granted at least to the more educated women of Egypt.

Huda was becoming interested in Freemasonry. In 1893, the wife of the late Senator George Martin, Marie Deraismes Martin, had founded a Masonic lodge that was intended to empower women alongside men, known as the Human Rights (Droits Humains) Lodge. Many of the guests at the Hotel Lutétia were Freemasons. Magd al-Din introduced Huda to French Freemasons who could help establish a dialogue with the Grand Lodge of England, where the Grand Master was the Prince of Wales. There was already an Arabic-speaking lodge in Egypt known as the Kawkab al-Sharq (Star of the East). This was affiliated to the Grand Lodge of England and counted among its members such figures as Khedive Tawfiq, Shaikh Muhammad Abduh, Saad Zaghlul, Boutros Pasha, Sherif Pasha, some members of the Egyptian parliament and even several members of the Ulema, the Islamic religious establishment. Huda was aware that her father, Sultan Pasha, and others he knew had been members of the Grand Orient of Alexandria. She recognised that Freemasonry could influence political decisions and could create bonds between powerful people of different races and religions, and that it could be of considerable help in overcoming racism, belligerence and discrimination.[14]

Huda and Céza travelled on to the United States in September. In New York, Carrie Chapman Catt met them off the boat. They were invited to lunch at the Woman's City Club of New York, a recently established and influential women's association whose board of governors included Eleanor Roosevelt. There was a third guest, Mrs Munch, the first female member of parliament in Denmark. Huda was awed by Chapman Catt, who had led the struggle that resulted in 1920 in the nineteenth amendment to the American Constitution, by which American women obtained the full and unchallenged right to vote. She had created the IWSA as long before as 1904, after having been the President of the National Alliance for some years. Her special blend of gentle persuasiveness had enabled her to launch affiliated movements in no less than 30 countries over the years. Her view was that women's clubs were the best way for women to get to know each other and to discuss what they needed before adopting a course of action. The Woman's City Club was a meeting place for active feminists and most of its members were involved in public affairs.[15]

Chapman Catt arranged for Huda and Céza to stay during their visit at the Cosmopolitan Club in New York, where artists, writers and other intellectuals gathered to talk and become acquainted with each other and with each other's ideas. They would spend the little free time they had in the club's small courtyard, blessed with a fountain and adorned with a huge lantern, feeling very much at home. They also admired the Colony Club, whose members were the richest families in New York. The Colony Club's beautiful sitting rooms, bedrooms, dining rooms and libraries matched the modernity and comfort of the areas designed for sports. The club had an enormous swimming pool and a degree of luxury that spoke of the financial stature of its members.

While in New York, the two women were entertained by Charles Crane and his daughter. Crane was a source of amazement to Huda and Céza. His knowledge of the Arabs and his sympathy for Arab culture, from mosques to horses and from literature to date palms, was endless. With his alert expression and always smartly trimmed goatee beard, he was a striking figure. He was an industrial magnate turned politician who had spent several years in China as the head of the American Embassy in Beijing. Wealthy and powerful as he was, he was an egalitarian and was quite unaffected in his behaviour. He knew people in Cairo, and already had many friends in common with Huda. Crane had a specially decorated suite in his house, where Caucasian carpets vied with Chinese pottery, Syrian woodwork and furniture, Damascene cushions and couches, painted wooden ceilings and brass chests. He could thus step into his beloved oriental world at his leisure even when he did not travel to it.

Huda could not help comparing Crane's style of life with her own. Her house in Egypt was furnished according to the prevailing Westernised taste of her time. The idea began to take shape in her mind that she could also follow her own oriental inclinations. It was this that gave her the idea of transforming her own house into something more like the house she had grown up in at Jami Sharkas Street, into a palace of the thousand and one nights, which would make a more convincing and persuasive background for her political activities and her guests from both East and West.

Crane also told her more about his visit to Palestine in 1917, and about the report that he and Dr Henry King had written together during the trip, with which Huda was already acquainted, which questioned the advisability of setting up a Jewish state in Palestine in accordance with the Jewish Agency's project. These were new problems as far as Huda was concerned. She had not previously queried the idea of coexistence with the Jews. The fact that it was only the Jewish community of Palestine that participated in international feminist events had not hitherto been a source of concern to her. But coexistence between Jews and Arabs in the same country was quite different from the creation of a Jewish state through the obliteration of a Palestinian society that already existed. Crane and his Palestinian friend George Antonius, the author of *The Arab Awakening*, gave her a different view of what was happening in Palestine.[16] It was some time, however, before this began to be reflected in *L'Égyptienne*. Huda's attention remained for the moment on Egypt.

After their stay of a few days in New York, Huda and Céza went on to Washington, where Bassna seemed to lead a no less exciting life. The Secretary of State himself, she told her mother, had asked to meet her. This was probably a result both of her own efforts and her mother's spreading fame, for, as she said, 'I do my best to live up to you, my darling Mummy.' Her social life was hectic, and she had been unable so far to take breaks at the seaside or at mountain resorts because the Egyptian Foreign Ministry had not agreed to cover holiday expenses. Huda already knew about this problem, and had contacted Ziwar Pasha before leaving Egypt, but he seemed not to be aware of the difficulty and certainly made no effort to improve the situation. Huda loved to see the children. They had grown up a lot. She was very proud of her daughter.

She asked Bassna if she could use her position as the Ambassador's wife to help selling the products of the EFU's workshops in the United States. The embroideries and haberdasheries of the EFU's workshop and the beautiful pottery of Rod al-Farag seemed likely to sell well in Washington. Huda and Céza had brought along as many items as they conveniently could from Cairo as samples. Huda took some time off to sit and talk with Bassna about her life in Washington and their life in Egypt, to play with the children, to converse with Mahmud Sami Pasha.

Bassna avidly absorbed all the information Huda gave her about the progress of the feminist movement in Egypt, which she promised to pass on to her acquaintances in America. She also undertook to relay any interesting developments in the United States to her mother. She was enthusiastic about Huda's new ideas for the house in Cairo, and promised to help with the work on her return. Meanwhile, Huda's tour of intellectual clubs continued in Washington. There was a Woman's Press Club for journalists and writers, a University Club, and a Washington branch of the Woman's City Club, where Huda and Céza were again invited and warmly entertained. The most interesting club in Washington,

Bassna.

however, was the National Women's Party Club. Alice Paul was one of the co-founders of the National Women's Party, originally established in 1913. She was an earnest feminist who explained to Huda the mechanisms of women's participation in political life in the United States, and how they were not served by the existing major parties.

During her visit, Huda met an English feminist, Emmeline Pethick-Lawrence, who gave a talk at a gathering that was being held. She was a tall and beautiful woman, neither frivolous nor playful, who exuded sincerity and straightforwardness. She spoke simply. The role of women in promoting peace was essential, she said, since women, who are always first and foremost mothers, knew the value of individual life. She believed in the equal rights of all individuals belonging to all races in all parts of the world. 'The life of a human being,' she said 'is worth more than all the economic interests put together.'[17] Céza immediately interviewed Pethick-Lawrence after her talk. Her husband, Frederick Pethick-Lawrence, was a member of the British Labour Party and a member of parliament who would later be a minister. Huda did not miss the opportunity to express her regret that Ramsay McDonald had not been able to resolve Egypt's difficulties when he had been visited by Zaghlul.

When Huda was herself invited to speak at the National Women's Party Club a few days later, on 8 October 1925, she stressed that Egypt's women were not seeking blindly to emulate the West, and made a point of wearing her traditional headgear.[18] In Egypt, she said, the veil was no longer an obstacle to communication. However, women still wore it sometimes as a part of their traditional costume, as an embellishment. She emphasised the need for nations to become acquainted with each other's customs and habits. She told her audience about Qasim Amin, about the issue of polygamy, about the marriage contract in Islam, divorce and inheritance, equal salaries for men and women and other matters, making a point of drawing upon Islamic sources, the Qur'an and Hadith, to support her arguments. She made the point that men's injustice towards women was an inheritance from pre-Islamic tribal customs, and misinterpreted Islamic law, emphasising that Egyptian women lived as well and were as active as women in the West. Finally, she briefly outlined the modern history of Egypt, beginning with Muhammad Ali, and described the establishment of the EFU and its goals.

The speech was appreciated by the audience, and Huda accepted an invitation to become a member of the international committee of the Women's Party. Her belief was that support for internationalism would help disseminate a non-discriminatory and humanistic climate of ideas that would bring about the end of imperialism. By educating public opinion, as Pethick-Lawrence so eloquently put it, they would sharpen the necessary tools to excise every manifestation of racial discrimination.[19]

Once back in Cairo, after three months spent in Europe and America, Huda decided that she needed to spend time thinking over and evaluating the experience of her trip, and that the experience she had acquired should be exploited to the full. Meanwhile, a new arrival on the scene in Cairo as she returned added to Huda's range of potential collaborators. Henriette Devonshire, a French woman who was married to an Englishman living in Cairo, was appointed on 2 November 1925 to the French Institute of Oriental Archaeology in Cairo.[20] Céza was anxious to start cooperating with Henriette, as they immediately began to call her, to promote the protection of Islamic monuments in the capital. Henriette was a specialist in Islamic art and architecture, and was sincerely devoted to the preservation of the Islamic heritage.

There was one final political upheaval in Egypt in late 1925, when the parliamentarians, prevented from meeting since March, decided to assemble at the parliament building to protest against the unconstitutionality of parliament's suspension. On 21 November 1925, troops and police were deployed by the Government to prevent the meeting by blocking all points of entry to parliament. Elsewhere in Cairo, bridges were closed and troops were on the streets. The response of Zaghlul and others was to convene an unofficial assembly at the Continental Hotel, which became known as the Continental Hotel parliament. This assembly adopted a number of resolutions, including an expression of no confidence in the Government. A humorous sidelight was that Ziwar Pasha was at the time living at the Continental Hotel, and was seen to flee rapidly towards his official car when he saw the parliamentarians begin to foregather. The key feature of this meeting was that it was the first time the Wafd and the other main parties, the Liberal Constitutionalists and the Nationalists, effectively joined together in a common cause.[21] Each of the parties held meetings, delegations came and went from Zaghlul's house, still known as the Bait al-Umma, and speeches were made. A second assembly was later held at the home of Muhammad Mahmud Pasha, with the participation of Zaghlul, Adly Yakan, Husain Rushdi, Abd al-Khaliq Tharwat and Ismail Sidqi, in the course of which they decided to form at last the long-awaited coalition of the three main parties.[22]

Following the Continental Hotel parliament, the Egyptian Students Association in Paris, presided over by Magd al-Din Hifni Nasif, Huda's protégé, invited all the associations of Egyptian students in Europe to hold a plenary conference between 29 and 31 December 1925 in Paris, in the premises of the Sociétés Savantes at 8 rue Danton. Egyptian delegates came from all over France, from Britain, Switzerland, Germany and other countries to participate in the forum. They expressed their support for the Continental Hotel parliament, and proclaimed a number of resolutions almost revolutionary in tone, calling for a new constitution, an electoral boycott and the rejection of Ziwar Pasha's Government as illegitimate:

> This Congress invites the civilised world, and all the democracies and parliaments of Europe, America and Asia, to bear witness to the violation of the Egyptian Constitution, rejects Ziwar's new electoral decree and declares that the electoral bill voted and promulgated under Zaghlul Pasha's cabinet is the only legal and constitutional one.[23]

Huda had planned beforehand with Magd al-Din what the contents of the communiqué from his conference would be, and duly reported it all in L'Égyptienne. As she had during her clash with Zaghlul, Huda used her access to the media to criticise Ziwar Pasha's Government and its policies. She condemned what she described as his weakness, and what she deemed an undignified tendency to appease the British occupation forces rather than to defend Egypt's interests. In common with the representatives of international feminism she met at the various conferences she attended, she upheld the cause of peace and of a utopian society where justice and equality would be the order of the day. But she held her ground like a stateswoman when it came to immediate matters of Egyptian government and policy.

By December 1925, Huda had begun once more to write her articles in *L'Égyptienne*, resuming where she had left off with a piece on Egypt's political place in the world. Her recurrent theme was the damage caused by foreign occupation to the dismembered fragments of the Ottoman Empire. The first article, therefore, was called 'Appeal to the West', in which she took to task the Western powers for the devastation they caused in the Eastern countries:

> The East is suffering, the Orient is bleeding, and it alone draws all my sympathy and all my attention. It is the Rif set on fire and bathed in blood by the Spanish and French troops; it is Syria revolting against the massacres in Damascus; it is Palestine and Iraq where, ever since the British mandate was established, there has been no end to the fomentation of discord and hatred between populations that follow different creeds. It is divided Arabia, all these countries in mourning, whence the sobs of widows, the screams of orphans, the curses of old men who only yesterday were full of respect for the Western civilisation and had placed all their hope and trust in it, reach our ear.[24]

She contrasted the talk about disarmament and peace she had heard during three months in Europe and America with the reality of life in the occupied countries. She appealed in particular to America, that great country which had itself been a colony in the not-so-distant past, and where she now had so many powerful friends. Following the statement of President Woodrow Wilson's 14 points, which supported the small nations of the world, Huda had expected the Americans to respond favourably to her call for justice. She hoped that her article would trigger a positive dialogue.[25]

At this stage, Huda decided it was time for the EFU to heighten its profile by setting up a club. This was to be known as the Club of the Feminist Union, and would be an intellectual and social organisation for members and sponsors of the EFU. On 8 January 1926, the club was inaugurated. Princess Samiha was to be Honorary President, and Huda was elected chair of the club's executive committee. Huda invited more than two hundred high-society guests to the opening celebration at the villa built by Alexander Green in the smart area of Qasr al-Dubara, close to the British High Commissioner's residence at 1 Midan Qasr al-Dubara. For the occasion, she made a presentation on the subject of the feminist movement in the West based on what she had learned in Europe and the United States. Tables were set in the garden by the tennis court, and Groppi, the exclusive tearoom, was asked to cater for the tea party, during which a small orchestra played Turkish music, popular at the time in Egypt. After tea, there was a concert by the popular Askenase-Menasche-Orletti trio. The club's activities began with a talk by a Mr Le Breton the following Monday and a tennis tournament on 15 February. Visits to theatres and concert halls were also planned, together with talks and conferences on various subjects. Members enjoyed Mascagni's music at the Kursaal Theatre as well as seeing Charles le Bargy and his wife Simone at the Opera House.

During the absence of Huda and Céza, Jeanne Marquès had worked very hard at *L'Égyptienne*, and had kept it going in admirable style. In February 1926, no doubt with Huda's agreement, ironically as it turned out in view of Huda's later attitudes, a long article signed by Jeanne appeared in *L'Égyptienne* praising the Zionist women settlers in Palestine:

> We have been following very closely and with great sympathy the work accomplished by our Zionist sisters in Palestine, in America, in all countries… They have demonstrated their strong character and practical organisation everywhere. They are everywhere a living example of the extreme vitality of a people that did not lose hope despite centuries of servitude, and that has kept intact its respect for intelligence and faith.[26]

In April, Jeanne followed this up with praise of a speech by Rosa Aberson, the Secretary General of the League of Jewish Women at a conference on child care.[27] The speech advocated the implementation of a resolution on educating children for peace, but also called for the eradication of antisemitism. Jeanne's article applauded the Jewish sisters and their determination to show themselves as capable of physical work as the men, expressing the hope that this would lead to a 'more humane and fraternal world'.[28] Despite her acquaintance with Charles Crane,

Huda had not yet begun to develop what later became her passionate support of Palestine's Arab population.

Huda also took an interest when, in 1926, the American multimillionaire and philanthropist John D. Rockefeller offered Egypt a donation to pay for a new research institute and museum for Egyptology that was to have stood at the southern tip of the Gezira island. The plan, masterminded by the University of Chicago Egyptologist James Henry Breasted, was presented to the Egyptian Government in January 1926, and was finally turned down by Ziwar Pasha in mid-March.[29] Huda took the liberty of sending an open telegram of thanks and regret to the American tycoon on behalf of the EFU: 'We hope that you will not blame the Egyptian nation for this stupid policy that runs contrary to the interests of the country which has rejected it on the grounds that it is a project devised by and for the interests of foreigners.'

In fact, Ziwar knew that if he had agreed to a project which would in effect have handed Egyptian archaeology over to foreign control, the nationalists would have been enraged. Huda, on the other hand, saw the rejection of the plan as British-inspired, and interpreted it as just another instance of Britain's neglect of Egypt's welfare. As she saw it, the desert was full of treasures, whose excavation would enlighten humanity on its origins and on the civilisation of ancient Egypt. Rockefeller reacted to Huda's telegram with a declaration of solidarity with the Egyptian people. He thanked the EFU for their message, and expressed his sincerest wishes for the future and happiness of the Egyptian people. The French poet Gérard de Nerval, in a sonnet published in the same issue of *L'Égyptienne* as Rockefeller's telegram, paid tribute to ancient Egyptian culture.[30] Many other articles were published that highlighted pharaonic lore and wonders.

The tenth congress of the IWSA was held at the Sorbonne in Paris from 30 May to 6 June 1926. A key decision was to change the name of the organisation from the IWSA to the International Alliance of Women, IAW, recognising the broadening scope of the organisation. On 29 April 1926, at a regular business meeting of the EFU at Huda's house, she announced the names of the Egyptian delegation. These were once again mostly veterans of the 1919 demonstrations. Huda said she was confident that the delegation would be, as she put it in French, 'remarquable et remarquée' ('noteworthy and noticed'). The list to accompany Huda comprised Regina Khayat, Esther Fahmi Wissa, Wajida Khulusi, Sayba Garzuzi, Fikria Husni, and of course Céza Nabarawi. Day-to-day EFU business also went on as usual, with the financial statement and reports on the dispensary and other activities.[31]

Once in Paris, despite the preoccupations of the congress, the women were constantly concerned about the situation at home, where national elections had been held once more on 25 May, just after the departure of the women's delegation from Egypt. In Paris, Huda pressed Magd al-Din to exercise to the full his talent for obtaining news in order to keep her informed. Once more, and unsurprisingly, the Wafd and its allies prevailed, scoring a yet more resounding victory than ever before. Nevertheless, Ziwar did not immediately resign. On 27 May, it was rumoured that Lord Lloyd, the British High Commissioner, invited Zaghlul to the Residency. Apparently, a violent argument broke out between them, because Zaghlul insisted that if he formed a Government it must be a coalition of non-royalist forces, a proposal which the British refused to accept. Lloyd knew Zaghlul could summon up riots if he wished, but requested him to head off trouble to renouncing any further attempt to lead the country. To underline his point, Lloyd asked for a British gunboat, HMS *Resolute*, stationed in the Mediterranean, to be sent to Alexandria. Zaghlul had for some time been making statements saying he was too old and tired for office, and that rather than being Prime Minister he wanted to be seen as the father of the nation. He may have wished to pre-empt any British decision to prevent him taking office, making it seem his own idea to step aside. The King reportedly rejected his proposal that Nahhas Pasha, second-in-command of the Wafd, should be Prime Minister. Instead, the British and the King proposed that Adly Yakan return as head of a supposedly neutral government.

The pressure was becoming too heavy for Zaghlul to bear.[32] On 3 June, at a banquet at the Intercontinental Hotel, several speakers pressed him to renounce his prime ministerial ambitions. These speakers urged him, 'not to overstrain his health by undertaking the cares of office, but rather to conserve and cherish it in the interest of the country'.[33] Zaghlul was taken aback when he heard these statements, and paused for a moment to grasp what had just taken place. He then rose and hesitantly confirmed the precarious state of his health and his own reluctance to assume more power or responsibilities. He declared that he believed more than ever in the will of his people, and that the members of parliament had to decide whether he should resume the position of Prime Minister or not. It became evident at this point that he would withdraw from the prime ministerial race. He paid another visit to the Residency, followed by a last visit to the King, and assured both Lloyd and King Fuad that he had decided 'never to take office again in any circumstances', and that he would 'extend to Adly Yakan Pasha … the full support of his party'.[34] Ziwar Pasha, who had been acting as caretaker, finally stepped down on 7 June, and Yakan Pasha took over. All this Huda and her colleagues heard while they were in Paris.

Huda cabled home from Paris an article entitled 'The Egyptian question and universal peace', which she wanted published as soon as possible in *L'Égyptienne*. Once again, she stressed the incongruity of the current rhetoric on peace in international circles while Egypt and other colonised countries were being oppressed. She laid emphasis on the contrast between the cordial atmosphere of the congress on the one hand and the alarming news, on the other, of the arrival of HMS *Resolute* in Port Said, and Britain's threat to suspend once more the Egyptian constitution were Zaghlul to be re-appointed. 'We trust in the wisdom of the Egyptian people and the capacity of its leader,' she wrote.[35] She took the chance to thank Zaghlul for at last measuring up to her expectations, and was careful to express her trust in her English sisters, making the point that the perfidy of governments should not be allowed to cloud the goodwill of peoples.

On the opening day of the congress in Paris, the heads of the national delegations assembled in their full national dress behind the podium, where Corbett-Ashby spoke at 9 a.m. The French Minister of Public Education, Anatole de Monzie, and Édouard Herriot, the speaker of the French parliament, who was shortly once more to be Prime Minister, attended the opening. Huda sat in her place, clad in what had become accepted, thanks to her, as the national dress of Egypt, a navy-blue chiffon dress and a scarf that surrounded her face and fell smoothly on her shoulders. In her manner, Huda had deliberately adopted the measured poise and serious mien that would remain alive in people's memory later. The impression she gave was one of solidity and dignity, and her husky voice often added to the general air of authority that emanated from her. While the proceedings were underway, Huda hosted a dinner for delegates at the Hotel Lutétia, which had become her favourite.

Huda decided that Margery Corbett-Ashby, now the Acting President of the IAW, was a person on whom she could rely after the departure of Carrie Chapman Catt. The founder of the IAW, who had stepped down after suffering a stroke to become Honorary President and to devote what energy remained to her to the promotion of peace in the world.[36] Corbett-Ashby struck Huda as an excellent replacement.[37] It should perhaps be mentioned, however, that in 1926 Corbett-Ashby provided an interesting view of how Huda had struck her when she wrote to Chapman Catt on 9 June that Huda was 'terrifically nationalistic and tyrannical'.[38] A principal point of difference between Huda and Corbett-Ashby was Huda's passionate determination to achieve the abolition of the capitulatory laws and other international obligations to which Egypt was subjected. Even Britain's Lord Milner, writing in 1904, was in no doubt as to the burden on Egypt represented by these laws, which he described as 'the countless international fetters by which Egypt is bound'. Addressing the predicament of the Government of Egypt, he wrote,

> Wherever you turn, there is some obstruction in your path. Do you want to clear out a cesspool, to prevent the sale of noxious drugs, to suppress a seditious or immoral print, you are pulled up by the Capitulations ... You cannot borrow

without the consent of Turkey; you cannot draw upon the reserve fund without
the consent of the Caisse; you cannot exceed the Limit of Expenditure without
the consent of the Powers.[39]

Huda's statement, when her turn came to speak, covered in broad
outline the progress made by the feminist movement in Egypt and in the
rest of the oriental world, including Algeria, Syria, Tunisia and even
India, where the women had made clear their sympathy for and solidarity
with the Egyptians. The success of the Turkish revolution, in her
opinion, would certainly consolidate the movement. She ended with a
tribute to Chapman Catt and a welcome to Corbett-Ashby. Meanwhile,
Céza made two statements. In one speech to the whole assembly at
the Sorbonne, she spoke about the capitulations and their impact on
prostitution in Egypt, in the other, at the Sociétés Savantes on 2 June,
about women's rights in Egypt, the application of the Code Napoléon,
and the demands made by Egyptian women to their Government. One
of the French women rose at the end of Céza's talk to exclaim, 'I want
to be Egyptian!'

While in Paris, Huda made the acquaintance of the Romanian Elena
Vacarescu, who was later appointed one of Romania's delegates to the
League of Nations, an important figure on the international feminist
scene with whom Huda remained in contact over the years. Another
person Huda was able to see while she was in Paris was Odette Simon,
the young French lawyer whom Bassna had befriended in London during
the trial of Ali Fahmi Pasha's wife. Through Bassna, Odette had also
come to know Céza and Huda's son Muhammad. A handsome young
woman and naturally outgoing, she soon began to call Huda 'Tante',
like the other young women who surrounded her, expressing her
enthusiastic admiration. She had been writing to Huda regularly, and
had contributed articles to L'Égyptienne after joining the French Union
for Women's Suffrage. Huda enjoyed the very real affection of the young
people who surrounded her. Hawa and Huria, who had been brought to
her in Cairo as children, loved her like girls who have no one else in the
world to care for them. Céza never left her side.

It was at this meeting in 1926 that Huda became a member of the executive committee of the IAW, just three years after Egypt's first participation in the organisation, in a development that was undoubtedly an honour both for Egypt and for her personally. The only opposition came from two of her Egyptian colleagues, Esther Wissa and Regina Khayat. Both made the point that Huda was already the head of the EFU, and that if Egypt was represented on the IAW executive committee, the representative should be someone else. The difficulty with this view was that Huda was the only Egyptian delegate certain to be elected to the committee. If Huda were not the candidate, the place on the executive committee would probably go to the representative of some other country. In the event, Huda's general popularity and reputation meant that when she stood, she could not fail to be elected. She was supported by the host country, France, and by nine other national delegations, and she became a member of the executive committee with 131 votes. She was immediately invited to participate in two sub-committees, one on peace, the other on finance.[40]

On 7 June, immediately after the conference closed, Huda invited all the participants again to the Hotel Lutétia for a farewell party which Magd al-Din helped her to organise. Both gave farewell speeches, and other speakers included Corbett-Ashby. The event was a great success. An illustrated talk about the eternal beauty of the land of the Pharaohs seemed to be appreciated by the guests. 'Egyptomania', the craze for the ancient world that was being discovered through excavation and the wonderful art objects of the Pharaohs, was a coming thing. Huda was conscious of ancient Egypt's fascination for the West, and its persuasive power in attracting sympathy to Egypt.

7

The game of politics

When Huda returned from Paris with Céza in July 1926, she called a meeting of the editorial board of *L'Égyptienne* to talk over how to redress the dearth of information about Egypt abroad that Huda had observed during her various foreign trips. They felt sure this ignorance contributed to the difficulty of persuading other countries to bring pressure to bear on Britain finally to relinquish its domination over Egypt and the rights Britain arrogated to itself. The decision was that *L'Égyptienne* should redouble its efforts to inform the West about the oriental world. Articles would be written about the dynasty of Muhammad Ali, the founder of the present Egyptian state and the ancestor of King Fuad. French translations of Egyptian poems would be published. Huda's protégé, the poet Foulad Yeghen, would do new translations of writers not previously available in Western languages. Prince Haydar Fazil, the King's cousin, who wrote excellent French poetry himself, agreed to translate passages of the Qur'an into the French language.

Huda also turned her attention to the management and marketing of the pottery and carpet workshops. Her plan was to establish a local school of arts and crafts that would consolidate artistic creation as a way

149

of life in Egypt. Louis Marcerou, Director of the Librairie Française, later wrote an article for *L'Égyptienne* about the ancient art of pottery and its recent revival in the Nur al-Huda factory of Rod al-Farag. 'Nothing is so dead that it cannot be brought back to life again, and nothing so alive that it will not soon die,' he wrote.[1] Marcerou recalled the metaphor of Omar Khayyam, who said that men are themselves made of dust, and therefore thrive on creating objects made out of the same material. With the capable help of James Alfred Coulon, Huda was now successfully reviving this ancient art in Egypt. It was Huda's enthusiasm for this project that kept ablaze the kilns which fired the pottery made by Egyptian hands in Rod al-Farag. The workshop's products were to be sold in Cairo and Paris, as well as in Constantinople, Washington and New York. Coulon came to be a key member of Huda's little court.

Another contribution to renewed creative activity in Egypt had just been made by Badrawi Ashur Pasha, who put up 150,000 Egyptian pounds of his own money to help fund the construction of a textile factory. After the cotton crisis of 1927, the factories of Manchester had failed to buy Egypt's cotton crop. Talaat Harb's Banque Misr also helped fund the new factory, but Badrawi Ashur Pasha's initiative greatly contributed to the revitalisation of the Egyptian economy. Huda reported his gesture in *L'Égyptienne*. 'We are convinced,' she said, 'that this great patriot's fine gesture will be followed by similar initiatives on the part of all Egyptians, without exception.' Everyone in the country, she reaffirmed, would want to subscribe to this great project, in order to rescue Egypt from the perilous economic situation that had resulted from the total absence of local industry.[2] The textile industry was only one of a series of projects that Talaat Harb was able to help initiate using the resources of Banque Misr.

If development was one field of concern, conservation was another. The recently arrived Henriette Devonshire, a French woman married to an Englishman, who was also an Arabist in addition to speaking English and French, launched her own campaign to save the Mamluk and Ottoman houses of old Cairo. Mosques and other public and religious monuments had so far been spared. Other buildings were still endangered. 'What about the old private houses of Cairo?' wondered Céza, in an article almost certainly inspired by Henriette, who liked to take her friends on tours of historic Cairo's main streets and by-roads. Modern development was already spreading at great cost to the old city, and new buildings of a Westernised style of architecture were springing up everywhere. Roads were being widened to accommodate the motor car, while old trees and street features were disappearing. Henriette's argument was that with the loss of its traditional infrastructure the soul of Cairo was gradually fading away. She was a tireless advocate for the protection of the architectural resources of Cairo, though the tide seemed almost unstoppable.[3] If anything was to be done to save the capital's oriental identity, however, the widest possible support from the Egyptian public needed to be engaged.

Saving the fabric of Egypt had become another passion for Huda. The imperative was to preserve Egypt both from the depredations of the British and from itself, by convincing the authorities that civic duty should take precedence over private reward. This was to be her new mission. At issue were the preservation of architectural masterpieces from destruction, the construction of hospitals and schools, where appropriate and in keeping with their surroundings, as well as fostering the self-esteem of the Egyptian people, who needed to be convinced that what was foreign was not necessarily better. The development of industry and of the arts were both essential, as were books and magazines that would enhance communication between the West and the oriental world. All this required the hard work and goodwill of the battalions of young men and women who surrounded Huda and were faithfully devoted to her cause. A special issue of L'Égyptienne celebrated the magazine's second anniversary.

Huda had a somewhat ambiguous relationship with King Fuad. Since 1918, when he had succeeded his brother Sultan Husain Kamal al-Din, the King had at least broadly shared with the nationalists the view that it was desirable for the British ultimately to relinquish their grip on

Egypt. The elevated circles in which Huda's family moved meant that from the earliest days she had been accustomed to social interaction with the royal family. She admired the King for his position on nationalism, as well as for the backing he had given the Banque Misr project and his support for various charitable causes, including some close to her heart. On the other hand, King Fuad was not personally very popular with women because of his overt misogyny. In fact, the King virtually never appeared in public with his consort. His credo was that affairs of state were a strictly masculine occupation, and the Queen was certainly not invited to participate in decision-making.

Huda was of course keen to see changes in the law regarding the status of women in Egypt, and one aspect of this was the so-called 'house of submission' ('bayt al-ta'a'), the legal right of a husband to imprison his wife within the confines of his household for an unlimited amount of time to compel her to obey his will. For Huda and her feminist friends, the fact that King Fuad not infrequently resorted to this legal right to punish no less a person than Queen Nazli for disobeying him was extremely irritating. Queen Nazli in fact spent much of her time confined to the palace. The fact that a wife of such elevated stature could be confined within four walls at the whim of her angry husband was, as they saw it, clearly unacceptable in the light of any humanitarian law, and set a very bad example, while Kings were meant to be role models for their people.

In 1926, a draft document was prepared by the EFU's justice committee proposing amendments to Egypt's legislation on marriage, in the light of the country's evolving economic conditions and modern thinking on women's rights. The EFU sent its proposals to the Ministry of Justice, which simply sent them on to the Ulema at Al-Azhar rather than giving consideration to a draft law to go before parliament. The women felt there was little likelihood that their suggestion would go forward. It was widely believed that the King himself wanted the present conservative law maintained rather than changes to be introduced that would protect women against their husbands. The rumour was that the King himself had called for the protests of the feminists to be disregarded.

All clouds have silver linings, however. In 1926, there was an unexpected and extremely welcome development for the women's movement under Adly Yakan Pasha's Government, when a government committee recommended that there should be controls on polygamous marriage and that divorce should be granted solely by the courts, and only after an equitable attempt to reconcile the two spouses as recommended by the Sharia. The mother's guardianship of children was to be extended beyond the current seven years for boys and nine years for girls, with the committee recommending that girls should remain under their mother's care until marriage, and boys until puberty. Finally, there came the long-awaited suppression of the house of submission. The EFU wrote to the Egyptian Government in support of these recommendations.[4]

Huda knew Queen Nazli, because the Queen, though kept on a short rein by Fuad, was sometimes permitted to attend cultural events for women. Huda therefore began deliberately to challenge King Fuad's behaviour by calling on the Queen whenever she was confined in the house of submission. On these occasions, Huda would of course be met by a protocol official to inform her that no visits were permitted. However, the gesture was the important thing, indicating as it did to the King that his action was not viewed as acceptable by others in society. Regardless of what the Queen did to irritate her royal husband, if she was to be confined in this manner, what would be the fate of other Egyptian women? Huda asked herself, how would women ever be respected, and how would women respect themselves, if the Queen herself could be so harshly humiliated and coerced into obedience?

From the early summer to the late autumn of 1927, King Fuad paid a four-month visit to Europe, sailing on the royal yacht *Al-Mahrusa* on 24 June. The declared purpose of the King's visit was to strengthen relations between Egypt and the various states of Europe, in addition to paying a month-long visit to the spa at Vichy for the benefit of his health. Newspapers hinted that while he was in London he would also seek a resolution of Egypt's paradoxical situation as an independent state that was still a de facto British protectorate. This did not especially gratify Egypt's nationalists, who were irritated that as a constitutional monarch he should presume to take it upon himself to embark on such an initiative. However, he was also supposed to be informing himself about aspects of modern European society, one of which was education, and it had been specifically stated that a subject in which he was interested was the education of girls. The King's spokesman, Ahmad Hasanain Pasha, said it was the King's firm belief that, since children were in general educated by their mothers, any reform should concentrate on improving the education of women. The King therefore intended to visit educational institutions for women in Europe, in order to acquire a clearer picture of the measures required for the education of this significant half of the Egyptian population.

Huda was ecstatic when Fuad indicated he was in favour of improving education for women. She commissioned a number of articles for *L'Égyptienne* in support of his plan. In a reference to the craze for ancient Egypt, which the recent discovery of King Tutankhamen's tomb had heightened still further, King Fuad was likened to an enlightened ancient Egyptian sovereign. Huda accepted that his mission was one of goodwill, and that if improved education for women in Egypt were to be its outcome it would certainly enhance Egypt's prospects for self-reliance and real independence. The King had already demonstrated his concern for education with his support of Cairo University, which his sister Princess Fatma Ismail had endowed through the donation of her jewels and lands. She felt that education, at least, was a subject he was qualified to tackle.

While the King sailed on the *Al-Mahrusa*, his ministers went on another ship that left Alexandria in late June, the *Mariette Pasha*. Gabrielle Rousseau happened to travel to France on the same sailing, with Gaillardot Bey, who was a member of the Institut d'Égypte and the secretary of the Société de Géographie. He had just created the

Bonaparte museum as well as a magazine entitled *L'Égypte*, and Gaby was delighted by his company. She was also thrilled to be on the same ship as Abd al-Khaliq Tharwat Pasha, who was once more Prime Minister, having taken over from Yakan Pasha on 26 April. Sirri Pasha and Midhat Yakan Pasha were also with the Government party.[5] The British had continued to be determined not to allow another Wafd Government, and in order to avoid a crisis Zaghlul had said the Wafd would accept Tharwat as Prime Minister.

On 4 July 1927, the King arrived in London, his first port of call. He was received by King George V, and welcomed by the Prime Minister, Stanley Baldwin, and the Foreign Secretary, Sir Austin Chamberlain. The same evening, there was a banquet in Fuad's honour at Buckingham Palace, at which the British monarch went out of his way to honour his Egyptian guest.[6] While he was in London, he also went to the theatre and undertook a round of visits to schools and colleges, including Eton, where he was greeted by Lord Lloyd, the British High Commissioner in Egypt, himself an Old Etonian, who was home on leave. He also visited the Royal Geographical Society and the Royal Children's Hospital, and travelled north to Manchester to look at various aspects of the cotton industry. On 18 July 1927, while Fuad was in London, an Anglo–Egyptian draft treaty was signed which pledged to end the British military occupation of Egypt within the coming ten years, transforming the protectorate into a treaty of 'friendship and alliance'. This was not welcome to the Wafd and other nationalists, who feared there would still be significant British reservations, and also suspected the treaty would be tantamount to the legalisation on a permanent basis of Britain's de facto dominance over Egypt. King Fuad left London on 26 July to sail to Italy.

King Fuad's next stop was Rome, where he arrived on 2 August to public enthusiasm and a popular ovation. He was given a grand welcome by King Victor Emmanuel III, and sumptuously entertained. On 7 August, he was received by the Pope at the Vatican. The King had studied at the military academy in Turin when he was a young man, and felt at home in Italy, whose language he spoke well. In Italy, his talks and those of his ministers related to trade across the Mediterranean. Italy was interested in the Egyptian market, and Egypt sought to diversify its trade partners. The following week he visited the spectacular city of Venice, where there was another grand reception. The King left Italy on 20 August to retire to the spa at Vichy for the part of his tour that was intended to be of benefit to his health.

He arrived in Paris by train on 20 October, and was given a 21-gun salute at the Quai d'Orsay, after which he was received privately by President Doumergue of France. He was then guest of honour at a banquet at the Elysée Palace. At this grand event, Haikal Pasha, who was spending his summer in France with his wife Aziza, was also a guest. Haikal asked Aziza to go to the banquet unveiled. Though she did so, she felt embarrassed, but the King himself welcomed her at the entrance with the kindest words, thus demonstrating to the world that Egyptian women had at least won that battle. The news was triumphantly sent by Magd al-Din and Gaby to Huda, who was by now once more in the United States. Huda felt that the King's appalling recourse to the house of submission might soon be abolished.

Queen Nazli had not sailed with the King in June, but joined him at last in France, after his visits to Britain and Italy were over. She had been educated in French schools in Egypt, and one of her ancestors was a French soldier, Joseph Anthelme Sève, later known as Soliman Pasha, who had served in Napoleon's army, afterwards remaining in Egypt, where he rose to be a general and then Chief-of-Staff. This was publicised by the press, with the result that she was fêted in France, where newspaper articles heaped encomia on her beauty and intelligence.

While he was in Paris the King made other visits, including to a reception at the Hotel de Ville, where he was accompanied by President Doumergue and given the gold medal of the city of Paris. It was noted by those who met him that he spoke good French with a slight Italian accent. On 24 October, he was guest of honour at a dinner given by French businessmen with interests in Egypt. Finally, between 26 and

28 October, he paid a short visit to Belgium. When Fuad eventually arrived back in Egypt on 14 November, triumphal arches were erected, and he was given a magnificent welcome home.

Meanwhile, Huda had been finding other issues to concern her. In June 1927, the British fleet had been exercising in Egyptian waters off Alexandria, and as President of the EFU, Huda dispatched a telegram of protest to the IAW. She demanded a feminist intervention in the face of what she described as the intimidation of Egypt by the presence of the British fleet in Alexandria's waters, which she declared a threat to peace.[7] The IAW, however, turned a deaf ear to her telegram, which it presumably saw as beyond its competence. Huda published an article in *L'Égyptienne*, deploring the alleged bilateral pact secretly agreed at the turn of the century by France and England, under whose terms France would supposedly leave England a free hand in Egypt in exchange for France being given free rein in Syria and elsewhere.[8] Huda had hitherto somewhat tended to set France up as a model of the defence of freedom, but this reputation she now saw as tarnished.

Conscious of his status as a member of the Shaarawi family, Muhammad continued to maintain his public duties. He had become the youngest elected member of the Egyptian senate, and Huda was always able to rely on his support in parliament and as a member of the Inter-parliamentary Association. In political and patriotic terms, he was steadfast. He was honest, direct and unswervingly loyal to his homeland, with a belief that he should do his utmost to serve it, even by pledging his own fortune in case of need. He regularly donated large sums of money to educational and health causes, and was one of the major landowners who participated in funding Egypt's budding industries through his investment in the Banque Misr.[9] When Egypt's interests needed defence, he fearlessly expressed his opinion. Huda therefore had many reasons to be proud of him, but she desperately wanted him to be steadier in his private life.

She had daily arguments with Muhammad during these days about why he should settle down. She felt passionately that her son should marry and lead a quiet and settled life. The solution still seemed to lie in her unspoken and long-standing pact with Fatma Fahmi Asim, the daughter of Munira Sabri, that Muhammad should be married to Fatma's eldest daughter Munira when they both reached a marriageable age. 'Mimi', as everyone called Munira, who was named after her grandmother, had grown into a beautiful young woman. Her father, Husain Asim, was an engineer, trained in England, handsome and genial, who was developing further the irrigation projects that had been initiated by European engineers. When he married Fatma, he had taken over the management of her extensive estates, and also managed the land belonging to her brother and sisters. After Ali Fahmi Pasha's death, he became their guardian.

Marriage with Mimi would be exactly what Huda sought for her son. It did not have to be a romantic relationship. She had not shared a passionate love affair with her own husband. Her marriage had been more of a practical affair, and she had only two children. Munira was a healthy girl with many siblings, and would surely have many children, including boys who would be Muhammad's heirs and the inheritors of his enormous fortune. Mimi was good-natured and unassuming, which would complement Muhammad's mercurial character. What Huda did not realise was that he was not ready for a peaceful life with a wife and many children by his side. Even had she sensed this, she was not ready to accept that Muhammad was unwilling to marry his beautiful cousin. Tragically, she had also failed to realise that Mimi would have done anything in the world not to marry Muhammad, and begged her mother day and night to set the idea aside and let her be.

Some time later, Huda was to prevail. The couple married, despite the reluctance of both young people, though it should have struck Huda as significant that Muhammad only agreed at long last to the marriage after a titanic confrontation between himself and his mother that had left him shaken and unnerved. However, she decided that for his own good he had to spend two years abroad before the marriage. With Mahmud Sami's help, he was sent to London to serve as an official at the Egyptian Embassy. The diplomatic service had been the making of Sami Pasha, and Huda was sure that this posting would shape Muhammad's character and make him stronger. She had also seen the benefit reaped by all the other young people she sent to study abroad, who had found maturity during the years they spent studying away from home. She thought that Muhammad would gain self-confidence after living on his own for a while, and could be more like his father, a capable man ready to be the head of a family.

She mentally compared her girls, the Cadettes, with Muhammad as she proudly watched them leave the house each week with their little baskets to dispense sugar, rice, soap and other products to the poor. She waited eagerly every time they went out for the news they brought home about people's health, and their reports about the lack of potable water, muddy streets and other problems. Based on this, lists of necessary restoration works could be prepared, and plans to submit to the Government could be drawn up. The girls were earnest and strong-willed because they had contact with the realities of life.

While Huda was in the United States in 1927, a national tragedy struck Egypt which rocked the whole country. This was the sudden death on 23 August of Saad Zaghlul. Huda was in Washington arranging to hold a pottery exhibition there and New York. The Egyptian press hinted that King Fuad, still taking the waters in Vichy, was not altogether displeased by the news. As Egyptian Ambassador in the United States, Mahmud Sami Pasha was swiftly informed, and passed the news on at once to Huda. Zaghlul had developed a very high temperature, caused by a flare-up of erysipelas of the ear, and was unable to fight it.[10] He apparently had an instinct from the moment he fell ill that it would be useless to fight, and he passed away without so much as a sign of anger. He kept repeating 'Ma fish fayda' ('It is no use'), no matter what was done to try to help him as he died. The whole country mourned Zaghlul's death. Huda tried to come to terms with the reality that he was no longer present. It was difficult. He seemed to have been there all her life, dominating Egypt's political landscape. His robust appearance, rough ways and powerful voice made him seem eternal, despite his old age. The political wisdom that he had recently displayed by accepting the principle of an all-party coalition made his loss even more of a calamity. He had been a forceful Prime Minister, but more recently had also been a strong and resolute speaker of parliament, and had developed an unusual ability to communicate with the British officials. Without him, at this point in the country's history, the frail vessel that was Egypt might drift into perilous waters. After all the travail and conflict, and after Zaghlul had finally found the role and the maturity that best suited him, he had passed away, and would be cruelly missed.

Back in Cairo, in Huda's absence, Céza went on with the business of producing *L'Égyptienne* as usual, exercising her eloquence and wit, and announcing that triumphal arches were waiting for the King, whom she called 'Fuad the Conqueror', who would return with innovative ideas about his country's needs. She added quizzically that 'time would show' whether that were true. For Huda, private life and politics were again closely linked. For her, politics always made life more exciting, neutralising the boredom of humdrum existence. Huda's house at 2 Qasr al-Nil Street had become a focal point for many different kinds of absorbing activities, and the little community that revolved in and around it was entirely taken up by its multiple tasks.

The pottery exhibition in Washington and New York was an enormous success. The exhibits sold very well, and substantial funds were collected for Huda's charities. She once more met Carrie Chapman Catt as well as seeking out Charles Crane. Huda delayed her return from the United States until late in the autumn because she planned to attend the IAW peace committee's meeting due to be held at the Colonial Institute in Amsterdam between 17 and 19 November 1927 in conjunction with the League of Nations. The mood was ripe for discussion of peace in these tense inter-war years. On 19 September, for example, in the Dutch city of the Hague, seat of the Dutch parliament, 80,000 people had demonstrated for peace in the streets. Huda would be the sole Egyptian participant in Amsterdam, and she was keen to go.

The House of the Egyptian Woman.

She wanted to take the opportunity of an international forum to remind as many people as possible about the unique injustice still suffered by Egypt in the shape of the capitulatory laws. She had been promised help by the lawyer Odette Simon, and support from a former German Reichstag member, Adèle Schreiber. The Dutch cold in November did not deter her, bent as she was on serving the cause of justice, peace and disarmament. Even Chapman Catt was planning to attend, despite her fading health, and it was therefore incumbent upon Huda to participate. In any case, she would need to stop over in Europe on the way back to Egypt to rest during the journey, so the conference would be a useful way to break her journey. It would also give her the opportunity to become better acquainted with Rosa Manus, the Dutch activist who had been newly elected as secretary of the IAW peace committee.[11]

The conference was by all accounts effective in emphasising the women's support for disarmament and peace. However, when Huda advocated the abolition of Egypt's capitulatory laws, she did not meet with great success.[12] Instead, she was asked to submit a report about what was described as 'this obscure issue' to an ad hoc committee for further examination. The issue loomed large in Huda's mind, but she may have been unable to see that for women with peace as their main concern it was perhaps not the most central of subjects. This did not prevent Céza from printing a condemnation of the IAW's attitude to her concerns in *L'Égyptienne*. While the members of the IAW committee were willing to ask Huda and her Egyptian colleagues to help them as usual with fundraising, Céza wrote, they were apparently not ready to support their Egyptian friends in such a crucial affair as the abolition of the unfair treaties that maintained the capitulations. This attitude, she said, was unfair and inconsistent. Huda appreciated Céza's efforts, but she realised she must be prudent and bide her time for the moment to bring the capitulatory laws to an end.

In another development in 1927, Muhammad Mahmud Pasha, Egypt's Minister of Finance, donated three plots of land in Qasr el-Aini Street to the EFU for the extension of their facilities.[13] The new sites would make possible the construction of a kindergarten and a permanent clubhouse. The Government had also, incidentally, decided to set up a Conservatory of Music in Egypt. For the earnest lover of music that Huda was, this news was thrilling. Music could not fail, as she saw it, to complement the efforts that were being deployed in the other arts and assist in promoting the spirit of a humanistic culture in the country and the world.

Before sailing for the United States in the summer of 1927, Huda had gone to visit the tomb of Adila Nabarawi, Céza's stepmother. Adila had been one of her two dearest friends from the strange days of her youth during the period of her unconsummated marriage with Ali Shaarawi, when she had been able to devote her teenage years to growing up instead of playing the young bride. In the autumn of 1927, Céza reminded her of this visit when she sent Huda news of the death in Syria of Subhi al-Nabarawi, Adila's former husband. The Egyptian newspaper *Al-Ahram* described him as a great Egyptian scientist who was also a member of the Lebanese Government's Public Education Committee. His funeral was attended by the Lebanese Minister of

Education and other distinguished personalities. Céza was appalled.[14] As far as she was concerned, Nabarawi had been dishonest all his life, and yet he had survived Adila by almost a quarter of a century. He was worthless, she thought, and did not deserve the posthumous tributes he received. Both Céza and Huda still mourned Adila, and this was an emotional bond they shared through their remembrance of the past.

After Zaghlul's death, it was necessary to choose a new leader for the Wafd. On 26 September, party members selected Mustafa al-Nahhas, who had been Zaghlul's right-hand man and had been serving as the party's Secretary. Nahhas immediately made clear his entrenched opposition to the current Prime Minister, Tharwat, despite the fact that Zaghlul had promised on behalf of the Wafd not to be hostile. Nahhas violently berated Tharwat for the talks he had held with the British Foreign Secretary, Austin Chamberlain, while he was in London with King Fuad, which had resulted in the draft agreement by which the British protectorate would be transformed over ten years into a treaty of alliance and friendship. The Wafd and other nationalists now said they regarded this agreement as tantamount to the legal perpetuation of the British protectorate. On 28 March 1928, this confrontation led to the resignation of Tharwat. The outcome was that Nahhas Pasha became Prime Minister and the Wafd returned to power, to the anger of Lord Lloyd. The British, however, were able to do little to prevent it, since the Egyptian political establishment, having been obliging to British whims on many occasion in the past, seemed unable or unwilling this time to come up with any viable alternative.

This was not to last for long, however. On 25 June 1928, the King found a pretext for dismissing Nahhas, and Muhammed Mahmud took office. On 19 July, he dissolved parliament and suspended elections for three years. The country would be ruled by royal decree. Worst of all, in October 1928 he suspended the 1923 constitution and proposed new arrangements so that when the democratic process resumed there would be a curious electoral procedure with indirect polls, in which parliamentary candidates would be elected by individuals chosen by carefully selected groups from the broader electorate.

Huda despaired of these assaults on the democratic process. Rather than plunge into politics, however, she kept her eyes this time focused on her charity work, which kept her increasingly busy. Funds were collected at the annual bazaar of the EFU to start building the planned new school for girls. More than three thousand people came to a bazaar held at a venue lent by the Levantine Lutfalla Princes. All the products of the various workshops were offered for sale, with the Rod al-Farag potteries exhibited alongside the carpets and needlework of the EFU workshops. Paintings donated by the members of the Les Amis de l'Art and La Chimère were also sold, while Abd al-Wahab and Umm-Kulthum sang their latest songs. There were, as usual, the remarkable *tableaux vivants*, in which Huda's girls participated. The tickets always sold very well for these events, so that there was a regular inflow of funds to support the schools and other projects.[15]

Huda's house at 2 Qasr al-Nil Street, which Ali had built, had by now come to play its own role in Huda's social and professional life. Inspired by Charles Crane's oriental salon, she decided it needed to be redecorated to live up to its purpose. If the house was to be the headquarters of Huda's journal and the social movement it represented, and to be worthy of the name of Bait al-Misria (House of the Egyptian Woman), as many people were already calling it, it had to look the part. It needed to be oriental in its appearance, while reconciling Western and Eastern styles. It had hitherto been decorated in the liberty style that prevailed in Egypt at the time. Huda realised that foreign visitors needed to see something more Egyptian. As her architect, she chose Antonio Lasciac, the well-known Italian who had been commissioned by Huda's brother Umar to build his *salamlik* in the garden of the Sultan family house in Jami Sharkas Street. He had designed many buildings in Cairo, and seemed the person best qualified for the job.

She was given heart to embark on the task by a promise from Mahmud Sami Pasha and Bassna to give their unstinting help when they returned from their diplomatic posting in Washington. Their help in supervising the work would be invaluable when Huda, as always, had so much to do. The house needed to become a symbol of freedom of speech and justice, not only in Egypt, but also in the whole world, and an emblem of understanding between East and West. She would use it to reinforce relations between people of goodwill. Lasciac's task was to change the style of the mansion from liberty to traditional Arabian by totally refurbishing the façade, the terrace and the balconies using the different elements of Cairene Arabic architecture. Thanks to the carved woodwork, battlements, little columns and stalactites that would echo those of the renowned Zogheb house next door, the façade would present the desired Moorish look. It would be in many ways similar to the Sultan house in Jami Sharkas Street. When future visitors arrived in these evocative settings every Tuesday evening, they were meant to feel as if they had been plunged into the *Thousand and One Nights*. The house itself, she hoped, would be a source of inspiration, stimulating creativity and thought.

Carved woodwork was chosen for the ceilings, doors and shutters. Huda found Syrian wooden ceilings that were painted in the best tradition, carved wooden doors inset with ivory, specially designed wooden floors, as well as huge brass chandeliers, marble columns, marble floors and fountains, and Turkish ceramics. These were to be the starting point for a personalised oriental style. A whole new salon was to be added to the ground floor, adjacent to and communicating with the dining-room. This famous Oriental Salon, as it became known, communicated with another salon in the Western style. This served to symbolise the magazine, which was meant to be a bridge of peace between the East and the West, like the Suez Canal: 'un trait d'union entre l'Orient et l'Occident' ('a link between East and West'). In these rooms, Huda was to hold many vital meetings.

In the centre of the Oriental Salon there was a fountain. The water flowed from the centre of the fountain out of an ancient carved stone in such a way that four jets sprang out to meet another four jets from the four

corners that emerged through the mouths of small marble representations
of frogs and mythical animals. The floor of the sitting-room was made of
coloured marble mosaics, and the walls were lined with sofas and couches.
Two windows were glazed in stained glass. Four pink marble columns
delicately divided the hall into three areas without obstructing its open
space. One end was framed by large windows, overlooking the garden on
the outside. The other end was separated from what became known as

The Oriental Salon.

the European Salon next door by a door made up of four panels lined with mirrors that were firmly fixed to the wood by large brass nails. The mirrors were inside the European Salon while, on the Arab side, the door was entirely made of Persian woodwork, inset with ivory arabesques and carved miniatures. An enormous brass chandelier hung down from the middle of the painted wooden ceiling honeycombed with beams.

The elegant wooden floor of the European Salon contrasted with the elaborate arabesques of the marble tiles of the Oriental Salon. The European Salon was decorated in the purest Western style, with sofas and gilded armchairs of the Louis XV period, a beautiful piano in light wood, and vast carpets especially woven to fit the huge spaces of the double sitting-room, which were, like the other salon, divided by pillars into separate areas. Paintings and tapestries hung on the walls. The two salons complemented each other, and each was meant to provide a soothing setting for the day's needs and moods. Going from one to the other was a demonstration of how the passage from one culture to the other could be simple, enriching and nourishing to the soul. A sense of adventure emanated, like passing from one world to another. They demonstrated how differences could be reconciled, and generated a sense of harmony between the two worlds.

The rest of the house, as Lasciac designed it, was also divided between Eastern and Western styles. The large entrance and the hall were decorated in an oriental style involving boxed-in painted planks for the ceiling, endless carpets and huge brass chests, with sofas nonchalantly covered with tapestries and cushions that smacked of the *Thousand and One Nights*. On the other hand, the large dining-hall accommodated a long table, chairs and cupboards in the best sixteenth-century Italian style, including dressers and glass cabinets bedecked with wooden carvings. Even the bedrooms were decorated in two ways, according to the European taste on the first floor and in an oriental manner on the upper floor, with wooden ceilings, chimneys covered by ceramic tiles, wooden furniture and beds inlaid with mother of pearl and ivory, echoing the style of all the doors in the house. The shutters were of handmade *mashrabia* woodwork to match the oriental façade.

Her guests continued to come faithfully on Tuesdays. All the usual people were still at her elbow, the Liberal Constitutionalists, the poets and artists who surrounded her, the interesting foreign visitors, and her extended family and their friends. In these days, King Fuad's brother, Prince Muhammad Ali Tawfiq, who was so attentive that he had become known as 'Huda Shaarawi's Prince Charming', was a faithful standby, frequently attending her evenings. The poet Khalil Mutran was another regular visitor, and later, in a poem dedicated to Huda and her feminist colleagues, he described her house.

Huda continued to write a stream of articles for *L'Égyptienne* even while she was away from home. On 27 August 1928, an important agreement for international peace was signed in Paris. This was the Kellogg-Briand pact, signed by 15 nations, which committed its signatories to a total renunciation of war, with the hope that their example would be followed by all nations.[16] The idea of the pact had been proposed by Aristide Briand, the French Minister of Foreign Affairs, and promoted by the American Under-secretary of State, Frank Kellogg. When she wrote about the pact in *'L'Égyptienne'*, Huda seized the opportunity to raise the question of Egypt's demand for membership at the League of Nations. Egypt, as she pointed out, was at the crossroads of three continents. It was therefore a key country whose neutrality needed to be respected, not least because its role in the history of civilisation bore witness to its capacity to consolidate peace.

On 25 September 1928, Tharwat Pasha died in Paris, not long after finally leaving office, and his funeral took place there. The obituary Huda wrote was published in *L'Égyptienne*. She conjured up a picture of Tharwat, having laid down the cares of office, returning to his beloved France. She described him briskly walking by the Seine, looking for books at the pavement stalls by the river while chatting and laughing in his own quiet way with whoever was his companion.[17] Si Kaddur Bin-Ghabrit, a Morrocan writer and high official who was the rector of the

Mosque of Paris, organised the funeral procession, which set off from the mosque, and Egyptians came from all parts of France and Europe to accompany Tharwat on his last walk through the French capital. Tharwat's family, representatives of the French Government and the British Ambassador in Paris also walked in the cortège, together with many of Tharwat's old friends and political colleagues. In another article, Huda lamented Tharwat's unexpected death, and recalled his courageous deeds in government and his achievements. He was a man, she said, who had worked hard for the restoration of peace. She did not herself take part in the funeral because it was not the custom for women to do so, but she spent a long time with his widow, seeking to comfort her. She admired Tharwat, and was appreciative of his achievements in his peace talks with the British, hoping that he would achieve after death the recognition that was his due as a statesman when he was alive.

8

The question of Greater Syria

Huda was less militant on some issues relating to equality between the sexes than on others. In 1928, the journalist Salama Musa urged her to advocate equal shares for both genders in such matters as inheritance. In response, she published an article in *L'Égyptienne* in which she insisted that she had not been mandated by the other members of the EFU to take up this cause and that, in her own opinion, the issue should not be raised at all.[1] Her contention was that Egyptian women were not capable of earning a living for themselves or their children, with the result that they needed to rely on their men for the material necessities of life. For this reason, she never questioned the soundness of the Sharia law that granted men double the women's share of inheritance. In addition, she took the view that, while in the case of the veil and of polygamy the relevant verses of the Qur'an were open to alternative interpretations, such was not the case with inheritance, where the rules were clear.

In 1929, Salama Musa, himself a Coptic Christian, invited Huda to lecture on Islam and feminism at the Cairo YMCA. She reaffirmed her belief in the basic values of Islam, pointing out that were the rules on inheritance to be questioned, the outcome might be that husbands might avoid their commitment to their wives and children. This in turn could have the effect that poorer women deprived of any fortune or any inheritance of their own, might be doomed to a yet more miserable fate. On the other hand, she noted that it should not be forgotten that in some respects women living in Muslim countries were better off than their sisters in the West. Though Muslim women were permitted to inherit only half the share allotted to their male siblings, many Western women were obliged by the law to hand over their property and money to their husbands until 1883. She published these views in an article in *L'Égyptienne*.[2]

Huda clearly took the view that civil rights could be broadened within an Islamic context through discussion of the issues with the Ulamas and with Muslim legislators. To take the issue of polygamy, for instance, the verse allowing for polygamy embodies the condition that the husband should love his four wives equally and treat them on a par, adding 'and thou shalt not be able to do it'. This may be taken as an expression of God's will to either limit or wholly negate the rights apparently granted by the preceding verse. She certainly believed it was possible to amend the interpretation of verses that seemed to indicate the permissibility of the use of *waqf* endowments to prevent girls from receiving their rightful inheritance and to find canonical justification for women to be given the right to an education, a job and participation in political life. While reinterpretation might not be feasible in certain fields, the reformulation of the law related to marriage, divorce, the custody of children and the use of the house of submission was practicable and would, as she put it, 'promote the welfare and happiness of families' as a whole.

All this was in line with her opinions concerning the veil. She had taken the matter into her own hands and uncovered her face with the dramatic gesture that became so famous because there was no verse in the Qur'an stipulating that women had to cover their faces, though some contend that such a regulation did apply specifically to the wives of the Prophet Muhammad. No similar latitude was available in relation to the verses concerning inheritance, so any attempt to reinterpret the Sharia laws on this issue would be unacceptable in the eyes of the Ulema, and would be seen as a challenge to Islam.

Prince Umar Tusun was a man of culture and learning, and an ardent nationalist, but was very conservative in matters of religion. He sent Huda a letter commenting on her article in *L'Égyptienne* on these issues:

> I have had the pleasure ... of seeing that wisdom and level-headedness have guided you in all your undertakings for the emancipation of Egyptian women, as well as all the efforts you unceasingly deploy for reform, with your advocacy of the observance of our religious laws and attachment to our most useful customs and morals which constitute the true characteristics of our nation and its spirit. Some of us, alarmed by the extent of the divide between the Western peoples and our own have sought, no doubt in good faith, to preach the abandonment of our national traditions, and have attempted to divert us from the principles of our religion. Such persons evidently believe they could lead us to become, abruptly and without evolution, a part of the West, because they are convinced that nothing can rid us of the backward situation in which we find ourselves, other than the destruction of our morals, our customs and our religion. Such principles can only lead to the most disastrous results, and those who propagate them will themselves realise some day that they are on the wrong road.[3]

This letter confirmed Huda's belief that the only path to change in Egypt was gradual reform rather than revolution, and that it was within the tradition and the customs of the Muslim world that Egypt would find its inspiration. Islamic art and architecture, the mystic approach to religion, and every characteristic of the opulent and graceful Islamic civilisation of the past should be cherished, exploited and refined. With this in mind, she commissioned Céza to write an article about Prince Muhammad Ali Tawfiq's Manial Palace on the island of Rhoda, situated in the heart of Cairo, which invited Egyptians to build, 'rather than banal constructions in the modern taste, ... elegant and original houses in the country's native style'. Preserving the spirit of Cairo as an oriental city became the duty of the women of Egypt.[4]

By 1929, Huda's health had begun noticeably to deteriorate, with circulation problems and her varicose veins becoming chronic. Her energy no longer seemed boundless, and it was becoming harder for her to include any other new activities on her agenda, though her existing commitments were already wide enough. Her charitable efforts in Egypt and her political presence on the international scene through her active membership of the IAW left her little time. Céza and Jeanne were pillars of strength, but others such as Hawa and Huria were still too young to be fully relied on, and were still in any case in full-time education as boarders at the Cairo American College for Girls. However, they and their friends had begun to take part in the annual events of the EFU. Huda was enchanted by their Circassian beauty, the standard of feminine pulchritude imprinted upon her from childhood.

The most painful task for Huda, as 1929 began, was self-imposed. She had decided that a mosque and mausoleum was to be built for Ali on his native soil, at Minya. She therefore had to face up to the process of overseeing the transfer of Ali's mortal remains from Cairo to the purpose-built mosque.[5] The exhumation of his body was an ordeal for Huda and Muhammad, who were both present at this dramatic operation. All the old regrets flooded back. She wished she could tell Ali that she had finally understood his motivations when he left the Wafd party. She felt she had been rash and immature when she quarrelled with him, and had hurt his feelings at a time when they might have discussed the matter more freely together. But, like everyone else at the time, she had been captivated by Zaghlul's charisma. Ali had never been inclined to articulate his emotions, while she always demanded clarity from her interlocutors, especially the ones closest to her heart.

This was a trait for which Muhammad had recently begun to chide her. He had always been inclined to open his heart to her, but had suddenly begun to refrain from expressing his deepest thoughts. During an angry argument, he said he knew she had no time for him, that she would never really listen, and that it was no use trying to communicate with her. However, he still dutifully made large contributions to the EFU. He gave her 500 pounds on the occasion of the annual fair in 1929 for the construction of the EFU's planned new vocational school for girls in Qasr el-Aini Street.[6] Bassna also made a charitable gesture on the occasion of her father's exhumation and reburial, by donating 100 pounds to the young girls of the workshop.

Many women Huda knew in Egypt were doing very well in the late twenties. A source of pride for Huda in early 1929 was Mayy Ziadé's nomination as a member of the selection committee for the Government's awards to playwrights.[7] All the other members of this committee were men of letters and high officials, and Mayy's inclusion was a good omen for the feminists. On the eve of the Berlin congress of the IAW in June 1929, Huda wrote an article about women's suffrage in England. The women of England had just obtained the right to vote on the same terms as men, which Huda interpreted as a victory for all women in the world. Huda deplored the fact that despite this progress, change was still obstructed in the countries under British occupation. Wherever men were not free, she argued, they were unable to grant their women rights that they themselves did not exercise. Under British control, Egypt's men certainly were not allowed to take their destiny into their own hands.

As the preparations got under way for the congress, Huda was asked as an executive-committee member to go to Berlin early to take part in the preliminary planning. The theme of the Berlin congress was to be support for the Kellogg-Briand pact and advocacy for the cause of universal peace. Most of the speeches at the preparatory meeting emphasised the role of women in promoting peace measures. Mothers, said Huda and the other women, were the natural enemies of war, and peace would best be served by promoting justice. She believed that women were best qualified to identify injustice, and were thus best placed to guide men on the tracks of peace. She argued that it was logical that the congress should address not only women's issues but also the theme of peace, since peace was a crucial issue for women. The echoes of the world war were still strong, and fear of another was mounting.

Huda was enchanted by the German capital, to which this was her first visit. Berlin was an elegant city with broad avenues, fine buildings and verdant open spaces, as well as its famous alleys of lime trees. The city was hospitable to visitors, and Baroness Katharina von Kardorff, the wife of the Vice President of the Reichstag and herself a former Reichstag member, had in any case recently visited Egypt, where she had met Egyptian feminist activists and published several articles about Egypt. The Baroness seems to have taken Huda up during this visit. Huda also had time to begin to admire the German spirit and to appreciate Germany's poets and writers.[8]

In another development in the run-up to the congress, the EFU appointed an advisory committee of sympathetic men to assist Huda and her colleagues in policy formation ahead of the meeting. The EFU had always benefited informally from the advice of male well-wishers, in the main Huda's old Liberal Constitutionalist friends, who participated in planning the organisation's various projects, bringing to bear their own various brands of expertise. Huda and Céza both supported the idea of setting up a formal advisory committee. These were men who would provide a strong moral support to the EFU, in return for which they would obtain an indirect platform for their own ideas at international gatherings where Huda and Céza participated. Among the members of the committee as it came into existence were some of Ali's closest friends. These included Muhammad Husain Haikal, Ahmad Lutfi al-Sayid, Muhammad Ali Alluba, Shaikh Mustafa Abd al-Raziq, Dr Muhammad Shahin, Mansur Fahmi, Ali Umar, Taha Husain Pasha, Murad Bey Sid Ahmad, Muhammad Fahmi al-Amrussi, Antoun Gemayel and Zaki Ali Bey. These were men of ability in whom Huda had confidence, and most of them were, or had been, high officials in the Egyptian Government or elsewhere. They were men of the world, who sensibly supported the empowerment of women.

On 17 June 1929, the eleventh IAW congress opened at last in the Reichstag building in Berlin. Margery Corbett-Ashby delivered the opening address, on the theme of women and peace. She focused on the women's past victories, when the feminist struggle was greeted by what she described as persecution, ridicule and caricature. Women were the first underprivileged group to struggle for their rights and win, though the battle would be long. Corbett-Ashby stressed the value of women's experience. Having welcomed delegates from Japan, China, India and the Dutch Indies, who were attending the congress for the first time, she drew attention to the presence of two women pilots who had flown across the African continent. These were Sophie Heath, who had flown from London to South Africa and back in a Tiger Moth, and Mary Bailey who was similarly intrepid. She ended on a hopeful note, pointing out that serious work might seem dull to the onlooker but is exciting to those absorbed in it. Rather than 'wine, women and song', she opined, let there be 'peace, women, humanity'.[9]

When Huda's turn came to speak, she said that women, as mothers, were the natural enemies of war, and that peace would best be promoted if justice prevailed in the world. By now, Huda had developed a powerful talent for oratory, and she put her deep, husky voice to use to great effect. She believed that women were best qualified to identify injustice, and that they could help their powerful men to pave the way to peaceful settlements wherever violence or injustice had broken out. Racial discrimination must also be abolished, she said. 'As long as mutual fraternal trust does not exist between all the peoples of different colour – there will be no peace.'[10]

It was in Berlin that Huda discovered more about India's struggle for independence, and the example it could set for Egypt. When Sarojini Naidu spoke on behalf of India, Huda felt an instinctive sympathy. Huda saw there was much in common between Egypt and India. Indian women, like the women of Egypt, participated in the struggle against colonialism. Naidu, an influential feminist, was also a staunch Indian nationalist who was close to Mahatma Gandhi and Jawaharlal Nehru, and was destined after independence to become Governor of Uttar Pradesh, one of India's states. In Naidu and Huda herself, the Eastern world had two remarkable representatives. Like Huda, Naidu also had a strong, warm voice. Both women conveyed their message with grace and elegance. Each had the decisive advantage of total sincerity. Both wholeheartedly believed in the causes they defended and were ready to pay for their beliefs. The two women's views were indeed very much alike.[11] Each insisted there was no truth in Rudyard Kipling's dictum that East and West shall never meet. Strong and dedicated individuals could make communication possible against the odds. Women from the ends of the earth, such as those meeting at the Congress, could stand face to face and speak with each other. Huda began to read more about India, and in particular to study the ideas of Gandhi, the so-called 'Great Soul'.

A source of personal happiness at the time, which buoyed Huda up during the proceedings, was that she was aware before she set off for Berlin that Bassna was definitely coming back to Cairo, since Sami Pasha had completed his tour of duty at the Egyptian Embassy in Washington. To know that her daughter and her daughter's husband would soon be back in Egypt was for Huda a source of joy. Mahmud Sami Pasha was a physically large man, perhaps to an extent that cannot have been good for his health. However, he was cheerful, outgoing and a considerate husband. Bassna throve in her beloved giant's presence, like a flower in the diligent care of its able gardener. The couple had built solid friendships in the United States and, as Egypt's Ambassador, Mahmud Sami Pasha had won wide confidence and respect. From Berlin, Huda travelled cheerfully back to Cairo, where she knew that love and support from her daughter and son-in-law would now be freely available to her. She also needed love, believe it or not.

The offices of *L'Égyptienne* at this time often rang to the sound of spirited arguments between Hawa and Céza about Russia, as the communist state took shape. Céza could not hide her enthusiasm for the Russian Revolution, while Hawa, who had been born in the Caucasus and brought up with the story of the massacres perpetrated by the Russian army against her people, passionately hated Russia and the Russians in any form because of her family's past history. For her, the overthrow of the Tsar had made no difference, since the country had not changed. In any case, as to communism, Hawa could not imagine how such a system might be successful. In her opinion, it was a utopian philosophy that human beings could never successfully implement. Huda went on with her work, and listened cheerfully to their stormy discussions. In support of Céza, she sometimes played devil's advocate against Hawa, asserting that she would not mind being stripped of her fortune by a communist government, and would happily live on a small plot of land, as little as five acres, if need be. Hawa, who was unable ever to hold her tongue, sharply replied, 'Do you really think, Tante Huda, that you could have financed all your activities with a few acres of land?' Of course, Huda knew well, in reality, that despite what she might say to tease Hawa, her enormous fortune, which was her source of empowerment, had to be preserved to sustain her activities.

All Huda's instincts told her she should try to do something to improve the political situation in Egypt, but her instinct for self-preservation intervened. With the passage of time, and with not merely Ali, but also Zaghlul having now disappeared from the scene, her political leverage had diminished. She therefore turned her back on politics, and looked instead towards her charity work. So much of her time in the immediately previous years had been spent travelling and in the international feminist movement that she felt she had neglected this aspect of her self-imposed duty. The time had come once more to raise funds and take steps to ensure that the EFU's planned vocational school for girls would at last be built, and she also needed to keep a closer eye on the artists and the affairs of the pottery.

She always felt obliged to develop talent where she saw it, and had found a promising young man named Abd al-Badi Abd al-Hayy, who was working for her as a cook, and seemed a potential artist. She had seen him carving pieces of wood outside the kitchen after his working hours, and he appeared to have skills that could make him a sculptor. She talked to him about his hobby, and how it could become his profession, but succeeded at first only in making him angry, because he misjudged her tone. With Gandhi's ideas about the dignity of labour in her mind, she pointed out to him that there was nothing wrong with being a cook. After all, she told him, a good cook can also be a good artist. To which he sharply retorted, 'Yes, but once the product of his art is digested, there is nothing left of it in the mind.'[12] She had perhaps neglected the truth that the dignity of labour is sometimes not so obvious to the labourer.

Abd al-Badi seemed so irritated that she felt sorry for having been so outspoken. She had, frankly, been unable truly to imagine what it was like to be poor. It was a fault of hers, she was aware, to lecture people from the point of view of theory without taking into account the practical situation. To set matters straight, she felt she had to make practical recompense for her own lack of sensitivity. The young man could not study formally, due to his lack of qualifications, so she sent him to be taught by Boris Friedman Klüzel, a Swedish artist who had established himself in Egypt. Abd al-Badi did not disappoint her expectations, and began to display real talent. Huda was proud of her new protégé.

Time seemed to run as swiftly as ever, and death regularly took its toll on people whom Huda knew. Prince Haidar Fazil, described by Ronald Storrs as 'stout and good-natured', died on 25 November 1929 at the relatively young age of 51, another of Huda's old acquaintance to depart. This stirred once more Huda's remembrance of the cruise to Upper Egypt with her late and still much lamented brother Umar, when the Prince had accompanied Juliette Adam and Mustapha Kamil on Umar's Nile boat, talking about Kamil's nationalist ambitions, in the days when he had seemed Egypt's brightest hope. Prince Haidar was a family connection of Huda's, a mystic who had become a Sufi. He often visited the Bektashi dervishes at their monastery perched on an outer ridge of the Muqattam Hills near Cairo. It was said in the family that he drank wine with the dervishes and was quarrelsome when he went home, so that long since, in 1909, Zainab Fahmi had separated from him. This story may well have been defamatory. Huda, however, had always enjoyed Prince Haidar's collaboration with *L'Égyptienne*, and regretted his absence when he died.

She was busy as always, however, and had little time for grieving. She was preparing a lecture she had promised to deliver at the Ewart Hall of the American University in Cairo on 12 November 1929. Huda had been a founding benefactor of the AUC, a fact that the institution did not fail to acknowledge in its records.[13] In her address, she spoke about the liberation of women in the United States, the great feminist figures of France, the feminist movement in Egypt, and other issues related to gender empowerment and to education. She did not fail to mention the philosophy of the Saint Simonians, a social movement which had originated in France and was appreciative of the role played by women in social development. She had not forgotten her childhood friend Mme Richard and her Saint Simonian relatives and friends.[14]

In 1929, a darker cloud appeared on the horizon when events in Palestine first began to attract her attention. She began to hear from visitors to Cairo and acquaintances in Palestine that the Arab Palestinians were deeply apprehensive of the consequences of massive immigration of largely Ashkenazi Jews from outside the Middle East into the region. These were an alien element, from Russia, Germany and Eastern Europe, and had little understanding of local customs and conditions. The arrival of Mizrahi Jews from the Arab world would come later. The Palestinians also viewed with suspicion the policies of the West concerning the settlement of the Jews in a tiny country that had hitherto been undivided and peaceful. *L'Égyptienne* followed developments faithfully, and reported the outbreak of disturbances in Palestine, where both Muslim and Christian Arab women had gone unveiled to the British High Commissioner to demand justice. Céza emphatically underlined the significance of this development: 'With this gesture of freedom, they demonstrated that nobody, not even women, should hide when it comes to demanding what any man, or any population, has not only the right, but also the duty to demand, namely impartiality and justice.'[15]

Huda followed closely the distressing events that were about to rend Greater Syria apart. Old King Hussein of the Hejaz, better known as Sharif Hussein, because he was a descendant of the Prophet Muhammad, incessantly proclaimed his despair at the false promises made to his family by the British Government. Resentment and anger prevailed across the former Greater Syria as it became clear that occupation by France and Britain was turning out to be more oppressive than the rule of the Ottoman Turks had ever been. The unjustly imposed mandates in the region had been blessed by the international community, despite the promise by the Western powers to free these lands from Ottoman rule. Through Palestinian friends like Auni Abd al-Hadi, the mayor of Jerusalem, and his wife Tarab, Huda gradually pieced together a clearer idea of developments in the recently established mandated territories, where Syria and Iraq had become in effect French and British possessions, while Palestine had also been placed under a British mandate. The steady influx of Jewish immigrants into Palestine continued to cause deep concern.

One of her informants on Palestine was a Maitre Sayba Garzouzi, a Palestinian woman lawyer resident in Egypt who worked at the mixed tribunals in Cairo where the capitulatory laws were applied. She was a frequent visitor to Huda's Tuesday evenings. Sayba Garzouzi sometimes visited the United States, where she had lectured at New York University and at Williams College, Massachusetts, together with the Turkish feminist Halidé Edib. These two women had met some of the most powerful men in America, like Curtis James, Morgan Prentiss and, of course, Charles Crane, discussing with them all the vital issues that concerned the Middle East.[16] She was also incidentally able to give Huda news about Carrie Chapman Catt's declining health, which saddened her.

Huda's erstwhile admiration for the energy and dynamism of the Zionist settlers in Palestine now gave way to profound misgivings. What she and her staff at *L'Égyptienne* had perhaps naively seen as practical measures on the part of the Jewish immigrants to develop Palestine for the benefit of all now seemed increasingly to be taking on the shape of an organised scheme to bring in Jews to replace the local Arab population, both Muslims and Christians. The first phase of the Zionist plan of action seemed to be to reinforce and consolidate the Jewish community in Palestine through systematic immigration. The second step would apparently be to dispossess the Arab inhabitants of Palestine of their villages and lands, replacing the Palestinian community and its infrastructure with something new and different. Despite elements of lingering incredulity that such events could truly be taking place, Huda decided that *L'Égyptienne* must report faithfully the plight of the threatened Arab population of Palestine.

Huda believed that the EFU must henceforth express a clear position in support of the beleaguered Palestinians, both Christian and Muslim, in whatever international forums were available to it. The goals of the EFU could in general terms be said to be expressions of a general desire to save the world from its own destructive hatred and madness. Huda could see no alternative than to support the Palestinians, the Syrians and the Iraqis in their struggle against the continuing occupation of their countries by Western military forces. In her eyes, these newly created nations in the Middle East were suffering the same oppression which Egypt had undergone for years. The inescapable conclusion as far as Palestine was concerned was that force was being brought to bear to change the reality of the country through violent action, against the will of the local population.

Sadly for Huda, the struggle this time was to be against the French as well as the British. France had regrettably demonstrated that it was not the reliable friend it seemed to be when represented by people like Juliette Adam, Victor Hugo, Pierre Loti and other republican thinkers. Such people, she concluded with regret, had obscured the true intentions of the French Government like a smokescreen hiding the unpleasant reality and masking the intentions of the French Government from Egyptian patriots who had always trusted in France. Lessons were to be learned from these developments, and yet at the same time there was a need to keep in touch with French and English friends, fellow feminists and sympathetic politicians, in order to keep a dialogue open. It was indeed sad for Huda, who was both Francophone and Francophile, to contemplate that at the beginning of the 1930s, the French mandates in Greater Syria, as in North Africa, were taking on an even more destructive character than the British mandate in Iraq. In Syria, the country was being dismembered, the education of the rising younger generation was being curtailed or manipulated, natural borders were disregarded, and communities of different religious faiths were set against each other. At the inauguration of the Arab Academy by King Fuad in December 1929, Huda met the President of the Lebanese Academy, Muhammad Jamil Beyhum, who was the President of the University of Beirut at the time and deeply versed in the regional situation. He agreed to write articles in Huda's magazine about the French mandate in Syria and the British mandate in Iraq. He would continue to be an influence in her life in years to come.[17]

At around this time, Huda began to feel something akin to a mystical sensation that her life no longer belonged to herself alone. She had the sensation of being a part of something larger than one individual alone. The French writer André Lichtenberger visited her a month later to interview her for an article, in which he commented that there was a shade of mystery in her wistful smile, and that she showed great restraint in her demeanour. He sat in her company in the spacious Oriental Salon, where he reported that he strove to read her mind but feared that she might make fun of him for trying. His article about Huda's smile was published in *L'Égyptienne*. When Huda read it, she said it was nonsense. Céza disagreed, saying the article would serve to intensify publicity about Egypt in France, and would conquer more hearts in the West.[18] Her smile was the inpenetrable smile of the *Mona Lisa*, of a sphinx, he said.

Prosaically, the everyday affairs of the EFU went on. The new year, 1930, began as usual with the EFU's annual fair, held that year at the Kursaal Dalbagni Theatre. The profits from the event were destined once more to be put towards the construction of the EFU's school, which now at least had the site that had been secured for the building in Qasr el-Aini Street. A contract had been signed with the architect Mustafa Fahmi, who was to draw up plans. The building would be undertaken by an Italian firm, Messrs Santo and Bianchi. Huda planned to lay the foundation stone on 2 April 1930.

The well-known conservative beliefs of King Fuad were shared by his personal physician, Dr Muhammad Shahin Pasha, who was also the Under-secretary of State for the Ministry of Health. In 1930,[19] Dr Shahin inaugurated an Egyptian Museum of Health, housed at the magnificent rococo Sakakini Palace adjacent to the mosque of Baybars I in Abbasiya. The house had been donated to the Ministry of Health by the family of Habib Sakakini Pasha, a Syrian merchant who had built it in 1897. Shahin regarded the Museum of Health as an educational project, and despite his antipathy to the feminist movement he approached Huda to give it publicity. She commissioned Céza to write an article about it.[20] When she came to visit the museum, Shahin Pasha showed Céza personally through the halls of the palace. He seems to have been impressed by Céza, and perhaps this was the reason he later accepted an invitation from Huda to be an EFU adviser, despite his reputed misogyny. In years to come, he would introduce a number of measures that met with Huda's approval.

More than ten years had elapsed since the women's march in 1919, and Huda had become calmer and more philosophical. She was less quick to take up the cudgels, and more willing to cooperate on pragmatic grounds with those who did not wholly share her opinions. She had even settled her differences with Russell Pasha, the police chief who had deliberately humiliated her and her friends. He had now thrown himself into a campaign against the opium trade in Egypt, of which she approved, and also shared the women's belief that prostitution must be eradicated in order to halt the spread of syphilis and other venereal diseases in the country. Russell Pasha and Mrs Russell were therefore now included in her list of guests, not necessarily in his capacity as the commander of the Egyptian Police Force, but certainly as an ally in advocating crucial campaigns.

The Samis, Bassna and Mahmud, now thoroughly settled back in Cairo, often helped to host her social events, which she found a great help. Huda's health was becoming yet more problematic. She felt strangely tired at times. Her legs, which had always given her trouble, tended to swell and hurt if she stood for any length of time. Her chest was often heavy and, at night, she sometimes gasped for air while waiting for sleep to come. But she told herself she really had no time to worry about such matters during the day, when she gave her time unstintingly to people who needed her and to her social and political work. Huda had sometimes said that she had never consciously thought of having a life 'of her own'. She would turn this sentence over in her mind, wondering what it might mean. Was her life not a life of her own? Was there a special way to live that was in some way one's own? Her active, restless way of life was all she knew. She accepted people and events as they came, and pursued a course of dutiful service to others without questioning its necessity. That this might be an abnormal way of life, or that her activities might be disturbing to others in her immediate environment, had never occurred to her. Egypt stood above all else, and she was its devoted servant.

By 1930, women in Egypt and elsewhere were beginning to play a part in professions and activities that had hitherto been closed to them. Huda always sought to encourage such bold representatives of her gender. In February 1930, she held a reception for two British policewomen, Commander Mary Allen, one of the first women in the world to be a senior police officer, who visited Egypt with her colleague Inspector Helen Taggart. Another phenomenon was that women pilots were being trained in various countries, and one such, Egypt's Lutfia al-Nadi, was sponsored and supported by the EFU. Women drivers participated in racing tournaments, and a motor rally for women was launched from the Mena House Hotel. Bassna and Sami Pasha assisted Huda to entertain these intrepid women and others at 2 Qasr al-Nil Street and elsewhere.[21]

Huda was now 50 years old. She was a woman of great self-discipline, though it might also be said that she knew little of the pathways of temptation. She led a very regular life. Her days began around 6.30 a.m., with a copious breakfast. She generally felt hungry when she woke up, pining for her cup of tea, followed by fried eggs, toast and marmalade.

Mabruk, her faithful dog, a trusty German shepherd, brought her the newspapers every morning and spent a few moments with her. Having eaten her breakfast and read the newspapers, she would dress. Her customary clothes were very sober, and she preferred grey and navy blue. She often wore ethnic black dresses, on the other hand, when she went to dinner parties, and felt more elegant in these than in any other garments. She ran the house herself, together with the head *suffragi*. Her routine when not travelling was to entertain friends in the morning, then settle down to work on the magazine or go out if need be. She would visit the workshops or the factory, and sometimes she would go shopping if there was the occasion. After that, there were often guests to lunch, and of course her close helpers and friends were always there every day, including Céza, Hawa, Huria, Salih Hashim, who had been Muhammad's Arabic teacher, Gaby, occasionally Valentine, and others, as well as, naturally, her son Muhammad and daughter Bassna whenever they wished to come. She would also entertain at tea, or have guests for dinner. When the occasion called for it, she might travel to Minya to see for herself that all was well at her estates, and take care of any business there that called for her personal attention.

An important development in Huda's personal life that year was that Muhammad at long last agreed to marry Munira. He had run across Munira by chance one day when Fatma Asim brought her to Qasr al-Nil Street, and perceived that now she had grown up she was a beautiful young woman. He therefore consented at last to the marriage his mother so much desired. The plan was that the couple would live with Huda at Qasr al-Nil Street, in a private section of the house. This required a complete rearrangement of the living area. Huda decided to transfer her quarters to the top floor, where there was room to keep Céza and all her girls around her, and for the business of *L'Égyptienne* to be carried on. As well as her private living quarters, she would also have a study of her own, where she would keep her own desk. In this organised atmosphere, she and her young assistants would be able to go on giving their maximum effort to the feminist and political movement, without interfering with the young couple on the floor below.

The decoration of the top floor of the house was still in an oriental style, as Lasciac had designed it, so she could enjoy the comfort of couches, cushions, carpets, tapestries and delicate woodwork, all of which reminded her pleasantly, as she had intended, of Jami Sharkas Street. Some of the rooms were arranged as duplexes with integrated wooden staircases, with a sleeping area above and a living area below. She selected one of these for herself. There was a profusion of silk in the cushions and precious tapestries, bedspreads and curtains, with richly coloured carpets on the wooden floors. One of the other rooms became her library, packed with books, just as her late father's library had been. The plan was to keep Céza, Hawa and Huria as close as possible, while Muhammad and Munira would reign over the whole first floor with their children and staff.

On the Egyptian political scene, Adly Yakan had once again been called back as Prime Minister in October 1929 to head a caretaker Government that would once more oversee democratic elections. In December 1929, the Wafd yet again won their usual convincing majority, and Nahhas Pasha took over again. The resulting interlude of Wafdist Government was not to last long, however. The King wanted a pro-palace government headed by Ismail Sidqi, who took office on 19 June 1930 and would serve until 1933. Huda was soon appalled by the direction his administration took. He had been one of the original Wafdists deported to Malta with Zaghlul, but had left the Wafd after the War and retired from politics entirely in 1925 at the age of 50. He was brought back by the King, at the instigation of the British, simply to attempt to amend the constitution in such a way as to ensure the Wafd did not return to power. He suspended the constitution on 22 October 1930 and brought in new rules for elections that were extremely indirect and set property and education qualifications on the right to vote that ruled out four Egyptians in five. Ministers were made responsible to the King, not to parliament, and bizarre restrictions were introduced on who could be a candidate for parliament that would have ruled out virtually all the Wafdists. Huda was implacably hostile towards him, and Céza launched a formidable campaign against him in *L'Égyptienne*. He was a strange, albeit brilliant man, and was in many ways a dandy, very conscious of his public figure. He was also a very modern man with progressive ideas, and an able economist. Nevertheless, he struck the women's movement as a ruthless and brutal Prime Minister.[22]

Huda started to feel she was now facing two political adversaries in Egypt. Not merely was there still the British presence, but also developments were taking place within the Egyptian Government that were leading it closer to a dictatorship. The stated reason for Sidqi's 'iron fist' regime, as commentators began to call it, was to give the Government scope to improve the country's living conditions and infrastructure, even in the remotest rural areas, at a time of global economic crisis. This Huda would have been prepared to accept. However, she was still opposed to Sidqi for a number of different reasons. He seemed to be a tool of the British, he was proposing irrevocable change to the constitution, and he did not shrink from using force against the people. She believed he was no more than an instrument of the King and had been brought back into politics to do a specific job. If Sidqi was King Fuad's man, the brutality of his style of government was a disgrace to them both.[23]

A positive effect for Huda of Sidqi's rule was that common opposition to his Government brought her closer once more to Safia Zaghlul, Saad's widow, with whom her relations had long been chilly. Huda's renewed friendship with Safia led her to begin to express support for her through *L'Égyptienne* and other means as Safia continued her Wafdist activism. It also inaugurated a new détente between the Liberal Constitutionalists and the Wafdists, who now had a joint interest in opposing Sidqi. Many people Huda knew were being personally affected. Taha Husain had been persecuted by the regime for criticising Sidqi, and Safia was banned from political activity.[24]

In the autumn of 1930, however, the confrontation between Sidqi and the opposition forces led indirectly to a disappointment for Huda. On 6 September, Mahatma Gandhi, whom Huda had come so greatly to admire, had passed through the Suez Canal en route for London, and was greeted on board ship by a welcoming party representative of Egypt's nationalists. Nahhas Pasha invited the Mahatma to visit Cairo as he returned to India later in the year. Sidqi was clearly unhappy at this, since a visit by such an enormously well-known figure, if exploited by the nationalists, could spark an outbreak of popular antagonism to his Government. Gandhi's ship arrived in Port Said again on 18 December on the return journey to India, but he was prevented from leaving the vessel by the captain, who insisted he could not delay his sailing schedule. There was no doubt that Sidqi's Government was instrumental in this. Nahhas Pasha had intended to entertain Gandhi in Cairo, and Safia had been ready to hold a reception at her house in Gandhi's honour, to which Huda would have been invited. As it was the celebration planned for Gandhi was nipped in the bud, and Huda lost the opportunity to meet in person a figure who had become one of her heroes. Instead, only the male Wafdist leaders went to Suez to greet Gandhi aboard ship.

On the other hand, Céza was able to be among the Egyptian press contingent who went to Suez with them. She returned with rapturous descriptions of the great man and his ascetic ways, telling of his exiguous cotton clothes, and of how he slept on the ship's deck. She brought back with her a message addressed to Egypt's women by the Mahatma, which read as follows: 'I hope that our Egyptian sisters will play the same part as their Indian sisters in the liberation movement of their respective lands. For I believe that non-violence is the special prerogative of women.'[25]

On 11 June 1931, elections were held under Sidqi's revised constitution, where the system of indirect elections minimised the possibility of a victory by the Wafd. The EFU joined other groups in protesting against the elections, but Sidqi was ruthless with anyone who demonstrated. Jailings and beatings had become common practice. There was a well-articulated protest by the Egyptian women's movement against restrictions placed on the press under Sidqi's new constitution, and Céza wrote an indignant article, couched in ironical terms, entitled 'Freedom under the New Constitution'.[26] The opposition boycotted the polls, and even certain members of the royal family spoke out against the new electoral system. The women went onto the streets to demonstrate their support for the electoral boycott, and the police behaved badly, assaulting demonstrators and onlookers alike, including children.[27] Visitors to Safia's house, still known as the Bait al-Umma, were harassed, and many of Safia's guests were arrested and interrogated. Céza was thus given a golden opportunity to speak out in *L'Égyptienne* against the regime. She did not mince her words, and frequently referred to Sidqi's regime as 'the dictatorship' in her articles. The elections were won by Sidqi, who had sufficiently gerrymandered the electoral system to be able to outflank the Wafd.

On 18 June 1931, the EFU lost a powerful supporter when their longstanding patron Princess Amina Ilhami, the Khediva Mother, passed away. She was the mother of Abbas II, and was known as 'Umm Abbas'. Her death deprived not merely the EFU but also the country of a generous and compassionate soul. Her elegant waterfront palace in Bebek in Istanbul was donated to the Egyptian Government for the use of its diplomatic mission in Turkey. Huda had known the Khediva Mother well. She had been involved with many charitable activities, and Huda hoped that her son, Prince Muhammad Ali Tawfiq, whom she knew well, would agree to replace her as a sponsor for EFU, though he was at heart no feminist and was reputedly opposed to girls studying at the university. This was another instance where Huda found herself having recourse to a man's support for feminist activities. Huda composed an elegy for the late Khediva Mother that was published in *L'Égyptienne*:

Mère des orphelins, Reine des Bienfaiteurs,
Son règne, parmi nous, fut celui d'une Sainte
A qui dans le malheur on adresse des plaintes
Et qui, seule, savait calmer notre douleur.

Souveraine bénie, sans soldats, sans armes,
Elle avait le grand don de conquérir les cœurs,
Et si ses derniers jours ont connu tant d'honneurs,
Dans l'épreuve et l'exil, ce fut grâce à son charme.

C'est grâce au noble cœur, bien plus qu'au noble sang,
Que Dieu lui décerna pour marquer sa puissance,
Qu'elle pouvait, aux jours de pire intolérance,
Puiser dans notre amour un courage incessant.

D'un regard, d'un beau geste, ou bien d'un doux sourire
Elle semait la vie partout où la mort
Menaçait de frapper le faible avant le fort
Par la faim, l'ignorance – et cela sans rien dire.

Mais le pieux secret gardé sur ses bienfaits
S'exhalait de toute âme aux heures de prière
Pour lui former de quoi la rendre heureuse et fière
Au Royaume des Cieux immuable et parfait.

('In Memoriam', Huda Shaarawi)

In 1931, *L'Égyptienne* published the appeal for world peace and disarmament launched by the Women's International League for Peace and Freedom (WILPF), by the IAW and by individual scientists and intellectuals such as Albert Einstein and the French writer Romain Rolland.[28] Against the background of the economic slump of 1929–32, and the rise in xenophobia around the world, social strife and political upheaval were becoming more widespread. Huda, like other feminists, became an ever more fervent advocate of peace and disarmament. The rise of Hitler and the Nazis in Germany was rapidly becoming another major source of concern.

As Huda girded herself up to make an appropriate response to the increasingly alarming international situation, as well as continuing her opposition to Sidqi at home, an unexpected and somewhat gratuitous complication in her family life placed her in a difficult position. Huria, who had become very close to Huda, accepted a proposal of marriage made to her by a young man called Ibrahim Hilmi, who was a cousin of Sidqi's wife. Hilmi was an official in the Department of Urban Planning in Alexandria responsible for landscaping and parks. The idea of a match between him and Huria made the whole group of women cringe, because it created a family link with Sidqi. Huria, however, seemed interested in her suitor, and Hilmi was obviously madly in love with her. Huda could do no other than be moved by their courtship and wish them well.[29]

9

The natural enemies of war

The spring of 1932 saw a key development in the affairs of the EFU when the organisation moved at last into its new and spacious headquarters in Qasr el-Aini Street. The EFU seemed to go from strength to strength. Over two days, on 28 and 29 April 1932, official opening ceremonies took place. The building at once became known as the dar al-mar'a (the House of the Woman), but the fear of offending public false modesty made it impossible to emblazon the word 'Woman' on the façade, which caused Céza great amusement.[1] There had been years of energetic fundraising to reach this point, after hopes of a subsidy from the Government evaporated due to the hostility between the EFU and Sidqi. It must be said that Huda had been to some extent personally responsible for this, not having concealed her animosity towards Sidqi. Huda paid tribute to the late Khediva Mother in her inaugural speech at the opening, while thanking the Khediva Mother's son, Prince Muhammad Ali, for sponsoring the event in her place. A charity ball was held, with a performance of a play, A Night at the Foot of the Pyramids by Tawfiq Ackad. There was the customary tableau *vivant* by the Cadettes, this time on the subject of the Caucasus, featuring Hawa, Huria and Suad

Rashid, Fatma Nimat Rashid's beautiful sister, as well as a performance by Circassian dancers. Umm-Kulthum performed, as she had done on previous EFU occasions. The EFU's Housekeeping and Professional School (École Ménagère et Professionnelle) had already been opened in the new building on 7 April 1932.

At the same time, Huda's attention was focused on the impending marriage between Muhammad and Munira. The wedding took place in the summer of 1932 at a private ceremony with only a few guests, at Husain and Fatma Asim's house in Zamalek. Munira was then brought to the big house at 2 Qasr al-Nil Street. Her maids of honour were her own sisters Aisha and Zainab, together with Hawa and Huria. The little girls who followed the bride and groom to carry the train of the wedding dress down the staircase were Munira's younger sister Huda Asim, and her cousin, Qadria Rifaat, daughter of Aziza Fahmi. Huda was certain that this was the inauguration of a new and happier era for the family.

Muhammad and Munira's wedding.

~ The natural enemies of war ~

As far as Huda was concerned, her son was at last settled satisfactorily with his cousin, and would no doubt soon become a father. Munira was taken straight back to the mansion as soon as the ceremony was over. Huda would not let her go to a house of her own, and intended her always to regard it in future as her own home.

Huda's relentless schedule of work and travel continued regardless. She went as usual to Europe in the summer of 1932. She spent July in London and August at the French spa town of Evian for the treatment she now liked to have each year for her legs. Céza remained with the rest of Huda's family in Egypt, who all went to the house she now owned in the Laurent district of Alexandria, entertaining themselves with visits to various places of amusement. There were always new beaches and resorts as the Corniche project developed along the sea shore, adding to the already cosmopolitan and fashionable life of the city. Muhammad and Munira seemed happy together during this early phase of their married life. Céza regularly briefed Huda about their outings, about Muhammad's good mood, which had become noticeable, and about the many places they visited:

> We are using our holidays to go each day to a different spot, to Stanley Bey, to Sidi Bishr, to the Pré Fleuri, or to the Casino cinema. Alexandria has become a vast and fashionable spot where there are plenty of walks. The beach at Stanley Bey is where all Cairo and Alexandria show themselves off. Pretty coloured sunshades make it all the more gay and elegant. From the café next to the cabins you can watch them all in their beach pyjamas of every sort and their ultra revealing bathing costumes…

In the same letter, Céza reported an invitation to lunch in Munira's parents' home in Zizinia. She recounted, tongue in cheek, that 'Daddy couldn't have been nicer, in fact it was really he who was the mistress of the house.'[2] Husain Asim, Munira's father, was tall, handsome and elegant, with a thoughtful expression and a gentle manner.

During the summer, Céza also had to give Huda some bad news. Huda's half-sister Luza had passed away. Luza was much older than Huda, and as she had been ill for a long time, her death had been half expected. Huda did not return to Egypt for the funeral. She had herself been suffering more from her various ailments, though she had not yet sought a proper diagnosis of what her illness might be. As far as she could, however, she chose to ignore her medical problems rather than face them, as she wanted nothing to interfere with her work. Aside from Luza's death, matters seemed to be unfolding on the home front as Huda had expected, and were causing her no concern, and she wanted to concentrate on her business in Europe.

A slight setback came when, in the course of the summer, Huda received a letter from Margery Corbett-Ashby. The IAW President wrote to remind her of her duties as a member of the IAW's executive committee, which Huda had to admit she had for some time been neglecting. Was Huda finding it difficult to make time for the IAW, and did she wish to be replaced? The direct question slapped Huda out of her forgetfulness. Corbett-Ashby was absolutely right. The demands of Huda's family and private life, the affairs of the magazine and the multiplication of her charitable activities in Egypt, not to mention her renewed concentration on political developments in Egypt in the Sidqi era had all distracted her attention from her role in the IAW, which she had allowed to slip into the background. While Huda was in England, she went to visit Corbett-Ashby at her home at Horsted Keynes in West Sussex to talk the matter over. Huda had not thought of leaving the executive committee. She now realised that she must either quit or resume in earnest her IAW responsibilities. She chose the IAW, and threw herself with a vengeance once more into the international world of women's affairs.

When she returned to Cairo, she made it clear that Céza would henceforth take total responsibility for *L'Égyptienne*, and delegated the EFU's fairs and other similar activities to Hawa and the little battalion of Cadettes, while she plunged once more into the international struggle for peace and justice. The girls were very keen, and Huda could see they would do well with less direction. New girls were always gravitating towards her. The Al-Said sisters, Karima and Amina, were very strongwilled, especially Amina, who had decided to become a journalist. Suhair al-Qalamawi, who had a great career before her, was clever and determined, as was Sherifa Lutfi. Duria Shafiq, who had done brilliantly at the Sorbonne, was ambitious and already bursting out of her bounds. She was reluctant to remain in Céza's shadow at *L'Égyptienne*, while Céza would never agree to share with anyone what had become in her eyes very much 'her' magazine. However, young Duria, who was close to Huda's heart, was impatient, and was obviously a very good writer. Eventually, she went to work elsewhere in order to escape from Céza, whom she felt was restricting her. This meant she also lost touch to some extent with Huda. With girls of such calibre coming up in the new generation, however, Huda felt confident for the future.

A further development in 1933 came when the French activist Camille Drevet, the Secretary of the Ligue Internationale des Femmes pour la Paix et la Liberté (LIFPL), contacted Huda and Céza to ask the EFU to collect signatures in Egypt in support of an international petition for disarmament that she had begun to organise. An irony was that with Sidqi as Prime Minister, the only way to collect signatures for such a cause was to obtain his signature first, since Government officials and others would then feel they were also able to sign. Huda would not speak to him. Céza therefore asked his office if she could come to talk to him, and he graciously granted her a moment of his time. He agreed to sign the petition, and while doing so, pen in hand, he asked her with a light, ironical, smile, 'Is there anything else I can do for you?' He was undoubtedly a charmer, and almost won Céza's sympathy. Government employees were all then able to sign without fear of the consequences for their careers. Many women also signed, and Drevet expressed her satisfaction with Egypt's contribution, hoping that a new LIFPL chapter in Egypt would be the outcome.

News coming out of Germany, as time went on, became more and more alarming. The women's movement there was hamstrung by political pressure. One of Huda's German commentators, whose identity was kept secret for obvious reasons, said, 'Any thinking individual may perceive the nature of a feminist movement that must submit itself unconditionally to dictators like Hitler, Goering and Goebbels.'[3] No one could fail to perceive and to be moved by the fate of the Jews in Europe, and Huda was certainly conscious of this. Articles published in *L'Égyptienne* also condemned the Italian Fascist aggression against Ethiopia and the mounting violence within Italy itself. The struggle against war, at this moment of world crisis, became the driving force of the women's movement. At the same time, the unrest in Palestine intensified, and Huda continued to condemn Britain's suppression of Palestinian protests, sending telegrams to the IAW on behalf of her Egyptian organisation. 'The EFU, deeply moved by the recent Palestinian events, deplores the armed attacks of the authorities against a disarmed population that peacefully claims its right to exist. We call for an immediate intervention.'[4]

Huda's passionate belief was that by the efforts of a sufficient number of right-thinking people justice could be imposed throughout the whole world. In the 1930s, events were conspiring to prove her wrong. The widening scope of her reforming instinct was itself leading her towards her ultimate frustration. She found the manner in which the Hashemites had been misled by the British in regard to the future of Greater Syria was repugnant. The Hussein–MacMahon correspondence revealed by the Russian revolutionaries in 1917 had disclosed the entire negotiation, which had been intended to remain for ever secret. The British and the French had cynically divided the area between them, and Syria had then been further dismembered by the French to further their own interests. In Palestine, agreements were being made by the British government with the Zionist leadership that were very alarming. The leaders of women's movements in Palestine sent letters to Huda, who was by now a well-known international figure, pleading for her assistance. For the Palestinians, their fear of the Zionists was as much a cause of anguish as was the fear of the Jews in Europe about the intentions of the Nazis, later to be horrifyingly justified.

L'Égyptienne began regularly to describe and deplore the state of affairs in Palestine. Tarab Abd al-Hadi, the Mayor of Jerusalem's wife, told Huda about a discussion between her husband and David Ben Gurion, the Jewish leader in Palestine. The Mayor, Auni Abd al-Hadi, had asked about the number of Jews that the Zionists were planning to bring in. Ben Gurion apparently answered that they longed for a state 'within the borders of the biblical Israel with a population of four million Jews', thus making it clear that, given the limited land area of Palestine, the true objective of the Zionist leaders was to displace the Palestinians and replace them with Jews.[5]

The IAW congress to be held in Marseilles in April 1933 was intended to be an occasion for the women to advocate peace.[6] Huda decided to use it to bring her concern for Palestine directly to the attention of the IAW. In September 1931, an umbrella organisation known as the Women's International Organisations, to which the IAW was affiliated, had set up a standing disarmament committee, with Rosa Manus as its secretary. In February 1932, Margery Corbett-Ashby had gone as Britain's delegate to a conference on disarmament in Geneva held by this group. As member of the IAW executive committee, Huda put forward a proposal to the Women's International Organisation that its disarmament committee should support the Arab demand for an end to Jewish immigration in Palestine.[7] At such an early date, this was probably rather a lot for the international women's groups to swallow, however, focused as they were on the plight of European Jews in the face of the rising tide of Nazism. Huda found it hard to see how the persecution of Jews in Europe could justify aggression against another helpless population, in Palestine.

When the Women's International Organisations set up a committee to devise ways of assisting refugees from Germany, 'with no distinction as to race or opinion', the EFU nevertheless gave its support to the proposal. Huda wanted to draw a parallel between persecution in Germany and the plight of the Palestinians.[8] At around the same time, Huda received a letter from Corbett-Ashby, who had heard that the

Czech activist Frantiska Plaminkova, one of the executive committee members of the IAW, had been arrested by the Nazis. Corbett-Ashby knew that Huda had good contacts in Germany who might be able to find out what had happened to Plaminkova. Huda was able to forward to Corbett-Ashby a letter from the German Ambassador in Egypt assuring her that Plaminkova had not been arrested.[9] Alas, this turned out later not to be true, and Plaminkova was eventually to die at the hands of the Nazis.

Among all Huda's occupations and activity, art had increasingly become her solace. She liked to turn from her worries and cares to calmer and more cerebral pursuits. In March 1933, Huda saw an exhibition of orientalist paintings, including some by Kees van Dongen, that greatly impressed her.[10] She felt nevertheless that Egyptian artists now painted so well. Huda made a point of buying the work of Egyptian painters like Yusuf Kamil, Raghib Ayad and Mahmud Said. She also supported the Turkish painter Hidayat Dac who had established himself in Egypt and saw himself as part of the Egyptian school. Her Egyptian patriotism held sway in her artistic choices. Much though she admired Western art, she left it to the great collector Muhammad Mahmud Khalil, who despised Egyptian painters, to acquire the works of Western artists. On the other hand, Khalil did succeed in building up a fine collection that he eventually left to the Egyptian state.

Towards the end of March 1933, Huda and Céza travelled to France for the IAW congress. Before the proceedings proper began, they had arranged for themselves a short lecture tour in the cities of the French Mediterranean littoral, including Nice, Toulon, Hyères, Cannes, Grasse and Menton, where they addressed local audiences about peace and feminism. Huda talked about the vital need for peace, while Céza spoke about the enormous strides made in Egypt towards the evolution and empowerment of women. In her address at the Toulon Opera House, Huda made the point that men claimed they were justified in refusing to grant women the vote because women would not fight on the battlefield. Huda turned the argument on its head, saying that, 'Women, who have known all the anguish of war and cannot forget the horrors they have witnessed, are today granting themselves the right to work for the consolidation of peace and understanding between peoples.'[11]

In Marseilles, at the IAW congress itself, which began in April, the themes were labour and nationality in relation to the role of women. Céza also spoke about the role of motherhood in the struggle waged by women against the selfish violence of men. As she said, 'It is the women's duty to find in their motherly hearts the treasures of energy and love that will ultimately defeat the destructive forces of masculine selfishness.'[12] Huda meanwhile supported Maria Vérone when the latter urged the adoption of a resolution calling upon the women of the whole world to refuse to work in the 'factories of war', where weapons were produced, even if they had to incur legal sanctions by doing so. Corbett-Ashby had not been informed beforehand that this motion would be put, and feared it was too far-reaching and unrealistic. In the event, the peace committee was chaired by Rosa Manus, who drafted a very articulate and firm resolution that supported disarmament and peace and condemned the production of armaments, including military aircraft and chemical weapons, by private industry not under the control of the state.[13] The congress ended with a sumptuous reception at the Hotel de Ville of Marseilles, where the Mayor, who sympathised with feminist causes, gave a farewell speech.

When they attended such events, Huda and Céza now normally divided between them the subject matter about which they spoke. Huda dealt in general with political issues, Céza concentrated on the feminist movement in Egypt, including the Cadettes. On this occasion, Céza had pictures of the Cadettes to give to the French press, which were published by *La Française*. Céza told the women about the EFU's achievements, beginning with unveiling, then the imposition of a minimum age for marriage, followed by the establishment of secondary and vocational schools for girls, and finally the entry of young women into the university.[14]

Nazism's increasing momentum in Germany seemed now to be inexorable, and feminist associations were finding it harder to continue their work. The German women who came to Marseilles brought with them, as a last free gesture, Sigmund Freud's anti-war book *Civilization and its Discontents*. They also brought with them a list of the women's associations that had been dissolved, including the German chapter of the IAW. They also had a list of the names of women who had been driven out of their jobs on the sole account of being women.[15]

At home, as 1933 went on, more of the initiatives put forward by the EFU in Egypt were gratifyingly translated into legislative change. Huda and her colleagues persuaded the Government to pass labour laws to protect working women against the heavy and excessive hours of toil to which many had hitherto been subjected. They were to be allowed rest for at least eleven hours a day, seven of which must be during the night, from ten at night to five in the morning. In addition, Huda and her assistants were encouraged when Dr Shahin Pasha, as Minister of Health, who was far from being a feminist, showed himself determined to stamp out prostitution and began to take steps against it. By June 1933, brothels were closed in the three cities of Damanhur, Assiut and Mansura.[16] He also delivered a speech about venereal diseases at the general assembly of the International Medical Union, announcing that he was taking steps to combat this scourge in Egypt. Finally, Huda also persuaded the Ministry of Justice to declare that the legal sanctions against precocious marriage would be strictly enforced. In theory, the legal ages for marriage were already 18 years old for boys, 16 for girls, but these were often ignored.

At the EFU's new headquarters, lectures were given by senior figures from the circle sympathetic to the women's cause, including Haikal Pasha and Taha Husain, who was temporarily suspended from his post at Cairo University after a disagreement with the authorities. The Arab women of Palestine, having heard about the Rod al-Farag factory, whose wares had been exhibited to very good effect at an international exhibition at Cairo's Continental Hotel, invited Huda to bring her artisans to exhibit at an international exhibition in Jaffa in May 1933. Feminist movements, modelled at least in part on the Egyptian example, were also by now beginning to spread into the Levant, and women's conferences were held in Damascus and Baghdad.

On 20 May 1933, Muhammad and Munira had their first child, Malak, a granddaughter for Huda. Sadly, her enthusiasm was dampened by the fact that she had hoped for a son, who would be the heir the family needed. Muhammad was also disappointed. The arrival of a girl was greeted with a general lack of rejoicing that deeply hurt Munira, who loved her daughter. She felt she had been relegated to the role of nothing more than the producer of male children for Muhammad, and that she had failed even in that. She had been prevented by her husband from participating in the many feminist pursuits she saw going on around her, and had therefore felt marginalised in the big mansion, amidst a hive of women who were constantly involved in interesting and exciting activities.

While Huda averred that of course she was happy to have a new girl in the family, she also underlined the need for a boy in due course, and rather unfeelingly asked Munira to hurry up and have another child as soon as possible. Muhammad suffered from the family's disappointment at the birth of his daughter and by their evident desire for a son simply to inherit the family money. He began to go out on his own, leaving his young wife at home. She had plenty of company, he reasoned, in such a house full of women. Two of his friends in particular exercised a malign influence over him. They were only too happy to go with him every evening to the Auberge des Pyramides and to other such establishments, where he paid for everyone's food and drink while dancers and singers from all parts of the world performed for a very cosmopolitan audience.

The marriage between Muhammad and Munira had held together up to this point because Munira had worked hard to keep her husband and had refrained from speaking her mind. Nevertheless, her situation was extraordinarily difficult. She was not only subject to the stress of her husband's neglect, but was also embarrassed by her isolation in the midst of independent women such as Huda and Céza, who were not concerned with childbearing or bothered by demanding husbands. Céza was aware of her misery, but was always too busy to extend a hand of friendship. Huda's attitude was another problem for Munira, seeming to blame her both for her failure to produce a male child and her inability to control her husband.

By the autumn of 1934, Egypt's internal situation was preoccupying Huda and her assistants a great deal. Their hostility to Sidqi Pasha grew day by day. They believed he was consistently failing to act in Egypt's interests. Education was a disaster, with too many jobless graduates, stultifying Government control over the university, and unresolved issues in the field of secondary and higher education for girls. Murad Pasha Sid Ahmad, the Minister for Education in Sidqi's cabinet, had refused to implement Taha Husain's plan to found secondary schools for girls. Women graduates of the calibre of Suhair al-Qalamawi and Fatma Fahmi were denied Government posts, while Naima al-Ayubi, who had graduated as a lawyer in Paris, was being prevented from becoming a member of the Egyptian bar.

Even Sidqi's elegance, down to the carnation he always wore in his buttonhole, began to be taken as an insult by the women. They found it offensive that he should behave in what they saw as a frivolous way when serious questions demanded to be resolved. Sidqi's apparent indifference to national aspirations and pride was what upset them most. New legislation was needed in so many fields, but the Prime Minister seemed able only to see the needs of business. 'Egypt lives under a business government,' was the watchword, and Sidqi was described as 'the contrary of a nationalist'. Worst of all, with all this concentration on business, there were no jobs. In addition, Sidqi did not seem wholly straightforward. Even in the context of his most successful venture, the construction of the Alexandria Corniche, Sidqi had been accused of corrupt dealings with the contractor.[17]

Huda found this attitude unacceptable. She had grown up in a family that had always done everything in its power to promote the democratic process in the country, and had striven to free Egypt from the British occupation. As she saw it, her father, her brother and her husband had paid with their own assets, and ultimately with their lives if they had to, for the establishment of legal rule and for the promotion of democracy in all aspects of civil life in Egypt, and she herself had spent her life trying to do the same. Huda decided to fight Sidqi through her magazine and to throw her weight behind her Liberal Constitutionalist advisers and friends, even if they sometimes seemed to lack the necessary aggressiveness to take the political life of the country into their own hands.

After three years of unconstitutional rule, Sidqi was accused even by the King of having established a dictatorship. His constitutional proposals appeared to fail even to attempt to limit the powers of the British to interfere in Egypt, and the country was thoroughly disillusioned with him. Few gave him credit for the attempts he had indubitably made to mitigate the effects of the world slump on Egypt, and in particular to try to offset the disastrous effect of the fall in cotton prices. On 27 September 1933, his resignation was accepted by King Fuad, who apparently felt the need to appoint someone less controversial. Huda, Céza and their colleagues were immensely relieved. Huda felt that political life in Egypt could only be on a better footing without Sidqi as Prime Minister. After Sidqi's departure, Abd al-Fattah Yehia Pasha, an elegant, suave gentleman from Alexandria, was appointed as a supposedly uncontroversial Prime Minister, and remained for just over a year. This was a strange time in Egypt, when the King's health was beginning to deteriorate and the expectation of change was in the air.

In December 1933, to demonstrate that the Government did not have the last word in gender matters, Muhammad Ali Alluba Pasha, who owned one of the biggest law firms in the country, invited Naima al-Ayubi to work in his office as a trainee. Simultaneously, the EFU held a formal ceremony in honour of the first female university graduates, to celebrate their achievement. Alluba Pasha introduced Naima in very enthusiastic terms, speaking of her eagerness to serve the weak and oppressed people of her country. He ceremonially presented the young woman with the black robe worn by lawyers at court as a gift of the lawyers' union.[18]

Taha Husain then introduced his four graduates from Cairo University, among them Suhair al-Qalamawi. She had graduated from the Arabic Department, while the other three, Fatma Fahmi, Zahira Abd al-Aziz and Fatma Salim, had graduated in philosophy and classical languages. Husain asserted that these young women were as capable as any man at the Sorbonne, declaring he stood shoulder to shoulder with the feminists to make sure that the highest levels of education would be open to girls as well as boys. Dr Sami Kamil, one of the medical advisors of the EFU, then introduced the young women who had just completed their medical studies in England, including Kawkab Hifni Nasif, who had completed her postgraduate medical studies to become a qualified gynaecologist, making one of the Bahitha's dreams come true.[19] Another laureate was Lutfia al-Nadi, who was introduced by Fuad Bey Abaza, Director of the Royal Society of Agriculture. Khalil Mutran, the celebrated poet, read an ode he had written for the occasion. In her closing speech, Huda recalled the role played in the rise of women by Qasim Amin, and by the Bahitha, whose strong voice had been so influential in the early days of the struggle for women's advancement.[20]

The achievements of the Egyptian feminists in 1933 culminated in spectacular fashion with the triumph of the pilot Lutfia al-Nadi, who won an air race against all comers. The EFU had sponsored and paid for her training. Egyptair had begun its operations in 1932, and Misr Air Work was set up to teach young people to fly using Gypsy Moth aircraft. Lutfia was complimented on her performance by the British Minister of Aviation, Lord Londonderry.[21] Huda decided to encourage the young woman further by buying her an aircraft of her own, and set up a fund for her at the Banque Misr. Providing gifted young people with the means for their education was a personal policy that Huda believed in, and hoped to see applied in the country as a whole, at all levels and irrespective of gender.

In early 1934, a tragedy struck Huda's intellectual circle, when terminal illness hit the sculptor Mukhtar, creator of *Egypt's Awakening*. Huda decided that for as long as Mukhtar was ill she would visit him every day. Mukhtar was Egypt's master artist, in national terms as important a man as Rodin. What he had achieved was great by any reckoning, and he deserved gratitude. Huda felt she must perpetuate his reputation and make his name as famous as it deserved to be. Thanks to her efforts, a museum was later built to show his work, and a regular competition was established for a prize in his name to be awarded to a young Egyptian sculptor. She hoped that her protégé Abd al-Badi would one day be worthy.[22]

As she visited Mukhtar day by day, she knew in her heart that his soul was slowly abandoning his emaciated body. Suffering had demolished his wit and humiliated him. He still had his warm smile when she appeared in his hospital room every day, carrying fresh flowers. He hardly slept, reviewing his past work in his mind's eye. There was still so much to do! 'When I get well...' he kept saying, and his friends eagerly smiled at him, saying, 'Of course you will.'[23] To thank Huda for her daily visits, Mukhtar repeatedly told her that she personified the goddess Isis. She was always humbled by such affirmations, which made her feel ridiculous. Tragically, Huda missed Mukhtar's final moments, as she suddenly had to go to Alexandria with Huria. Huria's fiancé Hilmi had also been suddenly taken ill, and she could not let the young girl attend to him alone. Mukhtar died on 28 March 1934. Poor Hilmi also died.

A new focus of Huda's international concern by this time was the League of Nations. The League had been founded in 1919, but Egypt had not yet become a member. By the early 1930s, it was widely felt amongst the Nationalists and Liberal Constitutionalists that League membership could be a way to assist Egypt to rid itself of the British yoke and the capitulatory laws. By 1934, the link between the League of Nations and the Women's International League for Peace and Freedom, in whose activities Céza took an increasing interest, seemed an avenue worthy of exploitation in Huda's campaign against the capitulatory laws. Most Egyptians were in any case indignant that Egypt was not yet a League member state when other oriental countries such as Afghanistan, Iraq, Persia and Turkey had achieved membership. Huda committed herself to the goal of Egyptian membership, though she was also aware that the League of Nations had already begun to prove ineffectual as a peacekeeping mechanism.[24]

On 15 November 1934, when Muhammad Tawfiq Nessim Pasha again took office as Prime Minister in Egypt following the onset of what was to be King Fuad's final illness, there were immediate effects. Huda felt at that point that she could rely on the new Prime Minister, although she had disapproved of him in the past (when he failed to maintain the sentence 'King of Egypt and the Sudan' in the 1923 constitution), to be a support rather than an obstacle, and she believed that he might save the country from further deterioration. In one development that affected her own circle, she was certainly relieved when the new Minister of Public Education, Naguib Bey al-Hilali, reinstated Taha Husain in December 1934, and in April 1935 Lutfi al-Sayid was summoned to return to the University of Cairo, to resume his previous post as rector. Husain had been suspended from the university on 3 March 1932 because of his refusal to be dictated to by the Government, and Lutfi al-Sayid resigned on 9 March in protest against the severe punishment of a friend who had merely spoken his mind. They had thus both been victims of narrow-minded authorities.[25]

Nessim Pasha was almost at once able to persuade the King to abrogate the disastrously altered constitution of 1930 which had been the source of so much social unrest. Nessim Pasha hinted that the old constitution of 1923 would be re-enacted, with the restoration of direct elections, which attracted the support of the Wafd and other opposition parties in the country. In fact, on 18 April 1935, the King himself wrote to Nessim Pasha, expressing his desire to reinstitute constitutional rule, preferably on the basis of the 1923 constitution. Huda was able to inform herself of all this when she returned from the IAW congress in Istanbul. The King's letter to Nessim had been published in the newspapers. She herself fired off a letter to Nessim Pasha on her return, drawing his attention to three of the resolutions adopted by the IAW in Istanbul. These resolutions called for the elimination of polygamy, the recognition of women's political rights, and the adoption of equal moral standards for all.

In December 1934, Huda had heard the good news that Margery Corbett-Ashby and other members of the IAW bureau were planning to spend some time in Egypt as part of a tour in the Middle East before attending the twelfth congress in Istanbul. Corbett-Ashby had become Great Britain's delegate at the League of Nations for the conference on disarmament, which was also good news, though she was to resign from this position in 1935 because so little progress had been made. Over the years, Huda and Corbett-Ashby had become close friends, and her stay in Cairo would be a chance to deepen their friendship. Dr Christina Bakker-Van Bosse, the Deputy Chair of the IAW's committee for peace and for League of Nations affairs, was also planning to come to Cairo with the other members of the executive committee.

First there was the EFU's annual fair in January 1935 to be dealt with. This year, Hawa directed a performance of a play written by the famous 37-year-old playwright Tawfiq al-Hakim, *Maidens of my Country*. Its subject, in a clear reference to the exploits of Lutfia al-Nadi, was a woman aviator whose husband refused to accompany his wife on her flights. The fearful spouse is ultimately persuaded to fly with her because of her insistence, and the mockery of her two closest girlfriends, an able lawyer and a brilliant journalist. With Sherifa Lutfi as the aviator, Amina al-Said as the journalist, and the famous actor Suliman Naguib as the husband, the comedy was a great success. The programmes were printed free at Paul Barbey's press, where *L'Égyptienne* was still printed. Muhammad Shaarawi and his cousin Naila Sultan, Umar Sultan's daughter, provided flowers from their gardens for the guests' buttonholes.[26]

With the EFU fair over, Huda was ready to greet her guests, and geared herself up to give the IAW women, whom she was gratified to

209

have the chance to entertain, as exciting a time in Egypt as lay in her power. The French representative, Germaine Malaterre-Sellier, who was adventurous by nature, had already declared that she wanted to take the opportunity to visit Upper Egypt, before the war that now seemed inevitable made it impossible for her to do so. Hitler had become Germany's unchallenged Führer when Hindenburg died in August 1934. This was a new post into which the previous positions of Chancellor and President were both subsumed, seemingly an omen of what was to come. At all events, for the moment nothing could be simpler than to arrange an Upper Egyptian itinerary.

When the IAW women arrived, Huda enjoyed their company in Cairo as much as she had expected. She took pleasure in Corbett-Ashby's intelligence and charm, and Malaterre-Sellier's eloquence, and was inspired by the optimism, sincerity and energy of Rosa Manus of the Netherlands, and the competence of the other Dutch woman, Bakker-Van Bosse. Corbett-Ashby informed Huda that she had accepted an invitation from the Secretary of the Palestine Jewish Women's Equal Rights Association in Jerusalem, and that she and Rosa Manus, who was of course herself Jewish, would also visit Jerusalem and Syria before going on to Turkey.[27]

Mrs Esther Wissa Fahmi and other EFU members met the women when they arrived at Alexandria on 15 January 1935, and travelled with them by train to Cairo. From the station, they were taken straight to Huda's mansion. Corbett-Ashby was to arrive separately on 19 January 1935, arriving from India. During the visit, Huda entertained Corbett-Ashby, Malaterre-Sellier, Bakker-Van Bosse and Manus at her house, while another guest, Catherine Bompass, the IAW secretary, stayed at the EFU headquarters, where two delightful guest rooms overlooked the garden and the Nile. Others were lodged on a houseboat opposite the EFU building. Huda's programme of activities was carefully prepared.

On 16 January Mansur Fahmi, director of the Amira Fawzia Secondary School for Girls, gave the women a tour of the school. At a tea party in the afternoon, they met representatives from Egyptian women's organisations, as well as foreign women's groups represented in Cairo, and gave a press conference. The next day, there was a tour of the bazaars, souks and picturesque districts of the city. In the afternoon, they were taken to Saqqara and invited to tea at the home of Mme Lacau, wife of the Director of the Egyptian Antiquities Department. On 18 January, Huda arranged an excursion on a sailing boat to the gardens of the Qaliub Barrage, giving the guests an intimate view of the Nile. When Corbett-Ashby arrived on 19 January, the party went to the Egyptian Museum and visited an archaeological dig supervised by Professor Selim Hasan near the Pyramids. On the evening of 19 January, there was a grand reception at 2 Qasr al-Nil Street, attended by a guest list of important Egyptian and foreign personalities.

On 20 January, the women visited the Coptic Museum and churches, took tea at Maitre Garzouzi's chambers, finally attending a meeting at the headquarters of the Workers' Federation chaired by Prince Abbas Halim. A tiny replica of a statue by Mukhtar of a *fellaha*, a peasant woman, representing the eternal reality of Egypt, was distributed to celebrate the tenth anniversary of *L'Égyptienne*. On 21 January, everyone visited the Nur al-Huda factory in Rod al-Farag and the EFU's school before going to a grand lunch at the Semiramis, hosted jointly by the EFU and the IAW peace committee. This was attended by some seventy guests, including ex-prime ministers, ministers and ambassadors among a battery of senior political figures and journalists, as well as many of the EFU's faithful friends.

The more formal part of the agenda was a well-attended gathering in the EFU's conference hall, where Manus, in a keynote address, spoke about the history of the IAW since its inception in 1904. What she wanted most to talk about, however, was the importance of the forthcoming congress in Istanbul and its focus on peace. Bakker-Van Bosse then spoke about peace and the role of the League of Nations, while Malaterre-Sellier addressed the issue that mattered most to her Egyptian audience, the prospects for Egypt's admittance as a member of the League. Corbett-Ashby and Manus left for Palestine and Syria the next day, while Bakker-Van Bosse and Malaterre-Sellier set off on the journey to Upper Egypt Huda had planned for them. Huda felt that the effect of the visit had been to strengthen the bonds between the IAW and the EFU, as well as the personal ties between the foreign women and their Egyptian hosts.

In early 1935, soon after the departure of the guests, it happened that Charles Crane also spent a few days in Cairo, as he often did on his way to the other Arab countries. He was by now elderly, at 77, but still travelled relentlessly between New York and his farm in California, as well as between the United States and the Middle East. As he generally did, he called on Huda and spent some time chatting in the Oriental Salon which he loved so much. On this occasion, she offered him the gift of a *hawdaj*, an ornate camel saddle, so that he might keep a characteristic souvenir of Egypt at his farm. Crane was moved by this token of friendship, and decided that he also wanted to leave Huda a souvenir. He was aware of the trouble she had with her legs, and her difficulty in walking, so after he left Cairo he sent her a telegram by way of the Eastern Telegraph Company: 'Permit me to arrange for the installation of an elevator in your house in order to help you save your precious energy.'[28]

When the IAW congress in Istanbul opened in April 1935, the main subject was the burning question of how peace was to be preserved. Turkey had given women the right to vote in 1930, and the women who attended shared a firm belief that, as women, they were armed with a spirit of love that would show the way to a better world. Their objective as they met in Turkey was nothing less than a plan of action for the salvation of humanity and the reversal of the seemingly inexorable drift towards war. The Egyptian delegation was composed of 12 members, this time including some of the Cadettes. All were friends and family for Huda, so the journey aboard the *Izmir* across the Mediterranean was pleasant and relaxing. In addition to Huda, the Egyptian group included Muhammad Ali Alluba Pasha's wife, Nefissa, as well as Fuad Sultan's wife, Amina, in addition to Esther Fahmi Wissa, Fatma Nimet Rashid, and of course Céza. The Cadettes were represented by Hélène Sarruf,

The congress session in Istanbul, with Dame Margery reading the opening speech, the IWSA Vice Presidents, the Secretariat and the country representatives in the first row, including Céza.

Nelli de Shedid, Laila Thabit, and naturally Hawa and Huria. The selection of so many Cadettes was intended to be a demonstration that the younger generation could be relied on, and that they were being trained to shoulder responsibility in the future. The Egyptian delegation was popular in Istanbul. The Egyptian women were active, enthusiastic and effective, and the pretty and eloquent Cadettes charmed the other delegates.

There was a warm welcome for Huda and her delegation when they arrived on 12 April. The Turkish representatives, the members of the Kadin Birligi Committee, were there to greet them at the port. A number of the Egyptian women could speak Turkish, including Huda herself, as well as Hawa and Huria, which facilitated communication between them and their Turkish hosts. The two groups at once became firm friends, and this sympathy was to continue during the working sessions and social events that followed. Three days later,

Huda led the Egyptian delegation to visit the national monument commemorating the foundation of the Turkish Republic and pay tribute to this Turkish symbol of freedom and equality. Huda spoke a few words in Turkish to Mustafa Kemal Atatürk, to whom she declared that he was not merely, as his title indicated, the father of all Turks, but rather a father to the whole Orient. He was, she said, 'Atasharq', father of the whole East. Her personal bonds with Turkey inspired her to make this declaration. Huda sincerely believed, as had Mustapha Kamil and her brother in the past, that in the days of its strength the Ottoman Empire had been the best protection for the whole region. She also congratulated Atatürk for having granted women in the new Turkey the same rights as men. Corbett-Ashby, in her capacity as the President of the IAW then held a press conference for the Turkish journalists at the Pera Palace Hotel, where, over tea, many of the delegates spoke about their concerns and hopes for the outcome of the congress. Two days of preparatory sessions followed. Various items were added to the agenda arising out of the particular interests of the various delegations, but the six principal items on the agenda were peace, the civil status of women, equal working conditions for women and men, the abolition of double standards in morals, suffrage, and the nationality of married women.

On 18 April 1935, the opening session of the congress took place in the great hall of the Yildiz Palace, which was so full that some of the audience had to stand in a corridor outside listening to the speeches relayed on loudspeakers. No flags were deployed except the host country's flag and the white flag of the IAW, which had the word 'Justice' printed on a white background, 'as a symbol of unity and justice between races, nationalities and religions'.[29] The Governor of Istanbul spoke a few words of welcome, after which the opening address was given by Latifé Bekir, the great Turkish feminist and national heroine. Corbett-Ashby moved a motion of thanks to President Atatürk for his support to the feminist movement. The re-election of Margery Corbett-Ashby as President of the IAW, though a formality, was another cause for celebration. Corbett-Ashby then gave her own address, outlining the situation and achievements of the IAW.

Peace, however, was the main theme. Malaterre-Sellier reported that three members of the executive committee, Rosa Manus, Christina Bakker-Van Bosse and herself, had visited Egypt, Syria and Palestine to see for themselves the situation on the ground, and spread the culture of peace. One thing she had noticed, she said, was that, 'in the Arab countries, despite the fact that people suffer from the crisis as anybody else, they complain much less than the Europeans. On the other hand, their moral needs are articulated more acutely. There is less talk about demands, but more about justice and peace.'

She said she believed that the Western world had a great deal to learn from the East about the power of spiritual values, and that only on the basis of such values could peace be reached.[30]

Huda spoke about cooperation between East and West. She pointed to the city of Istanbul itself as an instance of such a possibility. 'In

Sailing from Istanbul, Fatma Rashid, Laila Thabit, Céza Nabarawi, Nefissa Alluba, Hawa Idris, Huda, Huria Idris-Shafik, Esther Wissa, Hasan Shafik.

Istanbul,' she said, 'the two continents, the European and the Asian, reflect every day their serene beauty in the limpid waters of the Bosphorus, thus perfectly symbolising the brotherliness of these two worlds.' She named the four Arab organisations that had joined the IAW since its last congress. She also praised Atatürk as his country's saviour, and added that she placed her hope in Turkey's capacity to act as a link between East and West, so that 'this sincere and fraternal cooperation that we all ardently desire, be effectively realised in a brief time for the greatest good of humanity.'[31] Over the following days, as the congress continued its work, Huda was particularly satisfied by the participation of the Arab associations newly affiliated to the IAW, which she felt could only help to identify a solution to the increasingly painful situation created by the arrival of more Jewish immigrants in Palestine. At the same time, she was conscious of the need to save the Jews of Europe by quelling the brutality that prevailed there.

Meanwhile, the magnificence of the park in which the Yildiz Palace stood was a constant source of pleasure and wonder, together with the weight of history of the Ottoman Empire associated with its palaces and pavilions. The delegates were in contact with nature in all its beauty, and felt simultaneously that they could almost reach out to touch history, at a time when the uncertain destiny of the world continued to unfold with no safe haven in view.

10

Turning Points

uda always took great pleasure in the affairs of her two young Circassian cousins. During the IAW congress in Istanbul a particularly exciting event occurred. She was elated to discover, when Huria came to confess, that the girl had found time to be swept off her feet by a dashing young Egyptian diplomat she had met in the Turkish capital, whom she said she was certain was the love of her life. This was Hasan Shafik, one of Ahmad Shafik Pasha's sons, Vice Consul at Egypt's Embassy. This was a great relief for Huda after Huria's tragic and brief liaison with the ill-fated Ibrahim Hilmi, which had left Huria devastated. Huria wanted the wedding to take place in Alexandria as soon as possible, as Hasan could not be absent for long from his position in Turkey, and Huda agreed to make the arrangements. What Huda did not know was that Hasan had persuaded Huria to spend their honeymoon on his own yacht, which he would sail from Alexandria to Istanbul himself with the help of only the single young crewman who looked after the boat for him. This was a secret between the young couple, which Huria bravely kept to herself, despite the fear of being lost at sea that paralysed her whenever she thought about it. But, in theory at least, she liked to live dangerously, and she was thrilled by the idea of such

217

adventure. Huda would have been alarmed had she known, but the return voyage to Istanbul went off well when the time came.

The wedding took place at Huda's home in Alexandria in May 1935. The house was flooded with flowers for the occasion. The proceedings were simple but sophisticated. The bridegroom was a modern man, after all, who needed to get back to his job, and there was no time for lengthy ceremonies and preparations. Had anyone known about Hasan Shafik's nautical intentions, there might have been some protest, but the secret was too well kept for any objection to arise. Hawa was there for her sister's marriage, as well as Céza, with her new fiancé, the young sculptor Mustafa Naguib, who had just graduated from the Accademia delle Belle Arti, the art school in Rome. All the young crowd from the EFU were present, in addition to the staff of *L'Égyptienne*. Huda's Liberal Constitutionalist friends turned out with their wives, and of course, last but not least, Huda's family members. All agreed that the mercurial Mukhtar was seriously missed, and speculated what he might have said or done.

When the time came for the young couple to return to Istanbul, they were unable to take all their luggage on the yacht, and there remained several trunks in Cairo that needed to be sent to Istanbul. Huda agreed to send them off. Queen Marie of Romania, the mother of Romania's King Carol II, happened to be returning to Turkey after a brief stay in Egypt. Huda, who had met the Queen, described in *L'Égyptienne* as 'The Queen of Flowers', through her feminist circles, asked if she could help. Huda had first been introduced to the Queen, a granddaughter of Queen Victoria, by the Romanian Princess Alexandrina Cantacuzino, a stalwart of the IAW. The Queen obligingly despatched the young couple's luggage with her own. Hasan and Huria therefore found themselves taken by the Egyptian Ambassador, Amin Abusba Pasha, whose wife Attia was a friend of Queen Marie, to meet the Queen when she arrived in Istanbul. They found her to be a charming woman. For the two young people, this outcome of Huda's intervention seemed like a fairy-tale episode.

~ Turning points ~

Huria and Hasan's marriage was also an occasion for a small gesture in the direction of social reform. Huda believed that aspects of the Egyptian marriage contract needed to be amended to conform with feminist ideals. Conventionally, a large dowry was paid by the bridegroom, of up to 1000 Egyptian pounds, which in some cases even became a barrier to the marriage taking place at all. Huria shared Huda's beliefs in such matters, and agreed to ask for no more than 25 piastres from Hasan. He, in his turn, fixed at 300 pounds the amount to be paid in the event of a divorce. The symbolic choice of these sums was meant to show that marriage should be easy while divorce should be penalised. Other couples in Huda's circle who planned to marry soon after agreed to follow this example, and to include similar clauses in their own contracts.

Munira was also missed at the wedding, which she was unable to attend because on 2 May 1935 she had given birth to a second little girl. This child was named Muna, 'Hope'. The birth changed nothing in what Munira and those around her were coming to regard as her predicament. Her role was to produce an heir, which she was failing to do. Meanwhile, she found herself isolated. She could not indulge in the amusements of other young people her age, as she was a married woman. She was increasingly excluded from Muhammad's social life, as he had now taken to going out every night with his friends while she stayed at home with the children. Even her little girls were not left to her sole care, as she had to put up with the constant interference of a parade of foreign nannies and Egyptian wet nurses. Huda was too involved in her political and social activities to notice that things had gone amiss with her son's life, even though they lived in the same house. Munira still felt that Huda blamed her for a situation that was not of her own making.

Huda was busy, as always, with the welfare of some far-off countries. In the summer of 1935, she was concerned over the fate of Ethiopia, a country that was in fact important to Egypt, since it was in the Nile Valley and adjacent to Sudan. As the African ambitions of the Italian leader Mussolini escalated in May and June 1935, she addressed a direct appeal to the people of Italy, urging them to address an immediate

219

demand to their Government to halt Italy's onslaught on Ethiopia. She directed a further appeal to the League of Nations, calling for the League's intervention to preserve Ethiopia's independence. *L'Égyptienne*, as usual, was the means of expression of Huda's calls for peace. Articles were published about the ancient Queen of Sheba and Queen Menen of Ethiopia that were intended to promote sympathy in the West for Ethiopia's plight. She also wrote to the French writers Henri Barbusse and Romain Rolland, conveying her strong sympathy for the International Committee for the Struggle against the War and Fascism they had set up, and supporting their condemnation of the Italian aggression against East Africa. It should not be forgotten, she argued, that Ethiopia was the only truly independent country in Africa, and a member of the League of Nations, so that it was essential that it should be saved from occupation. Huda was eager, in her capacity as a member of the IAW's executive committee, to emulate her international colleagues in their campaign for peace.[1]

Huda's health continued to deteriorate. Her activities were now limited by attacks of malaise that unpredictably afflicted her. Her energy was sapped, a strange heaviness seemed to occupy her limbs, and an acute pain often struck her chest, almost choking her and sometimes seeming to paralyse her. She took this as a warning of difficult times ahead. She still demanded and expected much of herself, but faced by her incapacity she sometimes began to feel defeated. Would she ever succeed in carrying out all her ambitions, or was there no end but failure? She wrote a poem, entitled 'Pessimisme', about her state of mind. Poetry had often been her safety valve in moments of distress.

> On voudrait parer la vie de fleurs
> Et refouler au fond du cœur ses larmes
> Mais les fleurs cachent souvent sous leurs charmes
> Des épines qui font couler nos pleurs.
>
> On voudrait pardonner toutes les fautes
> En trouvant à chacune sa raison,
> Ouvrir à ses ennemis sa maison
> Et de ses agresseurs faire ses hôtes.

Mais on a beau prêcher la douce paix
Et condamner tout haut l'horrible guerre,
L'homme attaché par sa chair à sa terre
Lui doit son sang, c'est elle qui l'a fait.

On voudrait s'élever avec son âme
Au-dessus des misères des humains
Pour se frayer, parmi tous les chemins,
Celui qui n'aboutit jamais au blâme.

Mais hélas ! Qu'ils soient courbés ou droits,
Tous les chemins qui traversent la vie
Furent tracés par la haine ou l'envie
Des grands tyrans – ou bien des maladroits.

Est-elle une vallée de larmes
Cette terre à laquelle nous tenons
Et l'être humain cache-t-il un démon
Sous ses attraits de douceur et de charmes?

'Pessimisme', *L'Égyptienne*, September 1935

Despite the travails she underwent, however, Huda refused to give in to depression of the kind that had sometimes beset her when she was much younger. She had far too many causes to defend, too many wrongs to right, and all in all too much to do, to afford time to indulge her moods.

This was an era of political turmoil. By 1935, the Wafd, which with much justification regarded itself as the natural governing party of Egypt, had endured enough of Nessim Pasha's bland Government, and on 13 November, Nahhas Pasha called on him to resign. There were calls for all-party reconciliation as the way to form a new Government. There was a crescendo of demonstrations organised by the Wafd, and in the rioting that followed one student was killed and many others wounded.[2] On 12 December 1935, a royal decree finally reinstated the 1923 constitution. However, a rumour was spread that Sir Samuel Hoare (British Foreign Secretary) had pointed out in a public statement that Britain was in reality opposed to the re-establishment of the constitution.[3] Huda's mouthpiece, *L'Égyptienne*, was quick to take its cue. The magazine closely covered the November crisis. Huda made it a point to disclose the identity of the 20-year-old victim of the security forces, Abd al-Hakim al-Girahi. He had written a statement on his deathbed, saying that he willingly sacrificed his life to defend his country's freedom. *L'Égyptienne* published the letter.[4] Huda also sent her usual open letters to the British High Commissioner and to the Prime Minister of Egypt, denouncing their hypocrisy and unjust policies. The students continued to riot, demanding an end to British interference, until the University of Cairo was in the end closed by the police. The upheaval led to an outcome that at least in the feminists' opinion was positive. On 30 January 1936, the King appointed his Chief of the Royal Cabinet, Ali Maher Pasha, as Prime Minister, and yet another supposedly neutral government was installed, this time with the specific brief of negotiating a successful outcome with the British.

The British Government was at last brought to see that the situation in Egypt was deteriorating beyond repair, to the extent that seeking to maintain the British presence in Egypt on its existing basis seemed likely in future always to have more negative than positive consequences for the British themselves. On 4 February 1936, there was a momentous development in London. The new British Foreign Secretary, Anthony Eden, informed the House of Commons that Sir Miles Lampson, the British High Commissioner in Egypt, had been

> instructed to state that His Majesty's Government were prepared to enter forthwith into conversations with the Egyptian Government with the object of arriving at an Anglo–Egyptian treaty settlement. With a view to promoting the prospects of a comprehensive settlement, His Majesty's Government thought it desirable to begin with the categories which have given most difficulty in 1930. They felt that, if these difficulties were surmounted, the prospects of reaching a settlement would clearly be favourable.[5]

By 'categories which have given most difficulty', he referred to the administration of the Sudan and the other matters previously reserved to Britain.

When he took over as Prime Minister, Ali Maher Pasha was seen as a saviour by many Egyptians. All, from the highest to the lowest social class, were of one accord that there must be freedom from British interference. Most, on the other hand, were by now sick of riots and disturbances, and the disruption and lost income they represented. Ali Maher's smooth elegance, his earthen complexion, his love of perfumes were known to all, as were his intellect, his punctiliousness and his efficiency.[6] He had not always been popular, but this was largely due to the fact that he was a staunch monarchist. He had been Minister of Education in 1925, Minister of Finance under the Liberal Constitutionalists in 1928, and Minister of Justice under Sidqi between 1930 and 1932. His background was in the law, and he had long served as a judge in both the national and the mixed courts. He was a realist, and knew by instinct and experience that government could not be carried on by attempting to crush opposing interests, whether those of the people, the Crown or the British, but by seeking compromise. There was much hope that he might find the way forward with the British.

On 28 April 1936, King Fuad, whose health had steadily been deteriorating, finally passed away. His son and heir Farouk was aged only 16 and was therefore still a minor. Farouk was called urgently back to Egypt from the Royal Military Academy at Woolwich, in London, where he was studying. He travelled to Marseilles by train, and then by ship to Alexandria. On 9 May, Ali Maher summoned both houses of parliament to a joint session so that he could inform them of the late King's wishes as to who would be responsible for the necessary regency. Prince Muhammad Ali Tawfiq, his brother, was to be President of the Regency Council, which was to consist of three members, with Aziz Izzet Pasha and Sherif Sabri Pasha as the other two. King Fuad's funeral was a vast and chaotic affair. Some mourned for the sake of form, while the grief of others was heartfelt, but for the people the paramount concern was to know what the consequences would be for their already troubled lives. Afterwards, however, normality was swift to return, and negotiations with the British resumed. Despite the King's death, elections were held on 2 May

1936, resulting in a huge majority for the Wafd, which won 166 seats, with only 66 for all the other parties. Ali Maher resigned on 9 May 1936, and Nahhas Pasha became Prime Minister once more, of an entirely Wafdist Government.

Huda's attention, meanwhile, was increasingly monopolised by Palestine and the plight of the Arab women there. Céza published an article in L'Égyptienne including the text of the latest statement issued on 2 June 1936 by the Committee of Arab Women in Jerusalem. This was framed as an appeal to all British women, wherever they might be. In the words of the statement, 'the present critical situation...does not reflect a spirit of rebellion against the British authorities, nor a movement supported by foreign agencies, but a simple struggle on the part of the nation to obtain its natural rights.'[7] On 9 June 1936, Huda held a meeting with her colleagues at the EFU at which they decided that Palestine must henceforth be their first priority. This was a difficult moment for many of them, who had in the past admired the courage and determination of the Jewish immigrants in Palestine. Many had also given their instinctive support to the Jews against those who had oppressed them in the West. They insisted that Jews had always been welcome in the Ottoman Empire and in its different provinces, and that they would continue to be welcome in the post-Ottoman states. But the news from Palestine was alarming, with escalating violence against the local population.

The women were dismayed. Many were torn by conflicting emotions. Nevertheless, they resolved to take a number of practical steps. These were, first, to collect funds to assist the victims of the recent troubles in Palestine; second, to send telegrams to the British Colonial Secretary and to the speaker of the House of Commons; and third, to address an appropriate appeal to all the women of the world.[8] The text of the telegram, dated 17 June 1936, which was drafted in English, probably with the help of Esther Wissa, who was an English speaker, was published in English in the magazine. It was signed by Huda, in her capacity as President of the EFU:

Egyptian women show their heartfelt sympathy towards their friends and neighbours, the Arabs of Palestine, in the drastic ordeal they are going through. In the meantime, they are distressed by the weak and vacillating attitude of Britain and its robbing all the peoples of the Near East of their faith in Britain's fairness and readiness to meet righteousness and justice. The Egyptian Feminist Union, in its sincere desire for universal peace, exhorts the British Government to live up to its claim of championing the cause of the weak by putting an end to Jewish immigration to Palestine. By doing so the British Government divorces its policy of hesitation and ambiguity which is still responsible for all the troubles in the Near East.[9]

On 12 August 1936, at the Antoniadis Palace in Alexandria, a provisional agreement, drawn up on the basis of the negotiations undertaken by Ali Maher, was signed by Britain and Egypt. The agreement severely curtailed Britain's rights to interfere in Egyptian affairs. The long awaited Anglo–Egyptian treaty was signed in Cairo on 26 August, bringing with it the prospect of real independence for Egypt. The complete solution was still tantalisingly out of reach, however. The crucial issue of Sudan was avoided, and to the rage of Egyptian nationalists the terms of the treaty implied that Sudan was effectively lost to Egypt. In addition, the capitulations, another of Huda's bugbears, still remained in force.

At home at 2 Qasr al-Nil Street, Huda continued to treat Muhammad and Munira's growing problems too lightly. Munira had just had a third little girl. This one she named Huda, perhaps in an attempt to placate her mother-in-law. Despite the continued absence of a male heir, Huda still wanted to see the marriage succeed, and hoped her daughter-in-law would sooner or later be able to steady her husband. In the early summer of 1936, Munira was drawn into the intellectual activities of the household. Muhammad had been invited to participate at the conference of the Inter-Parliamentary Union (IPU) in Budapest from 3 to 8 July, and Munira busied herself collecting newspaper cuttings about the subject that was to be the conference's main theme, collective migration. Muhammad was moved by his wife's application to this task, and was more considerate towards her than had been his wont. Huda mistook this improvement for happiness.

Huda was interested in the topic of Muhammad's IPU conference, collective migration, with its relevance to Palestine. She therefore decided to go to Budapest to attend as an auditor, in preference to staying in Cairo to attend the EFU's own meeting on peace and the League of Nations, due to be held at the same time at the Qasr al-Aini Street headquarters. The EFU meeting was intended as a preparatory session for a conference to be held by the International Peace Campaign created by Robert Cecil and Pierre Cot and due to take place in Brussels between 3 and 6 September 1936, and to which the EFU had accepted an invitation.[10] The Egyptian women were sent their invitation to attend the Brussels meeting by the indefatigable Rosa Manus, the Dutch campaigner who was, in addition to her position in the IAW, also involved with the International Peace Campaign, created by Lord Robert Cecil and Pierre Cot. The four points to be discussed in Brussels were the inviolability of treaty commitments, agreement on the restriction of the production of arms, the reinforcement of the League of Nations, and finally the establishment of an effective mechanism by which the League would bring about the peaceful resolution of situations liable to provoke conflict.[11] These were not themselves to be open to discussion, and the purpose of the conference would be to identify the most effective means for their implementation.

When Muhammad set off for Budapest at the end of June, Huda travelled with him. At home, her agricultural produce from the estates at Minya had just won prizes at the Agricultural and Industrial Fair, whose final ceremony had taken place on 15 April. In addition, the Rod al-Farag potteries had won medals that spoke of the quality of the work being done at the factory.[12] She felt that she had achieved enough to afford the time for a summer break. Huda had in any case always gone to Europe when she could in the summer for medical purposes, and welcomed the benefit of a spell in a cooler climate. The plan was to stay on in Budapest for some time after the conference was over.

However, in place of enjoying a quiet summer, she was fated to face a major domestic tragedy. While Muhammad and Huda were still in

Budapest, they received the news that on 16 July Mahmud Sami Pasha had suddenly and unexpectedly passed away. There had been some minor problems with his health, and he had been treated for kidney trouble. Nothing, however, had led anyone to anticipate his death. He had been a pillar on whom not only Bassna but the whole family had come to depend. All relied on him for advice and moral support. His support for the feminist struggle had been unconditional since the outset, when, it should not be forgotten, he had gallantly stood by Huda's side in public as she took the veil from her face in 1923.

The journey home was agony for Huda. First there was the interminable train across Europe, then a ship from Istanbul that had never seemed slower. She felt guilty for having left Cairo when Mahmud had not been in perfect health, even though his death was so unexpected. When she at last left the ship in Alexandria, Huda ran towards Bassna, who was waiting for her. She wanted to hold her daughter in her arms and to reassure her that she would always be with her and would do all in her power to help. She wanted Bassna to know that she was not alone. She ran up the flight of stairs, at the top of which Bassna waited for her, as motionless as a stone. But when Huda tried to embrace her, Bassna pulled back and pushed her mother away. Huda stumbled and fell on the staircase. She could not believe what had happened, and began at last to understand how angry her daughter was. She understood that Bassna felt betrayed, believing her mother should have been by her side rather than out of Egypt. The warmth of the relationship Huda always had with her daughter seemed to have suddenly evaporated, and she did not know how to cope with this new and disturbing situation.

Luckily, Munira and her three little girls had also come to Alexandria. This must have been the first time Huda realised how compassionate and kind her daughter-in-law could be. Perhaps she had never until now seen Munira as she really was, or tried properly to communicate with her. This was the first occasion on which Munira was able to show how helpful her presence was, and how soothing she could be, when the unthinkable happened and this mythical woman, this pillar of strength and composure, as Huda was universally seen, broke down with emotion. Huda herself had come to believe she was totally imperturbable and, in the unexpected crisis, she could not cope with her emotions. She was baffled and upset, and did not know what to do or say to atone to Bassna for her absence. It was Munira who acted as an intermediary, helping the two women, mother and daughter, to communicate, and attempting to explain each to the other.

Sami Pasha's death had many consequences, but the new and unexpected tension to which it gave rise within the family was the most disturbing. Bassna came to live with Huda, and suddenly began to perceive as an irritation the constant presence of Céza, Hawa and some of the other women in Huda's little group. She had been accustomed to privacy in her own home, where she had been the mistress. What she now saw as the constant infringement of privacy in her mother's house filled her with resentment. Bassna discussed this with Muhammad, and discovered that he had long felt the same. However, all were enmeshed in the network Huda had constructed around herself in the course of her social and political activities, and were afforded little time to stop and think about their own lives, hopes or needs. There was always so much to do. To carry on the struggle was Huda's inflexible way.

When September came, Huda was not able to go to Brussels as planned because of Bassna's tragedy and her own need for once to concentrate her attention on her family situation. She also had a moment of private grief in September when she heard of the death of her old friend Juliette Adam. A further reason, incidentally, for Huda not going to the congress in Brussels, had she not been prevented from going in any case by her son-in-law's death, was that she had learned that Lord Robert Cecil was a Zionist sympathiser. She found it increasingly difficult to communicate with those who took this view. However, agonising though it was for her to be absent at this key international gathering, she felt sure that her colleagues would keep the flag flying for Egypt and make a valuable contribution. The Egyptian women were eager to take part. They had by now become well used to conference participation, and were not shy to address audiences. Fatma Nimet Rashid, Esther Fahmi Wissa, Duria Shafiq and others were prepared to speak whenever necessary in Arabic, French or English to support the League of Nations and put Egypt's case for becoming a member, as well as underlining Egypt's support for justice and peace.

In October, Huda's fears for Palestine reached new levels when the Palestinian Arab Ladies' Committee sent further news about recent events and the predicament of the indigenous population. The Jewish population in Palestine had increased from 174,000 in 1931 to 384,000 in 1936. The attitude of the Zionists towards the local population was undemocratic at best, and menacing at worst, since they despised the poor and helpless Palestinian Arabs and were ready to take any steps necessary to acquire more territory for themselves. Thanks to the Zionist lobby's effective advocacy in the West, they appeared to have the support of the British Government in Palestine, to the detriment of the Arabs, despite the claim in the White Paper of 1930 that the number of Jewish immigrants would be limited.

The Anglo–Egyptian treaty was ratified by the two houses of the Egyptian parliament on 18 November. On 26 August, when the treaty had first been signed, Huda had been one of those who still resented the humiliating acceptance of England's terms by the Egyptian negotiators. Both she and Céza clearly conveyed their disappointment. If Egypt's men could not secure its future, they argued, the solution to Egypt's problems must lie with its women. The women should rise up, Huda said, to protect their children and to demand a referendum for all Egyptian citizens, both men and women, on whether to accept the terms of the treaty or refuse them. But she also wanted to relate the issue to her other preoccupations of peace and Palestine:

> Women of Egypt, if I call upon your conscience, it is to preserve our country, while there is still time, against the sad fate of Palestine and Spain, the victims of foreign influence and civil war. For alas, though we are entitled to the constitutional regime for which we paid with our blood, I can see, rising at the horizon, the signs of political intolerance, the worst enemy of all individual freedom.[13]

Meanwhile, the focus on peace continued. One of Huda's regular European correspondents was Adèle Eidenschenk-Patin, a distinguished French educator who had founded the International League for Mothers and Educators in Peace (LIMEP). She had written repeatedly for *L'Égyptienne* about the need to control the European arms trade. In December 1936, she wrote, 'It is in the women's hands, with the help of men of good will, to chain the beast of war, and to restore a human soul to humanity.'[14]

By November 1936, Huda was actively planning a new publishing venture to stand next to *L'Égyptienne*. The plan was for a magazine in the Arabic language to demonstrate the solidarity of the Egyptian women's movement with the Arab world. *Al-Misria* (*The Egyptian Woman*) would target a new Arabic-speaking audience. Huda could thus reach Arab women in other countries where French was less understood, and would also be able to extend her audience in Egypt beyond the middle class to which its language unavoidably limited *L'Égyptienne's* circulation.

Huda tried hard to persuade Hawa to become the editor of the Arabic magazine. She pleaded with her, but Hawa would not hear of it. She maintained that she had no university degree and was not qualified for the post. Huda's response was to point out that she had no degree either, and yet she had never had any doubt of her intellectual ability. But Hawa would not yield. She enjoyed her work with the Cadettes, organising shows and balls for the EFU's annual fair, managing the nursery and sometimes the needlework in the workshop. She would not consider taking on a responsibility that she feared might be beyond her capacities. She saw Huda's faith in her as endearing but misplaced. In the end, Fatma Nimet Rashid took the position.

January 1937 saw the celebration of the twelfth anniversary of *L'Égyptienne*, along with the birth of the bi-monthly *Al-Misria*. In its early days, the new magazine lacked Céza's panache, but achieved its purpose. This was to inform Arabic speakers in Egypt and in the rest of the Arab world about the activities of the EFU, while offering them a wide variety of informative and educational articles by the best authors and poets of Egypt. Politics was central to its subject matter. At the party for the anniversary of *L'Égyptienne* and the launch of *Al-Misria*, more of the small pottery statuettes reproducing one of Mukhtar's sculptures of an Egyptian peasant woman were distributed to all the guests as souvenirs. It was clear from the start that *Al-Misria* would be a Liberal Constitutionalist magazine. Muhammad Ali Alluba, Hafiz Afifi and Muhammad Husain Haikal contributed to the first issue. International concerns were reflected in an article on peace and disarmament by Eidenschenk Patin, already published in *L'Égyptienne* and now translated into Arabic for *Al-Misria*.

As time passed, even Huda began to accept that the terms of the Anglo–Egyptian treaty were perhaps the best that could be obtained for Egypt in the circumstances. Many Egyptians had links with British business enterprises. Even the Wafdist leader, Nahhas Pasha, could see virtues in maintaining a relationship with Britain. Muhammad Mahmud, one of the most distinguished Liberal Constitutionalists, was an English-speaking alumnus of Balliol College, Oxford, which led him to feel special warmth towards Britain. Hafiz Afifi, Mahmud Sami's brother-in-law, made no secret of his pragmatic belief in the importance of British–Egyptian trade relations. In addition, she began to see there could be a real need for British protection against external aggression from other directions. Finally, Huda knew that it was not realistic to suppose the members of the negotiating committee really had any choice over the Treaty's terms.

The last issue to be settled was that of the capitulatory laws, and this was to be dealt with at the proposed conference at Montreux, in Switzerland, with all 12 states that had such agreements with Egypt participating. There was no disagreement in the event about the principle of dismantling the capitulations. Only the timetable and the length of the transitional period were at issue.[15] In the event, the Egyptian courts were soon able to cope with the additional responsibilities they would inherit from the mixed courts, and the Convention of Montreux came into force about 18 months later. Egypt had at last in principle recovered its full juridical and legislative sovereignty, though there was still to be a lengthy transition period. Egypt joined the League of Nations on 26 May 1937. Emilie Gourd, who was Secretary General of the IAW at the time, sent Huda a telegram of congratulations conveying her hope that there would be women in the Egyptian delegation to the League. Huda passed the message on to the Prime Minister.

There were spectacular celebrations for the return to Egypt of the country's new monarch, King Farouk, who had achieved his majority according to the Islamic calendar and was at last to take his place on the throne 15 months after inheriting it. Farouk arrived in Egypt on 25 July 1937, and was crowned King on 29 July. The scale of the ceremonies, the decorations, the illuminations and the pageantry were breathtaking. People thronged from all over the country like a rising tide of humanity, flooding the streets of Cairo to admire the handsome, charming, innocent, faithful and perfect young monarch. All sought to catch a glimpse of him or to hear his voice on the radio, to give a human shape at last to the hope they all invested in this adolescent boy. The Queen Mother, Queen Nazli, and her daughters, Farouk's sisters, were all present in parliament when he took the oath.

The young man found a place in his people's hearts in a way his father never had. He knew how to speak to the common man. When the three days of celebrations came to an end in Cairo, they started all over again in Alexandria, where the foreign communities had prepared the city for yet more festivities. The young King was adored by everyone, not least because he was handsome and elegant, which his father had certainly not been. He was a good Muslim, and could lead the prayers in Arabic, which Fuad had not been able to do, and that endowed him with the stature of a 'good King' ('Al-Malik al-Salih'). This could help him one day to become a leader not merely in Egypt but in a wider disintegrating post-Ottoman Islamic world where the need to stand up against foreign interference and manipulation was increasingly felt.[16]

Huda rejoiced in the knowledge that Queen Nazli was no longer a prisoner shifting aimlessly from palace to palace and from one strictly guarded harem to the other, with nothing but glamorous garments and jewels to keep her company. King Farouk himself had grown up in isolation, without any friends except for his sisters, meeting his mother only in accordance with a strictly regulated schedule, and King Fuad had been distant and severe with him throughout his childhood. The adolescent King was therefore obviously thriving on his sudden personal freedom and in the company of his family.[17] What seemed to be the return of the royal family to an almost normal family life was reassuring to Huda. It was another manifestation of a freedom which was gradually coming to pervade the life of Egypt's society.

It was a personal joy for Huda at this time when Céza and Mustafa Naguib announced their decision at last to wed. Céza was by now almost forty, and Huda had begun to feel guilty over her lack of a personal life, which she blamed on herself, for being too demanding, seeing it as a consequence of the selfless dedication Céza had shown towards furthering Huda's various causes. She recalled with a sense of guilt Céza's passing romance with Muhammad al-Saqqaf when she was a young girl, and how she had prevented her from going abroad to be with him because of Ali Saad al-Din's criticism of the young man's unruly behaviour. On the other hand, she could now compensate for the past and act as godmother to her spiritual daughter at the moment of her marriage.[18] Mustafa Naguib was a smart, vigorous and good-looking young man with a sunny disposition. His temperament matched that of Céza herself, with her acute insight into people and her sense of humour. On the other hand, Céza was more serious than Mustafa. For her, work was a vocation rather than merely an occupation. She felt passionate about what she did, while he on the other hand was whimsical and pursued whatever amused him. They were married at Huda's house, as was appropriate. However, sadly, in the long term they were not destined to stay together.

In 1937, Huda began once more to have misgivings about the Anglo–Egyptian treaty, as speculation spread in Egypt that under its terms the country could be dragged unwillingly as an ally of Britain into what now seemed an imminent world war. Huda was dejected by this prospect, and felt that it could be, after all, that the Egyptians had been outwitted by the British. The price for Egypt would be high if the country were to be dragged into the nightmare of global conflict. Huda had received a telegram from the International Peace Campaign promoted by Pierre Cot and Robert Cecil, asking her to join in a campaign for more effective action by the League of Nations, which was criticised for its failure to condemn the invasion of Ethiopia, the Spanish Civil War and Japan's war against China. Huda immediately gave her support. On 12 September 1937, she sent a telegram to Wasif Ghali Pasha, the Egyptian Minister of Foreign Affairs, which read, 'Alarmed by continuous violations of international law and by threats of war, Egyptian women demand from the League of Nations energetic action for full respect of the Pact in Abyssinia, Spain, the Near East and Far East.' However, Huda also added Palestine to her list of concerns. When Ghali Pasha took the floor for the first time at the League of Nations, he strongly criticised Britain's apparent intention to divide Palestine.[19]

Huda was increasingly aware that her interventions carried weight, and that she could use her magazines to publicise what she wished. She continued to underline the need for social reform in Egypt, and would often seek to shame the Government by writing about private initiatives that they were failing to emulate, such as an institute for the deaf and dumb that she visited in Alexandria, begun by a Greek charity. In power, the Wafd had not lived up to her expectations, and her battle against what she saw as the increasing corruption of Nahhas Pasha's Government became so virulent that some articles published in *L'Égyptienne* began to take a threatening tone. The detention of journalists in the same jails as common criminals, the general neglect of women, and an apparent disregard for the most needy segments of society all led her to declare that she was ready to withdraw her support from Nahhas's Government, and that this would be reflected in her magazines with a consequent impact on public opinion.

This was a high point for Huda's activism. Not content with her international interventions, her advocacy of the Palestinian cause, her concern over the Anglo–Egyptian treaty and her general political involvement, Huda chose to launch at this time her personal campaign against official corruption, a matter of principle that would continue to the end of her life. For example, when she was informed of the plan to generate electricity at the Aswan Dam, she published articles in both *Al-Misria* and *L'Égyptienne* underlining concerns that were being voiced over the possibility of corruption in the award of the tender. She sent a message to the Prime Minister demanding that he did more to curb corruption and that he should limit the state's disbursements by cutting down the Government's expenditure, for example on celebrations. Though she greatly approved of Farouk as an altogether more attractive successor to King Fuad, she felt that the expenses incurred at the time of his arrival might have been excessive at a time of financial stringency.

King Farouk was a young man of the modern era. Once installed on the throne, he needed a wife, and he proposed to his bride-to-be, Said Zulficar Pasha's daughter Safinaz, in an informal way, asking the girl, who was a friend of his sisters, if she would agree to be his Queen. Safinaz was the daughter of Queen Nazli's dearest friend and lady in waiting Zainab. She is said to have simply lowered her eyes and to have told Farouk that he should ask her father. He did not take offence at being treated in the same way as any ordinary young man would be, and subsequently made his proposal to her father in the proper form, as Safinaz had said he should.[20]

The story of the royal engagement was recounted by Céza in *L'Égyptienne* in very romantic terms. She portrayed the youthful King as charming and endearing. When Safinaz changed her Turkish name into an Egyptian name, Farida, so as to have the same initial as her husband, the gesture entered people's hearts. The couple were both young and attractive, and their wedding was intentionally reminiscent of the pomp and ceremony of the ancient Egyptian kings and queens. They were Egypt's crowned couple, and, as Céza put it, they were also the jewels in the crown. They added to the country's beauty and elegance, she averred, while endowing it with a much-needed youthful image.

11

Peace and justice

By 1938, Egypt not only had a new King, it also had yet another new Government. Farouk's first Prime Minister, Nahhas Pasha, had been given his marching orders by the King at the end of December 1937, when his cabinet was dissolved by royal decree. There had been a running confrontation between the King and the Wafd since Farouk's accession, and at a moment when the tide of popularity seemed to be running momentarily against the Wafd, the King took his opportunity. On 29 December 1937, Muhammad Mahmud took over once more as Prime Minister. As a Liberal Constitutionalist who believed in democracy, he successfully put together a Government from representatives of all the different parties as well as independent elements, among them Bahi al-Din Barakat Pasha, an independent member of parliament. He appointed Abd al-Fattah Yehia Pasha as his new Foreign Minister. Yehia, himself a former Prime Minister, was expected to manage tactfully Egypt's relations with the British Embassy. Egypt was once more in the hands of a political group of whom Huda approved.

Muhammad Mahmud made his own attempt to court popular approbation. As a landowner, he sought to show the reality of his concern for rural areas. He spent time in Upper Egypt, going up and down on his houseboat, meeting ordinary people and encouraging them to vote and to exercise their right to freedom and equality. Reforms were implemented to improve the lives of the *fellaheen* who made up the majority of Egypt's population. Bendari Pasha, his Minister for Public Health, had artesian wells dug in the villages in order to provide the rural areas with potable water. Two hundred vehicles were equipped as mobile schools and dispensaries for the outlying areas, in addition to the establishment of permanent health units managed by a medical doctor, a midwife and a nurse. The Egyptian feminists were unsatisfied, however, since he made no move to give women the right they demanded to vote and sit in parliament.[1]

It had begun to be painfully evident that Huda's son and daughter were now constantly critical of her way of life, and were frequently less than pleased with her activities. However, she still enjoyed her grandchildren's company. She would play with Muhammad's little girls whenever she had time. She sang Victor Hugo's 'Ronde enfantine' to them, clapping her hands, after arranging them in a circle: 'Dansez les petites filles/Dansez en rond/En vous voyant si gentilles/Les bois riront...' She knew the rhyme by heart, and soon the little girls learned it too. They loved Huda's husky voice, with its comforting strength. In addition, within the society of the big house, it was considered an honour to be in Huda's presence. If their father came in and began to argue, the girls were terrified and ran away. Clashes between Huda and Muhammad or Huda and Bassna often culminated in angry exchanges. The grandchildren were well aware that though their grandmother was always kindly in her dealings with them, she was also demanding and determined, and they knew she could be ferocious when roused. She was scrupulously careful never to hurt those who worked for her or those who needed her help, but she could on occasion be fiercely irate when she believed she was in the right.

By this time, sadly, Huda could no longer refuse to face up to the reality of her medical difficulties. She began to suffer more frequent

Huda in midlife.

chest pains. Angina pectoris was diagnosed, and her doctors insisted she take more rest. It was at this time that she began to contemplate seriously her own death, to which she was able to take a calm and philosophical attitude. As to the work, her assistants were able to help in many fields, though when Huda was unable to be at the helm it was evident that a sense of political direction was lacking. Business, however, went on as usual. Céza was fully capable of running *L'Égyptienne* and Eva Habib al-Masri, who had taken over as editor of *Al-Misria*, kept the Arabic magazine up to the same standard. Hawa took care of the practical activities of the EFU with the help of the other Cadettes. Sherifa Lutfi, Karima and Amina al-Said, Fatma Fahmi and sometimes even Huda's daughter-in-law Mimi, when Muhammad would permit, had become an excellent team, and were perfectly capable of running the business of 2 Qasr al-Nil Street and the EFU headquarters without help. Muhammad, ever dutiful in public affairs, donated the Mukhtar Prize.[2]

In early 1938, a committee of Chinese Muslims visited Cairo to seek Egypt's support against the aggression committed against China by the Japanese. This situation was one of the international flashpoints to which the international peace movement currently sought to draw attention, though it was little known in the West. For the Egyptian feminists, it was undoubtedly exotic. *L'Égyptienne* dutifully reported the visit, and once the interest of Huda's circle was aroused, it went further. Hawa became intrigued by the Hindu faith, to the point of organising a *tableau vivant* representing Krishna at the EFU's annual fair.[3] As Huda saw it, a pattern was emerging of colonised nations yearning for peace, while the preoccupation of the West was always simply the maintenance of its overseas possessions and influence.[4]

Closer to home, since the mandates had artificially divided up the Middle East it became obvious that Greater Syria, as much of the Middle Eastern region was known at that time, would inevitably come to suffer from the levels of instability that were evident in other colonised regions of the world. The terms under which Syria had recently acquired its independence raised concerns as to what France's plans were for the region. Huda asked Muhammad Jamil Beyhum to write a series of articles about the Franco–Syrian and Franco–Lebanese treaties, which were not dissimilar from the Anglo–Iraqi or the Anglo–Egyptian ones. Having divided the region's territories according to their own interests, the French were now about to leave the Syrians, in theory, to govern themselves after the country's independence in 1937, but intended to leave a military force in the country together with an agreement that Syria would be permanently allied to France. It was clear that the French plan to split off Lebanon from Syria would also result in unforeseeable problems in the future. Huda and her colleagues argued that the French, like the British, should be aware that Western-style political frontiers and Western priorities could not be forced on the whole world without giving rise to resentment.

In April 1938, Édouard Herriot, a former French Prime Minister who was a firm advocate of the League of Nations and the International World Order, visited Cairo. Huda, Céza, Fatma Nimet Rashid and Jeanne Marquès were invited to his press conference. The candid and reassuring approach of this great French pacifist was a source of solace to the journalists who met him.[5] He succeeded in presenting the possibility of peace as still feasible, and argued for a better understanding between the East and the countries of the West. The Egyptians felt they were justified in not entirely losing their faith in France.

King Farouk still seemed to have brought with him some hope for a better future in Egypt. Pictures of his wife, Queen Farida, wearing her vast diamond necklace, earrings and tiara, were published by Huda's magazines. The royal couple projected a vision of happiness. The young Queen was both intelligent and beautiful, and in her official pictures such was the breathtaking nature of her beauty that she appeared almost a benevolent spirit who had come to protect her country and her King merely through her radiant self. The feminists relished the idea that this was a King who allowed his royal consort and his mother to move freely in the world, and did not follow his father's bad example of imprisoning the women in the harem. Huda felt that there was a great improvement in the ways of the palace.

Huda still spent much time discussing political affairs with her group of advisers. Many had moved into powerful positions in Mahmud's Government. In 1938, Haikal Pasha became Minister of Education and Mustafa Abd al-Raziq was the Minister for Waqf. Her old friend Lutfi al-Sayid was still Rector of the University of Cairo, and Taha Husain was firmly ensconced as head of the Faculty of Letters. She also still took much advice from her old friend Muhammad Ali Alluba, Ali's faithful friend in the old Wafdist days and her preferred legal and political counsellor. Egypt's internal problems were as intractable as ever, and issues that currently interested Huda were the old questions of the education of women, the development of education in Egypt in general, and the broad issue of achieving social justice. Haikal Pasha had just conducted a survey in Egyptian schools, showing that many elementary-school children were either ill or malnourished. She hoped this could be addressed by providing meals in the schools while also progressively increasing the number of elementary schools in Cairo and elsewhere. The article of the 1923 constitution that made universal education compulsory would thus at last be implemented. Owing to the lack of schools, parents had not hitherto been forced to send their children, but if reform were to be successful, compulsion could be applied.

In May 1938, turning back again to Palestine, she used the pages of *L'Égyptienne* to launch an appeal to the countries of the Middle East, calling on them to help the Palestinian Arabs:

> All the Arab countries, which are painfully affected by the suffering of their Palestinian brothers, who valiantly defend their homeland and legitimate rights, have conveyed their indignation to the world. Egypt more than any other, however, is called upon to rise up against such injustice and to come to its neighbour's rescue. Has Egypt not been wounded by the same weapon with which England now pierces the very heart of Holy Palestine and did it not suffer yesterday from what this poor country is enduring today? In addition, when Egypt rose in revolt it had to defend its independence against only one usurper, whereas the unfortunate Palestine is defending its life against two audacious interlopers who have joined forces to exterminate its children and to take their place.[6]

As she embarked on this late phase of her journey through life, Huda remained true to her principles. There was nothing more odious in her eyes than violence and the unjust will to dominate others merely because they were politically, economically or militarily weak. This was what she had most passionately struggled against. She was determined to fight the battle to the bitter end with her customary weapons, reason and information. She saw in the issue of Palestine a growing regional, not to say global, tragedy. She continued to believe that non-Zionist Jews would side with the Christian and Muslim

Palestinians when the true situation in Palestine was known to them. Surely they could not look favourably upon the use of violence within the Holy Land?

A key moment for Huda came in September 1938, when the Palestinian women's organisations, together with women's organisations in Syria, Lebanon and Iraq, wrote to invite her to represent them in putting the Palestinian case to international organisations and in other appropriate forums.[7] In response, the EFU immediately put forward a plan to hold an international conference on Palestine in Cairo in October 1938. In her capacity as President of the EFU and of the Eastern Women's Conference, as the international meeting was to be known, Huda published an appeal in her two magazines to all the women of the world, in which she called for solidarity with the idea of the conference.

> We, the Eastern women, prompted by our conscience to save the martyred humanity of the Holy Lands have decided to hold a Conference in Cairo, in order to scrutinise the painful situation endured by Palestine for a number of years.
>
> What the Palestinians endure is increasingly alarming. Every rising day witnesses new orphans and widows, the death of old men, victims of both genders, fighting in the streets and markets. In brief, the cruellest savagery is manifested every day by the murder of innocent children, the destruction of homes and attacks launched against the Holy places during prayers.
>
> In the name of Justice and of humanity, I urge all feminist organisations, with no distinction as to religion or nationality, to join us by sending delegates, as a gesture of solidarity, to this Conference that will be held in Cairo in the middle of October.
>
> Together, we shall examine the Palestinian question and how it may be resolved. We shall then send our resolutions to the competent British authorities, because we are certain that we can convince them of the need to halt the shedding of innocent blood in a country where they are mandated to defend the people and where the provision of security is their responsibility.
>
> We shall do all in our power to provide the delegates with the necessary comfort and facilities for their transport.
>
> We are convinced that any noble hearted and just person must share the suffering we feel for the martyrdom and bloodshed of Palestine and will not hesitate to respond to our appeal by extending their hand to help us in the accomplishment of this humanitarian duty.
>
> Only thus can we stop the revolt that is breaking out everywhere from spreading even further in the Arab countries, that are indignantly reacting

against the injustice suffered by this unfortunate country.
    May God help us by making our just cause triumph.[8]

In October 1938, the planned conference duly took place. On 11
October, the Syrian–Lebanese delegation arrived at Cairo station, to
the cheers and applause of a large delegation of Egyptian and foreign
participants and onlookers. They were taken directly to Huda's house
for an evening reception.[9] The Palestinian delegation arrived during
the night. One of the participants was the wife of Hasan Sidqi al-
Dajani, who was murdered by a group of Zionist terrorists immediately
after the departure of the women's delegation, with the result that his
wife was obliged to return at once to Jerusalem on a special flight paid
for by the Egyptian Government.[10] The Palestinian women therefore
received an especially heartfelt and sympathetic welcome the following
morning at the EFU headquarters. On 12 October, a committee was
chosen to manage the conference. Huda had then organised a visit to
the Pyramids and a reception at the Actors' Studio in Giza close by,
aiming to give the women some leisure before the proceedings began.
The Iraqi delegation, which had farther to travel, arrived that night.

On 15 October, the conference opened. Egyptian political figures and
other distinguished male guests also attended. Huda gave the opening
address.[11] The Palestinian women spoke eloquently and movingly.
Akila Shukri Deeb talked of twenty years of suffering endured by her
people. Bahira Nabih al-Azama gave an account of how Palestinians
were being imprisoned and maltreated by the British, and persecuted
by the Zionists. She demanded to know why the Palestinians should
leave their homes to make way for Western Jewish immigrants who
could surely be given homes in other countries where an indigenous
population would not be displaced. The Secretary of the Arab Ladies'
Association in Jerusalem, Zulikha al-Shahabi, added that the hostility
of the British towards the local population was unacceptable. She also
accused these Jews of bringing with them the alien creed of communism.[12]
Most of them talked about the beauty of their beloved country, Palestine.
A second day of oratory followed the first. The next day, 17 October,

was taken as a rest day, with various visits and receptions. The Egyptian Government showed its solidarity with the spirit of the conference when the heads of delegations were invited to lunch at the home of the Prime Minister's wife.[13]

On 18 October, the conference held its third and final session. Huda again opened the proceedings. She had been silent so far, listening to the contributions of the visiting delegations, but now gave an impassioned address. She argued that strong measures must be adopted to resist Zionism and its agenda, and to protect Palestine and the region as a whole from penetration by Zionism and its communistic principles. 'Was there any greater, any more terrifying threat to the whole region than Bolshevik Zionism?' she asked. She also took the opportunity to mention the Anglo–Egyptian treaty and the burden of its provisions on Egypt, asking for wider Arab support for Egyptian efforts to throw off this remaining yoke.[14] After the conference was over, Huda tried at last to rest for a brief period, as her doctors advised, although she obviously felt the political situation provided little if any leeway for a respite.

On 1 October 1937, the British authorities in Palestine had arrested a number of members of the Palestinian Arab Higher Committee, established in April 1936 by a number of distinguished Palestinians to defend Palestinian interests, deporting them to the Seychelles. The Palestinian figures involved were Ahmad Hilmi, Yacub al-Ghasin, Fuad Saba, Husain al-Khalidi and Rashid al-Haj Ibrahim. Towards the end of 1938, when Egypt obtained the release of these Palestinian leaders, Huda took the opportunity of their passage through Cairo to invite them to her home, which was now being referred to by many as Bait al-Shark, the Orient House.[15] They told Huda about the rough treatment they had received, and recounted how they had been held under virtual house arrest while they were in the Seychelles.[16]

She also lectured again at the American University in Cairo, this time on world peace in relation to women's issues. Huda severely castigated the League of Nations and its repeated failure to act on flagrant issues.[17] Her statement was published in *L'Égyptienne*, in the same issue as a letter by Huda addressed to Sir Neville Chamberlain, Prime Minister of Great Britain, in which she maintained that in the talks recently held in London the Palestinian Arabs had been moderate in their demands. This was in contrast to the representatives of the Jewish Agency, who had clearly gone to London unwilling to listen to anything but their own agenda, ignoring any willingness on the part of the Arabs to compromise.[18]

Charles Crane's arrival once more in Cairo in October 1938 was a redeeming presence. Harun Al-Rashid, as he was called by his good friend George Antonius, the Arab nationalist, was a faithful friend, and when he was in Cairo his habit was now to visit Huda and her team every day at her house. He liked to sit in her Oriental salon for at least an hour a day, watching the water as it cascaded out of the marble fountain, which he said helped him to rest and meditate. He attempted to reassure Huda that President Roosevelt had considered the future of Palestine and was aware of the pitfalls of partition. He was confident that the American leader would find a just solution. Because Crane knew Roosevelt personally, his words mitigated the anguish of the situation. He gave Huda a copy of *The Arab Awakening*, the new book by George Antonius about the predicament of Palestine. After his departure, she sent him a handsomely bound album of pictures of Egypt in order to express her respect and affection towards him. She also sent a signed picture of herself, sitting at her desk, pen in hand, inscribed 'Au grand ami de notre chère Égypte'.

Another flicker of hope for Huda in a world inevitably destined for war was the arrival of an invitation to attend the thirteenth congress of the IAW, to be held from 8 to 13 July 1939, in Copenhagen. Huda would find a further opportunity there to advocate her causes in an international arena.[19] She promised herself that she would go, despite her failing health, together with the intensifying portents of imminent war and the associated fear she had of becoming stranded in Europe. She had, after all, been through that experience before, at the outset of the First World War, and knew what it entailed. Nevertheless, she felt duty bound to participate in the congress. The idea of seeing friends was enticing, especially Margery Corbett-Ashby and Germaine Malaterre-Sellier. Céza immediately declared she was also willing to go, and they asked Munira Thabit to join them. Meanwhile, Huda took a break to think of her family and of the cultural activities that mattered most to her.

She still maintained, as ever, her interest in Egypt's artistic scene and in young artists. She sponsored an exhibition by the painter Hussein Badawi,[20] whose hazy representations of other-worldly Pharaonic scenes were inspiring. She bought some of his paintings herself. In addition, at the Agricultural Museum, Husni al-Bannani exhibited a portrait of Nihad Khulusi, who was the museum's director and the son of Huda's Turkish friend Wajida Khulusi. Al-Bannani was the son-in-law of Yusuf Kamil, a painter whom Huda greatly appreciated, and he himself was a promising young artist. Céza also expressed enthusiasm about this portrait in *L'Égyptienne*, since it was an indication that Egyptian painters were at last confident that they could paint portraits and sculpt human and animal forms without being accused of religious apostasy. Shaikh Muhammad Abduh himself had expressed the belief that art and idolatry were two different things. According to Shaikh Mustafa Abd al-Raziq, he even wrote about art in a late stage of life, praising painting and sculpture as 'the receptacles of human attitudes' and as 'silent poetry'.[21]

A sad blow fell three months after what no one had realised at the time would be Charles Crane's last departure from Egypt. Huda received a telegram from his personal secretary, saying that Mr Crane was no longer of this world. She incredulously read and re-read the telegram:

> Villa Cornelia, Palm Springs, California, Feb. 24, 1939. My dear Madame Charaoui, I am so sorry that your beautiful 'Golden Book' of Egypt arrived after Mr Crane's death for I know how much it would have pleased and interested him to receive this gift from you. Sincerely yours, Helen K. Powell, Secretary.

His last postcard to her had come from Japan on November 22: 'Envoyez un mot, je vous prie, en Amérique, et quelques nouvelles. Elles me manquent beaucoup dernièrement. Je pars bientôt pour S. Francisco. Amitiés. CRC.'

When the Egyptian broadcasting system invited Huda to deliver a talk on the radio for the thirty-first anniversary of the death of the original Egyptian pro-feminist writer Qasim Amin, she spoke not only about his life but also about the need for women to participate in official activities and in the Government. Though she had achieved much in women's circles, she knew she could have worked side by side on a basis of equality with men, and she felt that her passion for the causes she found significant would have enabled her to be more effective than the majority of men. The obdurate refusal by most Egyptian men to allow women into political life, despite the level of their education, their intelligence and their eloquence, was disheartening.

On 23 May 1939, the second White Paper on Palestine, presented by Neville Chamberlain, was approved by parliament in London. Its main proposal was to limit the number of Jewish immigrants to Palestine to 75,000 for a five-year period until 1944. This was still a substantial figure, but the restriction infuriated the Jews. The transfer of property was also forbidden. The British authorities seemed to have recognised that Palestine's capacity to absorb more immigrants was limited, though their motivation may have been less than honest, since they may have calculated on the wisdom of not alienating Arab states whose assistance might be valuable in the war.[22] During that same month of May, Huda received a great number of appeals for help from desperate Palestinians who wanted the world to hear about their fate. Whole Arab villages were being attacked, and there were terrorist killings. The Mufti of Palestine, Amin al-Husaini, who had been persecuted by the British since the riots of 1933, had been obliged to flee the country.[23] Prisoners were left to languish in British jails, and alleged Arab insurgents faced death sentences.[24]

Huda protested, on behalf of all Arab women, against what she called 'the unfairness of the new White Paper', which 'merely reinforced the death sentence pronounced by Lord Balfour against the Palestinian Arabs'. Evidently, she believed that the terms of the White Paper, though apparently disadvantageous to the Zionists, would in the longer run redound more to the detriment of the Arabs. Addressing the British Colonial Secretary, she wrote,

> Arabs and Muslims all over the world are united by the indestructible bonds of their religion, origin and language. They form a single nation that will never agree to be enslaved or to undergo such suffering while supporting at its own expense the development, under your protection, of an entity that it rejects on the grounds of its intrigues, its ill-faith and its treachery.
>
> Palestine has always been Arab, your Excellency. It is therefore needed by the Arabs more than you might ever need the Jewish people. It will therefore remain Arab, despite Lord Balfour or any other person who might wish to make their own fantasies come true.
>
> This treacherous and hypocritical policy is far from honouring Great Britain. Your Statesmen, who have adopted it, must understand this fact. Not only will it not gain the friendship of the Arab peoples for the English people, it will also destroy whatever is left of their belief in British truthfulness or loyalty. Indeed, this policy stands in contradiction with the democratic principles that Britain simulates in the presence of the dictatorial governments, and upon which are based the bonds that led the Arabs to help you in difficult times.
>
> The clearest evidence of this is the eloquent silence of the Arab countries on the subject of your White Paper and the ridiculous and premeditated campaign launched by the Zionists to mislead the world into thinking that its conditions favour the Arabs at their expense.
>
> If you fail to understand the spirit of the Arabs, if you are unaware of their pride and courage as well as of their determination to preserve their unity, allow me then, Your Excellency, to call your attention to the silence that has met the publication of the White Paper.[25]

Huda's concern with Egyptian affairs also continued, and at a session of the Egyptian chamber of deputies in May 1939, Egypt's parliamentarians discussed the thorny issue of education for girls in an unexpected debate that Huda and her colleagues saw as insulting to all that the women had so far achieved. It seemed that hard-won steps forward would never cease to be challenged by reactionary men. The member of parliament who initiated the discussion, Abd al-Rahman Fahmi, was strongly critical of the Government's policy of providing education for women, maintaining that it only served to corrupt them. Fikri Abaza and Abbas Mahmud al-Aqqad spoke out in favour of the Government's policy. The ministerial spokesman, replying to the debate, eloquently defended the education the Government provided for girls on the grounds that no concrete evidence had been produced that education threatened their moral standards, while all its other benefits were undeniable.[26] Huda was furious at the attempt to curtail the advances that had been made in women's education, but unfortunately her illness was gaining ground, and prevented her from personally drafting a response, though she was pleased to see that what Céza and Eva wrote was more than satisfactory. Céza wondered rhetorically in her article why there was any necessity to have this argument, fifteen years after the education of girls had become a fact in Egypt. In another article, she asked why it should be thought that education would corrupt women and not men. Surely, she enquired, corruption was no respecter of gender.

From May 1939 onward, with two months remaining before the date of the IAW's congress in Copenhagen, Huda attempted consciously to rest and to regain her strength. The pain in her chest fluctuated while she prepared the statement she planned to make and as she tried hard to stay on top of her duties and obligations. She had, however, come to terms with her predicament, and knew that her angina was something she now had to accept. She found comfort in the prospect that hers would at least be a quick death when the time came.[27] For the moment, she had other matters on her mind.

By going to Copenhagen when she was not in the best of health and also in such troubled times, Huda demonstrated her courage and willpower, but was also risking her own welfare. This angered Muhammad and Bassna, who were concerned for her despite their anger at her over her way of life. They felt that they were given no say in her decisions and that she seemed sometimes to go out of her way to cause them needless worry. They felt it should have been sufficient for Huda's purposes to send Céza and Munira Thabit, who were younger and more able to cope. Huda should not imagine she was indispensable, they argued, but they failed to convince her. Meanwhile,

Huda learned that the Palestinian and Syrian women would not be allowed to travel by their respective authorities, which made her yet more determined to go herself. The Arab women's groups begged Huda to speak on their behalf, as her prestige and her charisma would make people listen. Huda was well aware, however, that the Danish hosts had insisted that at this sensitive time there should be no political discussion. Huda therefore planned to speak, when the moment for her intervention came on 12 July, about the subject that she had almost come to personify within the IAW, namely cooperation between East and West.

The opening session of the congress was held at the City Hall in Copenhagen. The congress was sponsored by the Queen of Denmark and opened by the Danish Prime Minister. The British delegate, Lady Astor, soon came close to breaching the injunction to avoid politics when she made a statement about the threat to world peace from the totalitarian states. Lady Astor also criticised the League of Nations for failing to live up to the expectations that had been placed on it, and concluded that it was up to women, through their spiritual influence, to find the means to unite male politicians and make peace the common ideal of all humanity.[28] As usual, Céza gave her talk about the progress made by the Egyptian feminists over the years, while, to Huda's pleasure, Munira spoke boldly about youth and feminism. When she was invited to take the floor, Huda delivered a speech that was rather brief and to the point. 'I have always believed,' she said, 'in the possibility of a fertile cooperation between the women of all the continents – since we share the same ideals: to build a better world, based on justice, equality and brotherly understanding between all peoples.'

However, emboldened perhaps by the political content of Lady Astor's intervention, Huda decided to ask for a message of sympathy to the Arab women of Palestine to be added to the proposed resolutions.[29] As worded by Huda, the effect of this would have been to condemn the displacement of the Palestinian Arabs and deplore the immigration into Palestine of the European Jews. This was stubbornly opposed by the Jewish delegation from Palestine, as were all other references to this or similar issues by the Egyptian delegation. The Jewish delegates insisted that the congress should instead endorse the right of Jews to migrate to Palestine. Huda realised that Corbett-Ashby and the other members of the executive committee intended to insist on agreement with the position of the Jewish delegates, and therefore decided to resign from the executive committee with immediate effect, to step down as an Honorary Vice-President of the IAW, and to leave Copenhagen with her Egyptian colleagues.[30] Corbett-Ashby called her urgently to a private meeting, where she said she would refuse to accept Huda's resignation, and urged her to continue to participate in the congress in order to avoid an incident that could be embarrassing for the IAW and attract undesirable publicity.

This was the first time the two had ever disagreed. Each woman was aware of the reasons for the position of the other, but neither was willing to yield. Both were left upset and miserable by the clash between them. Neither wished their disagreement to become personal. In the end, it had to be Huda who accepted that she could not force her resolution onto the agenda. This was her first real defeat. She decided she would bow to Corbett-Ashby and stay at the congress, though she would fight to the end for her principles. Despite the fact that the pain in her chest now ruled her days, she would shoulder her responsibilities. Though she could not introduce her resolution, she would not be seen to be reconciled with the opposing position. She would never cease to defend the women of Palestine. The strength of her personality was to leave a lasting impression on those present, even though she failed to change people's minds.[31]

Corbett-Ashby was grateful to Huda for her agreement to stay, and so were other key delegates. The congress showed its appreciation by re-electing her as an executive-committee member, against her will. She also felt concern for the Jewish delegates, many of whom she knew were about to return to insecure situations in their own countries and to face violence that they might not survive. The dark forebodings that threatened the world often invaded the atmosphere of the congress. Nevertheless, she continued to ask herself how a people who had suffered like the Jews could inflict suffering on others. She would always insist on standing up for the Palestinians, who were unjustly made to pay for the misdeeds of the totalitarian states in the West.

12

The Second
World War

On 3 September 1939, Britain and France at last declared war on Germany. The German invasion of Poland occurred two days earlier. In Egypt, however, the war was experienced quite differently from how it was in Europe. It was a distant phenomenon, to which people in Egypt related as lighthouse keepers might to a far-off tempest. They glimpsed a distant catastrophe and hoped they would avoid being involved. They feared, of course, that Britain might drag Egypt into the war. The most keenly felt repercussion of Europe's upheaval was the growing momentum of violence in Palestine. As the situation quickly deteriorated, Huda continued to send telegrams, like the following one, to the IAW: 'The Egyptian Feminist Union, deeply moved by recent Palestinian events, deplores the armed attacks by the authorities against a disarmed population that peacefully claims its right to existence, and demands immediate intervention.'[1]

Despite the provisions of the Anglo–Egyptian treaty, the Egyptian Government attempted to keep the country as much as possible from the war.[2] In November 1940, Husain Sirri Pasha, a new man, was appointed Prime Minister to replace Hasan Sabri, who had died in office after succeeding Ali Maher Pasha. This was a difficult time for Egypt. The

King was still very young, and Huda feared for the country's stability with an untested hand at the helm of government and a new King. She wished the royal family well and had high hopes for the young and apparently vulnerable monarch. At the same time, it was impossible to be unaware that the Queen Mother, Queen Nazli, was becoming a threat to the royal clan's stability. Huda, who had supported her when she was the maltreated wife of King Fuad, was deeply disappointed in her behaviour. She had spoiled her son, whom she actually encouraged to live a frivolous life. Queen Nazli's personal comportment was also hard for Huda to understand. She seemed oblivious of her own rank and the responsibilities it entailed. This, Huda sometimes said, was certainly the result of the years spent in seclusion in the harem and the house of submission. There were constant rumours about her unsuitable friends and pastimes.

In 1940, there was a crisis at the Banque Misr, and the ageing financier Talaat Harb, the bank's veteran chairman, was asked by the Government to resign after two decades at the helm. Fuad Sultan, who had been Umar's favourite nephew, also resigned. Dr Hafiz Afifi Pasha, the late Mahmud Sami Pasha's brother-in-law, was asked to step in. Hafiz Afifi recalled Huda's role in the inception of the bank, and again invited her to become a member of the bank's board of directors. Huda was immensely flattered, but her chest pains were now so frequent as to be virtually constant, and she felt she could not take the responsibility. However, she accepted the offer on an honorary basis, and attended the inaugural meeting of the new board.

On 19 October 1941, Huda's collaborator Mayy Ziadé, who had been ill for many years, died at Maadi hospital. On 4 December, Huda organised a commemoration for her after the mourning period of 40 days.[3] She gave a speech recalling Mayy's spirit and sharpness of wit in former days, when she had been one of the first feminist lecturers at Cairo University, regretting the passing of such a figure. Those close to Huda say she began at this time to think more about her own death. Though her father had passed away when she was no more than a child, her mother's death had been the first great loss in her adult life. Since then, she had thought philosophically about the issue. In her own seventh decade, she began to feel that separation from loved ones was the real tragedy.

The war came closer. In June 1942, with German forces just a hundred kilometres from Alexandria, there were air raids there that killed some six hundred and fifty people and caused a temporary flight from the city. Three hundred thousand people, or nearly half the population, left their homes. Food shortages began to affect people's lives. There were demands that the British navy should be used to evacuate Alexandria.[4] The lack of food led to riots and demonstrations, and Husain Sirri resigned when the demonstrators began to be heard shouting, 'Come on Rommel!' and 'We are all Rommel's soldiers!' With the British forces visibly in retreat, many in Egypt had evidently decided it was a better bet to back the Germans. The British authorities were very jumpy, but Sirri Pasha was unable to stop the disturbances.[5]

The British Ambassador, Sir Miles Lampson, told the King that the British Government wanted Nahhas Pasha to take over once more at the head of a coalition for the sake of stability. The British, whatever their underlying opinion of the Wafd, knew that Nahhas was best placed to attract popular support and quell unrest, if he would agree to cooperate. On 4 February 1942, the King asked Nahhas to be his Prime Minister. The plan was that other party leaders were to be included in the cabinet to ensure the Government's moderation. The King was aware that the people wanted Nahhas, which meant that he would swiftly provide some stability, but the Wafdist leader adamantly rejected the idea of a coalition, persistently reiterating his usual position that his Government had to be totally made up of Wafdists.[6] King Farouk started to look at other options, but the British insisted that he must appoint Nahhas or abdicate himself.

The situation became critical when British tanks took up positions outside the King's palace in Abdin, with their guns pointed at the building. The British Ambassador and a number of senior British officers, all armed, insisted on being shown to the King's office. Farouk had just held a meeting with his chief of cabinet and with Queen Nazli, who had both advised him to give in to the British ultimatum. The King had not yet agreed, but when he saw the abdication paper that Lampson had in his hand, he swiftly claimed he had already invited Nahhas to form the new cabinet. It was a bitter experience for all Egyptians to see their 22-year old monarch, in whom so much hope had been invested, so bullied and humiliated by the British. Everyone knew that Lampson had brandished a pistol and threatened to force the King to abdicate.

Huda was appalled by the British Ambassador's behaviour. On 9 February, she sent a telegram of protest to the British Prime Minister, Sir Winston Churchill, as well as an open letter to Sir Miles Lampson denouncing his interference in Egyptian affairs.[7] The same day, she sent the palace protocol chief a formal letter of support for the King on behalf of the women of Egypt. This conveyed the people's sadness and the women's request to visit the palace to offer their respect. Short of actual violence against Egypt, she declared, what had happened was the worst possible breach of the Anglo–Egyptian friendship agreement.

On 5 September 1942, Muhammad at last became the father of a son so that his inheritance was at long last safe from all possible contenders. He was still no more pleasant to Munira, however, saying that he now expected her to give him a second son to make the family position yet more secure. At the beginning of the war, Munira had decamped at Huda's suggestion to the family estates in Minya, where she had organised a life for herself. She had set up a clinic for the villagers, ensuring that they were fed and taken care of. She provided clothing for them, and endlessly listened to their complaints and demands. Living a rural life in Minya had brought her close to the poor and enabled her to understand their needs. Henceforth, she was to devote much of her time and money to the needy. With the five little girls she now had in addition to Muhammad's much-hoped-for son, her Croatian nurse Angelina, the Greek nanny Félicie and her Italian dressmaker Georgette, as well as her faithful Nubian servant

Saleh, she led a life dedicated to good works in a household mainly made up of women. Her situation was one that no other high-society lady in Egypt would have accepted, and her husband was hardly ever there. Huda found her way of life surprising, but kept her own counsel. She felt she was partly responsible for the isolation in which Munira now lived.

In 1942, King Farouk awarded Huda the highest Egyptian decoration, the Medal of the Highest Order of Perfection, during a ceremony held at the headquarters of the EFU. The King wanted to convey his gratitude for her support after the Abdin Palace siege of February 1942. The British authorities objected to the award, since Huda's severe criticism of British policies had not been welcomed, and they suspected she was a person who was intrinsically hostile to Britain rather than simply the patriot and activist she in fact was.

Nahhas held office through most of the war, but stepped down in October 1944, after factionalism began to pull the Wafd apart with the emergence of a group, formed by former Wafdists, that called itself the Saadist party. The King asked Ahmad Mahir Pasha to form a new coalition Government made up of four Saadist and four Liberal ministers while Makram Ubaid, leader of a new Wafdist group calling itself the Kutla (block), was suddenly released from jail and appointed Minister of Finance.[8] Huda was pleased when Muhammad, still the youngest senator in the Senate, backed Ahmad Mahir Pasha.

During the war, despite her failing health, Huda continued to travel to the neighbouring Arab countries when possible, where she received a number of medals and decorations. She was awarded the Honorary Golden Medal of High Merit from the Lebanese President Bishara al-Khuri in the summer of 1944, the Syrian First Grade Special Badge of Merit by Shukri al-Quwatli, the Syrian President, and finally King Abdullah of Transjordan awarded her the Badge of Liberation, an honour he had never bestowed before on a woman. The decorations Huda received were in recognition of the moral support she had offered the Arab leaders of these countries in

Huda on the threshold of her house.

their struggle to free their countries from foreign influence. She also went on pilgrimage to Mecca.

Habib al-Masri Pasha said in the eulogy he read after her death that towards the end of her life Huda had become not so much a person as an idea, and that she was for many people, especially women, the embodiment of the virtues of courage, pride, integrity and compassion.[9] Huda had become part of the ideological landscape of Egypt and the Arab world. She could not bear the thought that poor children could be deprived of food or comfort, that men should abuse their power over women, or violate their rights, or that stronger countries should use their power over weaker ones to serve their own interests. The very thought of injustice and coercion was intolerable to her, and she responded by feeding the hungry and protecting the weak with every means at her disposal, and protesting with all her authority against political and social injustice. During her journeys to Syria, Lebanon, Palestine and Transjordan, Huda did what she could to promote political, economic, social and educational activities in the region. The politicians were discussing the creation of a league of Arab states, and it came to Huda that the feminist movement should follow suit. Her plan was for all the feminist unions of the states of the former Greater Syria to participate in a second Cairo conference. The goal was the establishment of an international Arab Feminist Union.

On 15 March 1944, while the President of Lebanon was visiting Cairo, Huda invited Laure al-Khouri, the first lady of Lebanon, to a reception. On the eve of the party, while preparing for the following day, Huda had a fainting spell, but she decided to ignore it. The only alteration in her plans was that someone else had to read her speech on her behalf.[10] In the summer of 1944, the President and his wife invited her to their home at Alia, in Lebanon, and it was during this visit that the Golden Medal of High Merit of the Republic of Lebanon was bestowed on her. Representatives from women's organisations in other countries were also present, and it was at this gathering that they decided the planned Cairo conference would be held on 12 December

1944. The goal was to reinforce regional solidarity despite the externally imposed boundaries between states, and to recover something of the unity of Greater Syria under the Ottoman Empire. The purpose of an all-Arab organisation would be to help rebuild an Arab nation that would transcend the borders prescribed by the colonial powers. For Huda, this conference would be a final step forward, when she would take the lead in a feminist organisation that went beyond the frontiers of Egypt. Once she returned to Cairo, Huda threw herself into the organisation of the meeting and the process of identifying and inviting delegations. In the event, the conference was to be a triumph, with royal patronage and government endorsement. December came, and the finishing touches to the plan were put together by Huda and her team.

Delegates began to arrive in Cairo from Jordan and Syria by train on 8 December. Since the conference was sponsored by Queen Farida, all were invited first to the Abdin Palace. The King welcomed them in person, shaking hands with all, to their intense gratification. Lunch was served at 2 Qasr al-Nil Street. The Iraqi delegates arrived the next day, when there was a press conference. Some of the women stayed at Huda's house, others were given accommodation in the EFU headquarters guest rooms or in houseboats provided by the Government. Others stayed at Cairo's major hotels. On 11 December, there was a visit to Queen Farida at the Abdin Palace, where Huda introduced the heads of delegations to the Queen.

The conference proper began at the Royal Opera House on the afternoon of 12 December. Amina al-Said delivered Huda's inaugural statement and welcomed the heads and members of delegations who represented all the states of the former Greater Syria. Nazima al-Askari headed delegations from four Iraqi women's societies, eight Syrian organisations were led by the wife of the Emir Mukhtar Abd al-Qadir, and two organisations from Transjordan were headed by Luli Abu al-Huda. There were no less than 25 Palestinian organisations headed by Zulaikha al-Shahabi, and 27 Lebanese organisations headed by Rose Shahfa. There were also numerous Egyptian representatives.

'The two issues to be discussed by this conference are equally important,' Huda wrote in her statement, 'and they are the issue of women's rights and the question of Palestine. Both questions are related to violations of rights that must be redressed.' The Egyptian Government was also well represented at the opening session, which was attended by the Prime Minister, Ahmad Maher Pasha, and numerous ministers. There were also many other leading Egyptian figures.

The visiting women were all people of distinction. Lebanon's Najla Kfuri was a well-known writer and feminist activist in Beirut. She was associated with Lebanon's Feminist Revival Society and the Arab Feminist Union of Beirut. Adla Abd al-Qadir, the head of the Syrian delegation, was the daughter of Abd al-Rahim Beyhum Bey and the wife of the Emir Mukhtar Abd al-Qadir. Transjordan was represented by Luli Abu al-Huda, who had been at the 1938 conference. She was the daughter of Abu al-Huda Pasha, the Prime Minister of Transjordan, and had studied politics, philosophy and economics at Oxford University. The fourth speaker at the opening session was the leader of the Iraqi delegation, Nazima al-Askari. The Palestinian feminist Sazij Nassar, whom Huda had known for a long time, was the granddaughter of Al-Baha', the founder of the Baha'i religion. She was married to Najib Nassar, the owner of the newspaper *Al-Karmal*, where she also worked. They had both been arrested, detained and tortured by the British Government for almost a whole year, from 23 March 1939 to 22 February 1940. At the time of the Arab women's conference, she was the Secretary of the Feminist Union of Haifa. Rose Shahfa was the head of the Lebanese Feminist Union, which had been affiliated to the IAW since 1935. The first day ended with dinner at the Cairo house of Abu al-Huda Pasha, where his wife and daughters acted as hosts. Then all were invited to a play at the Royal Opera House at the invitation of Haikal Pasha, currently Minister of Education.

Each speaker, as the conference proceeded, dealt with her special subject. Nahid Sirri, as the Head of the Red Crescent, spoke about the earthquake that afflicted Turkey just before the war. She also touched on the role of the Red Crescent in aiding the Egyptian Government to offset the damage caused by air raids on Egyptian cities, especially Alexandria. They provided jobs for the unemployed, tended to the wounded and other sick, and provided shelter for the displaced and refugees. She praised the American Red Cross for its donations, and for helping to eradicate the causes of poverty. Suad Riad, chair of the Princess Ferial dispensary, emphasised the need for social solidarity, and recommended cooperation between men and women to further social development and to provide education for children. Nur Marzi of Egypt spoke about pre-natal care. Nimet Irfan also raised the subject of prostitution, once more a scourge because of the social circumstances of the war. Suraya al-Khuga of Iraq and Zahia Dughan of Lebanon both talked about improving women's education. Zahia Suliman of Lebanon also touched on the topic of education, and Emily Bisharat of Transjordan brought up the issue of the situation of Bedouin women. All the basic topics that came up at the 1938 conference were re-examined. These included poverty, illiteracy, education, social solidarity, social equality, and the laws on polygamy, divorce, alimony, childcare, guardianship, the house of submission and the nationality of married women. Nazima al-Askari reaffirmed Iraq's determination to help the women of Palestine, and the Palestinian Sazij Nassar said that Palestine, as a holy land, should not be the scene of conflict. At the close of the conference, all the delegates thanked Huda for organising the occasion, and also expressed their gratitude to the King and Queen of Egypt for being its patrons.

On 15 December, all the participants were invited by Safia Zaghlul to her home, the Bait al-Umma. There were also numerous other invitations and visits. On 17 December 1944, the King in person accompanied them on a journey by train to his farm at Inshas, where they were able to admire the lush Egyptian countryside. Later in the evening of the same day, Huda invited them to attend a performance of a comedy at one of Cairo's theatres. These recreational activities were a welcome respite from the hard work. During the conference, they also went to the Zaafaran Palace for an official reception, as well as paying other instructive visits to charities. There were visits to Princess Ferial's dispensary in Heliopolis, where they were met by its director and to the Red Crescent where Nahid Sirri took them on a tour of the hospital and the out-patient clinic; and finally to the Mabarrat Muhammad Ali, where they were received by Princess Shivekar. Social visits were paid to the Cairo Women's Club, and to the Arab Union, of which Fuad Abaza Pasha was President. The women also went to King Fuad's mausoleum in the Rifai mosque. Their days were full, and the time to depart came all too soon.

On 20 December 1944, a farewell party was held at the EFU Social Club. Sadly Huda was too ill to attend, and Amina al-Said once more read a statement on her behalf. Najla Kfuri of Lebanon delivered a significant political statement at the closing session. She declared that the Arabs had chivalrously suspended their revolutionary activities against the British after the outbreak of World War II, so that the British forces would not have to fight on two fronts. She also added, however, that their help to the British forces merely resulted in the victory of the Zionists. She also made the point that Palestine was not an uninhabited state before the arrival of the Zionists, and that an injustice was being committed to the Arab people.

Huda made a gigantic effort to attend the reading of the final resolutions, after a whole week of illness during which she had found hardly any time to rest. The conference had adamantly refused to adopt its resolutions in her absence, and the women waited for her to recover. They also wanted her to be there when the resolutions were adopted, since most believed her presence would be essential to the ultimate success of the meeting. Telegrams sent to the conference were read prior to Huda's closing speech, and included, among others, one from Eleanor Roosevelt, congratulating the women and encouraging them to continue their efforts. There were also good wishes from many Arab organisations.

In her closing statement, Huda made a point of conveying her thanks at the end of her statement to her friends and colleagues, and especially to Margery Corbett-Ashby, who had sent telegrams of support since she had begun to plan the conference, encouraging her to continue to serve as the link between Eastern and Western women.[11] She thanked Eleanor Roosevelt for her kind message to the conference, which 'relieved us of the effect of some statements made by American individuals and the American authorities on the question of Palestine'. She promised her that the Arab women would indeed do their utmost to promote peace in the world. Huda ended her message by inviting all the leaders of the Arab states 'seriously to examine the Resolutions adopted by this Conference, given the impact of women on the recent progress of the region and on the life of all nations'.

Huda then read the recommended resolutions to the participants for adoption. There was a certain difference between the resolutions adopted by the conference of 1938 and those adopted in 1944. In 1938, most were focused on Palestine and its problems. In 1944, the resolutions were in great part aligned with the recommendations of the IAW. They addressed feminist issues one by one, in the context of possibilities for reform. They mainly concerned women's rights, in politics and law, as well as in education and culture. These were followed by recommendations on the rights of mothers and children, including health issues and protection. These were followed by general recommendations on the protection of moral values, and economic cooperation, and finally a resolution exhorting the Arab nations as a whole to heed the voices of women and pay attention to women's concerns.

The Arab Feminist Union's constitutional act was signed a month later, in January 1945: it was drafted in legal form by Muhammad Ali Alluba Pasha and Zaki Ali Pasha.[12] Huda was confirmed as President, which was in many ways the culmination of her career as an Arab feminist. In that capacity she had the honour of representing the Arab Feminist Union at the inauguration of the Arab League in Cairo in March 1945.

In 1945, Egypt was approaching the delicate moment of actually having to agree, at least formally, to take part in the war, in order to be recognised as a full member of the post-war community of nations and be eligible for United Nations membership. Having dismissed Nahhas Pasha in October 1944, the King had appointed Ahmad Maher as Prime Minister, and to him fell the difficult task of announcing to parliament Egypt's decision to declare war against the Axis countries. This was not palatable to the Egyptian people, who resented the British army's presence in Egypt for many reasons. Throughout the war, they had been constantly harassed by British soldiers, who had behaved badly and often stopped people in the street to take money from them, or simply tormented them for the fun of it. An unwelcome rumour also circulated that Egyptians would be recruited to fight on the Asian front.

On 24 February 1945, Ahmad Maher held a closed session of parliament to explain that Egypt would not be required to fight, that Egyptians would not be recruited, and that the declaration of war was to be a technical one described as defensive, since the war was in any case coming to an end. His main point was that the declaration of war was necessary if Egypt was to qualify as a founder member of the United Nations, where it would be able to stand as a nation among the free nations of the world and would be able to militate for the right of the Palestinians to enjoy their independence and self-determination. After he had made his speech to the Chamber of Deputies, he was crossing the Pharaonic Hall towards the Senate when a young man called Mahmud al-Issawi took a gun out of his pocket and shot him. He barely had the time to say 'This is the end of me' as he died.

Huda was struggling against her illness, attempting to gain time for the battles she felt she still had to fight. Maher's assassination saddened her. He had tried to pacify the students during their demonstrations against the heavy presence of foreign soldiers when there was a danger that Egyptians might be harmed.[13] She appreciated his understanding of the common people, with whom he would fearlessly sit and talk. He had been murdered over a misunderstanding, by an impetuous fool. The irony was that he had just convinced Egypt's parliamentarians of all parties, even those passionately opposed to involvement in the war, that the declaration about to be made by Egypt, while no more than a formality, was also a necessary one. It was an irony that his best friend and colleague, Mahmud al-Nuqrashi, appointed by the King to replace him, made the declaration of war in his stead. Al-Nuqrashi had been steadfastly anti-war, and suffered for the duty imposed on him.

Egypt declared its 'defensive war' against Germany and Japan on 25 February 1945, the day after Mahir's assassination. On 7 March, Abd al-Hamid Badawi Pasha, one of the most brilliant thinkers, legislators and diplomats in Egypt, was made Minister of Foreign Affairs. On 26 June 1945, he led the Egyptian delegation in San Francisco that made its contribution to the adoption and signature of the United Nations Charter by the founding states of the new world body.[14] This gave Huda hope, but on 6 August, along with the rest of the world, she was appalled to hear the news of the dropping of the atomic bomb that day on Hiroshima, to be followed on 9 August by the bomb on Nagasaki. The United States explained that the bombs would foreshorten what was still a costly and bloody war with Japan. Egypt's Georges Henein, the gifted francophone Egyptian poet who had spoken so convincingly in 1935 against Mussolini's attack on Ethiopia,[15] swiftly wrote an impassioned tract entitled *The Prestige of Terror* (*Le prestige de la terreur*). Henein, a family friend of Huda's, expressed the dismay generated in the whole world by the apocalyptic explosions, and how they placed incidents of mass slaughter previously thought horrific in the shade:

> August 8, 1935 will remain an unbearable date for some of us to remember. An appointment with infamy has been placed on record by history...Such inhuman games suddenly seem absurd, now that the atomic bomb has been used and the democratic bombers have directly tried out its capacities on the Japanese people![16]

Huda, in common with the world's pacifists, who were growing in number, was of Henein's view. She saw the bombs as the beginning of a new and very ominous era for mankind.

A sad casualty of the war, as Huda was to learn in 1945, had been her Jewish colleague Rosa Manus, the Dutch IAW executive-committee member whom Huda had first met at the IAW's Paris congress in 1926, where she worked in conjunction with the Swiss representative Emily Gourd to organise the event. She was a buxom and plucky blonde with sparkling eyes, a lively smile and a sense of humour. In 1931, she had become chair of the peace committee of the Women's International Organisations. At the IAW congress in Marseilles in 1933, she had chaired the peace committee, drafting a very articulate and forthright resolution supporting disarmament and peace and condemning the manufacture of armaments by private industry. She had been made Officer of the Order of Orange Nassau by the Queen of Holland for services rendered to peace and to women, an event which Huda and Céza had celebrated. She had been subjected to an ordeal unbearable to think of. She had flatly refused to hear Huda's arguments about Palestine at the Copenhagen congress in July 1939, but this became understandable in the light of the cruel end put to her life by the Nazis. As a Jew, she had been arrested and questioned by the Gestapo in August 1941. She had friends and relatives in Germany and, long before the war, had been a co-founder of the Neutral Women's Committee for Refugees, helping those who fled Germany. She had been driven from one jail to another for weeks, and finally detained in Ravensbrück, where she died two years later in 1943.[17] It was a nightmare for Huda to think of the suffering Rosa had endured during her years in jail and in the concentration camp.

13

The UNGA divides Palestine

After the war, there was a final quarrel between Muhammad and Huda which resulted in his refusal ever to see her again. In the summer of 1946, he had taken Munira and the children away to the Lebanese mountains. Hafiza, the Sudanese nanny, came with them, as well as Salih the Nubian servant, and Georgette, so that the household that surrounded Mimi in Minya was almost complete. Mimi understandably hoped that this was to be the beginning of a happier time, but Muhammad was in a strange mood. He was cold and seemed not to want to see her. Then he suddenly declared that he had decided to return to Cairo alone before the planned end of the holiday. She pleaded to go with him, and wept. She said she would follow him in any case, but he would not hear of it, and threatened to divorce her if she dared to disobey him. He returned to Cairo alone, and when he communicated with her again it was to tell her he wanted a divorce.

Soon afterwards, he went privately to see Huda in her apartment to inform her that he intended to repudiate his wife, the mother of seven of his children, because he loved another woman whom he described as a younger woman of his own choice, and whom he would never give up. Huda lost all control over herself. She could not believe that

Muhammad would abandon his wife and family, apparently for another woman. She screamed at him, called him names and slapped his face. He left her, and she never saw him again. When Huda calmed down, her feelings were all for her daughter-in-law. She realised that Munira had been treated very unfairly, unloved and saddled with children. She had been both used and abused. Muhammad apparently resented her for her very patience and forbearance. Huda knew that the marriage could no longer be saved, and did the only thing she could do under the circumstances. She welcomed Mimi into her circle of feminist activists and asked her to run the EFU Social Club.

Huda was saved from despair by the fourteenth congress of the IAW in Interlaken, Switzerland, which took her mind off her family problems. Though she did not yet know it, this was to be her last journey. The congress took place on 11 August 1946, and Huda was accompanied by her most efficient assistants and representatives. These naturally included Céza, who was now divorced from Mustafa Naguib, and on this occasion, as she often did, she took her little girl, Huda, with her. Another of her closest aides was Ismat Asim, who was strongly committed to feminist causes. There were also young newcomers to the world of international conferences, such as Munira Salih Harb and Qut al-Qulub Mahir. Only 18 countries were represented at this gathering, and Huda was the sole delegate from the Middle East, officially representing Palestine, Syria and Lebanon as well as Egypt. In addition to Switzerland, the other participating countries were England and the United States; Austria, France, Italy, Greece and the Netherlands, representing continental Europe; the antipodean countries, Australia and New Zealand; and the Scandinavian states of Sweden, Norway and Denmark. There was also a Jewish delegation from Palestine. Huda had originally offered to host the gathering in Egypt, but the IAW officials had preferred Switzerland as the sole country in Western Europe that had not been devastated by the war, which was also, as it happened, a country where women had not yet obtained their political rights, so that there was local lobbying to be done.

Huda made the journey to Interlaken, despite the pain and difficulty it cost her, because she believed in the effectiveness of face-to-face meetings and because of her responsibility for the other countries that she would represent in addition to Egypt. She also went because Margery Corbett-Ashby and some of her other friends from the IAW were to be there. She had visited Switzerland with Ali in the distant past, and then at other times over the years, and was well acquainted with the country. Interlaken offered a fine setting, not least because of the beauty of the Swiss landscape. During the proceedings, the discussion focused on the familiar feminist themes that had gradually been identified and developed in the West over the years. The war and its hardships had brought some setbacks in fields where progress had previously been made, and prostitution was once more placed on the agenda as a central concern. The subject of the fate of displaced persons, especially Jews, was also of concern for the Europeans, and international migration was another source of anxiety. In the minds of the Egyptians, migration was certainly a problem in the Middle East, where a whole population of Palestinians was being dispossessed of its country.

It was as usual a source of great joy to meet Corbett-Ashby. The two women chatted together for hours. There was so much to share, and so much evil and violence to assuage through their mutual expression of friendship and generosity. However, Huda discovered that Corbett-Ashby had decided to leave the IAW in order to dedicate herself to reinforcing feminism in her own country. There was still a lot to do in Britain, she explained. Meanwhile, feminist efforts on the international scene were increasingly running foul of the national politics of different countries, and seemed fated to encounter fruitless complications. The incoming President was a Swedish woman called Hanna Rydh,[1] whom Corbett-Ashby introduced while taking her leave. Huda invited Rydh to visit her in Egypt during a forthcoming tour of the Middle East she had already planned, and began at once to work with her. She envied Corbett-Ashby for her bold decision to withdraw. Huda knew that after this meeting she would probably never see her again.

Huda had begun to feel she herself was now living on borrowed time because of the weakness of her heart. The heaviness in her chest now sometimes seemed to stifle her, and she felt that she could not breathe. She had also begun to feel pains in her arms and shoulders. She often thought about an Arabic poem which she had written about her own death that she wanted to be displayed in the mausoleum she had already built for herself in Minya. She knew that she would soon be unable to travel abroad again. However, once back in Cairo, she compensated by placing more responsibility on the shoulders of her young assistants, sending them on her behalf to represent the EFU at the international events to which she was invited. She was comforted that she could feel secure in sending her fearless young disciples to far-off countries to deputise for her. She sent Ismat Asim to Geneva, and Amina al-Said, who was increasingly active in the movement, to Hyderabad. She knew these young women were staunch feminists and that they would also defend the Arab cause.

On 11 February 1947, King Farouk repudiated Queen Farida, and Huda, angered by what she considered unacceptable behaviour on the part of a King, sent back to the Palace the decoration he had given her. On 31 March, however, she nevertheless took great pleasure in watching him raise his country's flag above the British barracks at Qasr al-Nil, where the British flag had flown for 65 years. She was gratified to have seen this with her own eyes, after all the years of struggle. King Farouk attended the ceremony in person, and Huda watched from her terrace in Qasr al-Nil Street, across the square, laughing joyfully as her grandchildren pushed and pulled each other, struggling over who would be first to raise the flag on the terrace of the Maison de L'Égyptienne.

Meanwhile, Huria's husband Hasan Shafik, the young diplomat from Istanbul, had been seconded to the service of the Royal Palace by the Ministry of Foreign Affairs after the war, where his task was to report on the situation in Palestine on the situation there. His reports, some of which she had read, were perceptive and to the point. In March 1947, Huria came to see her, and Huda took great pleasure in her visit. There was still huge affection between them. Huda put her guest in one of the rooms next to her own, decorated with tapestries from Bukhara, with its own inner wooden staircase, leading up to a small wooden platform and sleeping area, with a traditional mattress on top of a wooden bed and a chest of carved wood exuding the perfume of sandalwood. They breakfasted together in Huda's room, and Huda was able to confide in Huria about the sad turn her own life had taken and her difficulties with her own children. When Hawa and Céza joined them upstairs in Huda's room, the four women felt comfortable and serene together, and Huda silently recited a short prayer, placing her hand on Huria's head, to bless her before bidding her farewell. The few days Huria would spend in Cairo were quick to pass, and Huda saw her young cousin depart with an aching heart.

The conference of the Inter-Parliamentary Union, held in Cairo in April 1947 and which Huda attended, left her aware of how exhausted she was. To leave the house each day to attend the sessions was as much as she could do. On the other hand, she had some help at home. Mimi had come back from Minya without Muhammad, and naturally continued to live in the big house with her children. Huda had left the first floor to her estranged son's wife and children, and continued to live in her rooms on the upper floor of the mansion. As to the potential difficulty of being at the top of the house, Huda no longer had to climb any staircases thanks to the lift so presciently given to her by Charles Crane.

Haikal Pasha was responsible, in his capacity as the President of the Senate, for the organisation of the Inter-Parliamentary Union conference, and his wife Aziza helped him to receive and entertain the women. Aziza asked Mimi to work for the conference and receive guests at the airport, accompanying them to their accommodation and looking after them in case of need. At one point, Mimi crossed Huda's path in the large mansion, and was surprised when Huda timidly asked her, 'Why do you think they did not ask for my help?' Mimi was astonished, and immediately tried to comfort her by saying 'But Tante,'

which was what all the girls called her, 'you are above the level of such
simple activities and in fact what you might do, if you wish to make a
gesture, is to invite all the guests to dinner in this wonderful house.
Haikal Pasha would appreciate it.' Huda obligingly gave a party for
all the visiting parliamentarians, and took them on an outing to the
countryside. They were in any case having a fascinating time, visiting
Pharaonic, Coptic and Islamic museums and sites. But Huda had
started to feel that she was losing ground, and was somehow no longer
in the centre of things. Was she no longer anything more than a society
hostess? she asked herself. She felt she had so little time left before the
violence that was once more gaining momentum would overwhelm
the post-war world.

Nuqrashi Pasha had stepped down in February 1946, and in October,
after strikes and demonstrations that brought some Egyptian deaths,
his successor Ismail Sidqi attempted to reach a final agreement with
Britain to get British troops out of Egypt after the war, holding talks
with Ernest Bevin, the British Foreign Secretary. Sidqi effectively
conceded the Sudan to Britain, which the Wafd and the country could
not accept, and Sidqi's Government fell in December. Nuqrashi
returned, and Huda believed that Egypt was in good hands. His courage
later became evident when, as head of the Egyptian delegation to the
United Nations, he decided to take Britain to task before the Security
Council in August 1947. Nuqrashi took the commitment of the United
Nations to justice at face value, insisting that the UN Charter entitled
him to demand the withdrawal of Britain's forces from Egypt and the
renunciation of the treaty of 1936. He spoke at length, an unarmed
knight facing the representatives of the great powers, stressing that
the UN Charter stipulated the equality and equal treatment of all
nations, regardless of their power. Nuqrashi did not mince his words.[2]

Huda did not travel abroad again. At the All India Congress in
Delhi at the end of May 1947, Hawa and Karima al-Said represented
the women of Egypt.[3] She had long since begun to give Hawa particular
responsibility. As long before as 1945, when the French bombarded

Damascus after Syria's demand for the end of the French occupation and the withdrawal of French forces, Huda had sent Hawa on a quite dangerous assignment, to accompany the Egyptian Red Crescent mission that went to Syria to help care for the many casualties and report back to her.[4] Hawa was ecstatic when she returned from India, where she had spent a lot of time in Nehru's company and with his daughter Indira. Nehru had introduced Hawa to the Mahatma, pointing out that this was one of the prettiest women attending the conference, and Gandhi, smiling, had agreed with his remark. Gandhi had apologised to Hawa for not getting up to greet her because of his age and declining health, and she had replied that she was proud to meet him standing up or sitting down, because he was a symbol of rare heroism and just struggle. Then, following Nehru's example, she had taken off her shoes to sit on the straw mat that covered the floor of the tiny room where the Mahatma squatted, cross-legged, on the floor. She was awed by this tiny and weak man who had become one of the great legends of his time. Hawa also visited Agra and Bombay, and returned with a vision that would guide her life. She did not dream of marriage but had a vocation for militant feminism, and took a great interest in the protection and education of children.[5]

Early in 1947, Huda started a new magazine, *Al-Mar'a al-Arabia*. The lack of paper during the war had forced her to stop publishing *L'Égyptienne* in 1940 and *Al-Misria* shortly after that. The advent of *Al-Mar'a al-Arabia* heralded a more peaceful global situation, but it also addressed the very real problem of peace in the Middle East. Huda created the new magazine to inform Arab women about the resumption of feminist activities all over the world, and she judged Amina al-Said was exactly the right person for the job of editor. In May 1947, Sarojini Naidu sent Huda an invitation to attend another feminist conference in India, in the city of Hyderabad, and on this occasion Amina al-Said represented her. Huda wanted to test the mettle of the editor of her new magazine.[6]

Huda had struck up a good relationship with the Indian women who attended international feminist meetings, and insisted on playing host when she could to Indian women visiting Egypt. In the summer of 1947, on her way through the Suez Canal to represent the All India Women's Conference at a meeting in Europe, Kamaladevi Chattopadyay, Sarojini Naidu's sister-in-law, was met in Port Said by a group of young Wafdists who brought her to Huda's house in Cairo. Chattopadyay reported this visit in her memoirs:

> I was worn out after the stormy crossing across the Arabian sea in the early South-West monsoon. So when I landed I was allowed immediately to tumble into bed. When I woke up and looked around, I was sure I was dreaming, so I closed my eyes and dozed off again. Bright sun was pouring in when I got out of bed. No, I was not dreaming, I was wide awake but in an Arabian Nights Palace, so it seemed to me. An exquisite breakfast of sweet melon, russet red grapes, crisp melting toast, fresh dates that put me in mind of palm jaggery at home, was spread out before me. The only object that seemed real and not part of the hazy dream was my hostess sitting opposite me, solid, down to earth, in spite of her exquisitely chiseled face and statuesque figure, Madame Charaoui Pasha. With her keen sensitive nature, she had modeled her house on the traditional Arab architecture. The furniture was Syrian, with the fine lacy carved patterns. The tiniest, the most innocuous item was delicately chosen. But there was much more to learn than looking at a fancy mansion.[7]

The two women briefed each other at length about the political situation of their respective countries, and Chattopadyay talked about Gandhi, his way of life, his ideas, his asceticism and strength. It struck a chord with Huda when her Indian guest said, 'Gandhi had touched the global nerve centre when he proclaimed that India's freedom would mean the liberation of British colonies and by chain reaction, of other subject peoples. That the Indian struggle was crucial in a larger context...'[8]

Quite by chance, while she was entertaining her Indian colleague, Huda received a visit from the great Moroccan resistance hero, the Emir Abd al-Krim, who had struggled against France and Spain. He had then been imprisoned by France for many years on the island of Réunion, a French possession in the Indian Ocean. In May 1947, with the help of Egyptian nationalists, he had succeeded in jumping ship as a vessel carrying him back to France had passed through the Suez Canal, and had then been given asylum in Egypt. Chattopadyay described him in her memoirs:

> The man who extended a hand and said welcome with a most genial smile was short, solidly built, with the kindliest bead-like eyes which as we talked began to get shot through by sharp glints like sparks of steel. There was, however, an air of benevolence about him that was accentuated by his long creamy gown which characterized the seasoned warriors from the rugged mountains of the Riff, whose valiant battles and curving fortunes had made world history. His skin, so fair and untanned, shining in its delicacy, like a flower-like sheen, seemed to belie his warlike role.[9]

A topic the two women discussed at length was the role of handicrafts. These would become the foundation of the economy of liberated peoples, and had already been the basis of the new cottage industries in India. Huda had become an expert in the field of crafts, and was able to compare notes. Chattopadyay was in Cairo for Huda's Tuesday open house, where she talked to the guests about aspects of Gandhi's philosophy, as opposed to Tagore's. Tagore criticised Gandhi's condemnation of machines, and thought they could profit men, whereas Gandhi believed that machines would lead only to the destruction of human feelings and behaviour. With the spinning wheel as his only weapon, he had led a relentless war against the British textile industry that was destroying the economy of his country. Huda was enchanted by this visit and fascinated by the discussions that took place. What she enjoyed most in the life that she had chosen for herself, aside from the satisfaction of doing good, was the gradual development of knowledge and the gradual acquisition of learning.

There eventually came the sad day when the United Nations General Assembly ruled in favour of the partition of Palestine. Abd al-Rahman Azzam Pasha represented the Arab League, while Nuqrashi represented the Egyptian Government. The lobbying had been feverish, especially on the part of the Jewish Agency members, who did everything in their power to win the votes of all the member states of the General Assembly at the United Nations, against a background of daily acts of terrorism and counter-terrorism that constantly tore at the fabric of Palestine.[10] The Resolution on the Partition of Palestine was adopted by the United

Nations on 29 November 1947. Huda was told that tears streamed down Nuqrashi's face when the result of the vote was read out by the rapporteur. Nuqrashi could not hide his silent frustration and despair.

When Huda heard the news in Cairo, she felt it literally as a shock, despite the fact that she had in her heart expected this defeat. She felt instinctively that she needed to spring into action. The decision had to be revoked or the whole world would suffer for it indefinitely. There was of course nothing she could do. Nevertheless, she received visits from all her Palestinian friends, who still hoped that she could help them. She was in constant pain at that point, but was still ready to struggle, pen and paper in hand, ready to write down all the ideas that came to her mind. What she was to do, she did not know. She did know that she could not simply stand by and watch an injustice take place.

On 7 December 1947, Huda woke, as she often did, at four in the morning. The difference this time was that it was not an insomnia that nagged her, but a severe unmistakable pain from angina pectoris. This was surely a stroke, though it was mercifully brief. She went back to sleep, and woke up at seven in the morning, feeling much better. When she told Hawa about it, she wanted to call the doctors at once, but Huda refused. They would only tell her to rest, and there was no time for that. She needed every minute that remained to her. She would organise a boycott, the women would stand shoulder to shoulder with the Arab armies, she would raise funds, she would lobby. Palestine must not be divided.

The pain returned at noon, and treacherously began to escalate while she was alone, while the family was having lunch in the dining-room downstairs. She had been settled in Mimi's room, on the first floor, because of her serious condition. She perspired and her breast heaved. When Hawa returned, she told her what she knew: 'It's finished, Hawa... It's finished...' Hawa immediately called the doctor. In a minute, all the others were upstairs. Mimi's little girls, hidden behind a screen placed at the entrance of the room and almost climbing on each other's backs, saw Bassna kneeling on the floor, sobbing loudly.

277

Céza stood paralysed near Mimi, and Huda muttered again, as if she were asking a question, 'It is over? Khalas ["finished"]?' Hawa screamed out, 'No, you are fine, you'll be fine, it is nothing…' The doctor walked into the room and gave Huda an injection. She smiled at him, 'It is over,' she murmured, 'khalas.'

She seemed to recognise this last ordeal of the injection as the blow that marks the end. She had written a poem once about the relief provided by death. The storm that was raging within her seemed to be destroying the world as well as whatever remained of her body, but she believed in the survival of the soul. She was suffocating, and she thought she heard the beat of a racing horse's hooves nearby, as if in the freedom of the mountains of the Caucasus, seemingly galloping towards her. The little girls hidden behind the screen saw her look towards the window. She raised herself on her elbow, smiled as she had never been seen to smile in her entire life, and was gone.

Notes

Chapter 1

1   Wilfrid Scawen Blunt, *Secret History of the English Occupation of Egypt*, T. Fisher Unwin, London, 1882, p. 314.
2   Huda Shaarawi, *Mudhakkirat ra'idat al-Mar'a al-'Arabia al-haditha Huda Shaarawi*, Dar al-Hilal, Cairo, 1981, p. 40.
3   Hawa Idris, *Ana wa al-Sharq*, unpublished, printed in Cairo, 1973. In this book, Idris claims that Hadji Murad 'had been the surname of Sharaluqa Gwattish during the resistance to the Russian invasion of the Caucasus'.
4   Robert Hunter, 'The making of a notable politician: Muhammad Sultan Pasha (1825–84)', *International Journal of Middle Eastern Studies*, 15 (1983).
5   Abdel Azziz Ezzel Arab, *European Control and Egypt's Traditional Elites: A case study in elite economic nationalism*, Edwin Mellen Press, Lewiston, NY, 2002; Abd al-Azim Ramadan, 'Min tawdhif al-din ila tawdhif al-amwal', *October*, 611 (10 July 1988), Cairo.
6   Shaarawi, *Mudhakkirat*, p. 17.
7   Ibid., p. 20.
8   Blunt, *Secret History of the English Occupation of Egypt*, p. 314.
9   Ibid., p. 305.
10 Ibid., p. 314.
11 Now Sabri Abu Alam Street.
12 Shaarawi, *Mudhakkirat*, pp. 40–41.
13 Ibid., p. 41–42.
14 Ibid., p. 44.
15 Ibid., pp. 43, 44.
16 Ibid., p. 70.
17 Ibid., p. 45.
18 Ibid., p. 47.
19 Ibid., p. 68.

20   Ibid., p.69.
21   Ibid., p.71.
22   Ibid., p.71.
23   Ibid., pp.72–73.
24   Ibid., p.74.
25   Ibid., p.76.
26   Eugénie Lebrun (written as Niya Salima), *Harems et musulmanes d'Égypte*, Félix Juven Éditeur, Paris, n.d., p.91; Shaarawi, *Mudhakkirat*, pp.75, 77.
27   Shaarawi, *Mudhakkirat*, p.77.
28   Ibid., pp.79–80.
29   Ibid., pp.82–83.
30   Mercédès Volait, 'Un architecte face à l'Orient: Antoine Lasciac (1856–1946)', in Jean-Claude Vatin (ed.) *La Fuite en Égypte: supplément aux voyages européens en Orient*, Institut français d'archéologie orientale, CEDEJ, Cairo, 1986.
31   Letters, 3 December 1895 and 7 April 1897; see also Shaarawi, *Mudhakkirat*, p.84.
32   Letter, July 1897.
33   Shaarawi, *Mudhakkirat*, p.84.
34   Ibid., p.92.

Chapter 2

1   Huda Shaarawi, *Mudhakkirat ra'idat al-Mar'a al-'Arabia al-haditha Huda Shaarawi*, Dar al-Hilal, Cairo, 1981, p.86.
2   Ibid., p.87.
3   Ibid., p.80.
4   Ibid., p.105.
5   The site where more recently stood the Nile Hilton Hotel and the building of the Arab League.
6   Shaarawi, *Mudhakkirat*, p.107.
7   Interview with Suza Khulusi, 2003.
8   Shaarawi, *Mudhakkirat*, p.113.
9   Moustafa Kamel, *Égyptiens et Anglais*, Perrin et Co. Éditeurs, Paris, 1906, p.318.
10   Shaarawi, *Mudhakkirat*, p.118.
11   Eric Davis, *Challenging Colonialism: Banque Misr and Egyptian industrialization, 1920–41*, Princeton University Press, Princeton, NJ, 1983, pp.48–49.
12   Muhammad Husain Haikal, *Mudhakkirat fi al-Siyasa al-Misria*, Dar al-Maarif, Cairo, 1977, vol. I, p.29.
13   Jacques Berque, *L'Égypte, impérialisme et révolution*, Éditions Gallimard, Paris, 1967, p.258.

14 Shaarawi, *Mudhakkirat*, p.104.

15 Muhammad Husain Haikal, *Tarajim Misria wa gharbia*, Al-Siyasa Press, Cairo, 1929, p.164.

16 Hawa Idris, *Ana wa al-Sharq*, unpublished, printed in Cairo, 1973, p.541; Eric Davis, *Challenging Colonialism: Banque Misr and Egyptian industrialization, 1920–41*, Princeton University Press, Princeton, NJ, 1983, p.75.

17 Shaarawi, *Mudhakkirat*, p.117.

18 Ibid., p.121.

19 Letter, from Francine Daurat, dated 20 July 1912.

20 Shaarawi, *Mudhakkirat*, pp.124–31.

21 Malak Hifni Nasif, *Athar Bahithat al-Badia*, a collection of essays, poems and letters edited by Magd al-Din Hifni Nasif, with an introduction by Suhair al-Qalamawi, Al-Mu'assassa al-Misria al-'amma li al-ta'lif wa al-tarjama, wa al-Tiba'a wa al-nashr, Cairo, 1962.

22 Huda Shaarawi, opening speech for Mayy Ziadés memorial, *Dhikra Faqidat al-Adab al-Nabigha Mayy*, Al-Matba'a al-Misria, Cairo, 1941 (Mayy's commemorative publication), p.16.

23 Letter, 23 May 1913.

24 Shaarawi, *Mudhakkirat*, p.133.

25 Family stories.

26 Shaarawi, *Mudhakkirat*, p.139.

27 Ibid., p.135.

28 Ibid., p.138.

29 Ibid., p.145.

30 Ibid., p.147.

31 Ibid., p.151.

32 Ibid., p.152.

33 Muhammad Ali Alluba, *Dhikrayat Ijtima'ia wa Siyasia*, General Egyptian Book Organisation, Cairo, 1988, p.69.

34 Zaki Mubarak, *Ahmad Shawqi*, General Egyptian Book Organisation, Cairo, 1997, pp.305–6.

35 Shaarawi, *Mudhakkirat*, p.154.

36 Lami'i al-Moti'i, *Safwit al-'asr fi tarikh wa rusum mashahir rijal masr*, Matba'at al-I'timad bi Sharia Hasan al-Akbar, Cairo, 1926.

37 Letter, 19 June 1904.

38 Hifni Nasif, *Athar Bahithat al-Badia*, p.35.

39 Shaarawi, *Mudhakkirat*, p.159.

40 Ibid., p.160.

41 Davis, *Challenging Colonialism*, p.165.

42 Idris, *Ana wa al-Sharq*, p.383.

43 *Al-Muqattam*, 21 August 1924; Davis, *Challenging Colonialism*, p.170.

Chapter 3

1   Royal Institute of International Affairs, *Great Britain and Egypt 1914–1951*, Information Papers no 19, RIIA, Chatham House, London, 1952, p. 3.

2   Abd al-Rahman Fahmi, *Mudhakkirat Abd al-Rahman Fahmi*, General Egyptian Book Organisation, Cairo, 1988, vol. I, p. 50; see also Huda Shaarawi, *Mudhakkirat ra'idat al-Mar'a al-'Arabia al-haditha Huda Shaarawi*, Dar al-Hilal, Cairo, 1981, pp. 162–63.

3   Peter Mansfield, *The British in Egypt*, Weidenfeld & Nicholson, London, 1971, p. 219; Jacques Berque, *L'Égypte, impérialisme et révolution*, Éditions Gallimard, Paris, 1967, p. 315; Firmin Van Den Bosch, *Vingt années d'Égypte*, Librairie Académique Perrin, Paris, 1932, p. 33.

4   Shaarawi, *Mudhakkirat*, p. 194.

5   Ibid., p. 165.

6   Ibid., p. 179.

7   Ibid., p. 183.

8   Ibid., p. 181.

9   Ibid., p. 174; see also Berque, *L'Égypte, impérialisme et révolution*, p. 327.

10 *Al-Ahram*, 31 March, 6 April 1964; Shaarawi, *Mudhakkirat*, p. 186.

11 Russell, Sir Thomas (Pasha), *Egyptian Service, 1902–1946*, John Murray, London, 1949, p. 208.

12 Ibid.

13 Yunan Labib Rizk, *Al-Ahram*, 11–17 March 1999.

14 Shaarawi, *Mudhakkirat*, p. 190.

15 Ibid., p. 196.

16 Muhammad Ali Alluba, *Dhikrayat Ijtima'ia wa Siyasia*, General Egyptian Book Organisation, Cairo, 1988, p. 122.

17 Ibid., p. 122.

18 Family letter.

19 Berque, *L'Égypte, impérialisme et révolution*, p. 322.

20 Fahmi, *Mudhakkirat Abd al-Rahman Fahmi*, vol. II, p. 348.

21 Shaarawi, *Mudhakkirat*, p. 203.

22 Alluba, *Dhikrayat Ijtima'ia wa Siyasia*, p. 122.

23 Ibid., p. 131.

24 Lord Lloyd, *Egypt Since Cromer*, Macmillan and Co., London, 1934, vol. II, p. 71.

25 Alluba, *Dhikrayat Ijtima'ia wa Siyasia*, p. 132.

26 Interview with Gabrielle Rousseau, 1970.

~ Notes ~

Chapter 4

1 Jacques Berque, *L'Égypte, impérialisme et révolution*, Éditions Gallimard, Paris, 1967, p.333.

2 Badr al-Din Abu Ghazi and Gabriel Boctor, *Mouktar ou le réveil de l'Égypte*, H. Urwand et Fils, Cairo, 1949, p.26.

3 Margot Badran's translation. Quoted in Margot Badran, *Feminists, Islam, and Nation: Gender and the making of modern Egypt*, Princeton University Press, Princeton, NJ, 1995, p.84.

4 Family letter, 5 January 1922, Juliette Adam to Huda.

5 Family letter, 22 January 1922, Huda to Juliette Adam.

6 Family letter, 26 January 1922, Juliette Adam to Huda.

7 Huda Shaarawi, *Mudhakkirat ra'idat al-Mar'a al-'Arabia al-haditha Huda Shaarawi*, Dar al-Hilal, Cairo, 1981, pp.240–42.

8 Ibid., p.243.

9 Balsam Abd al-Malik, *Al-Mar'a al-Misria*, February 1921, p.70 and May 1923, p.272.

10 Ibid., May 1923, p.250.

11 Balsam Abd al-Malik, *Al-Mar'a al-Misria*, May 1923, pp.300–1.

12 Ibid., 297.

13 Esther Lombardo, 'Sorelle di terra lontana', *Giornale di Roma*.

14 Balsam Abd al-Malik, *Al-Mar'a al-Misria*, May 1923, p.361.

15 Balsam Abd al-Malik, *Al-Mar'a al-Misria*, October 1923, pp.361, 384, 425.

16 Shaarawi, *Mudhakkirat*, p.291.

17 Ibid., p.292.

18 Céza's interview notes.

Chapter 5

1 *L'Égyptienne*, March 1925, p.46.

2 *L'Égyptienne*, August 1925, p.202.

3 Muhammad Husain Haikal, *Mudhakkirat fi al-Siyasa al-Misria*, Dar al-Maarif, Cairo, 1977, vol.I, p.154.

4 Royal Institute of International Affairs, *Great Britain and Egypt 1914–1951*, Information Papers no 19, RIIA, Chatham House, London, 1952, p.8.

5 Huda Shaarawi, *Mudhakkirat ra'idat al-Mar'a al-'Arabia al-haditha Huda Shaarawi*, Dar al-Hilal, Cairo, 1981, p.310.

6 Ibid., p.315.

7 Ibid., p.315.

8 Haikal, *Mudhakkirat fi al-Siyasa al-Misria*, vol.I, pp.174–75.

9 Shaarawi, *Mudhakkirat*, pp.300–1.

10   *L'Égyptienne*, February 1925, p. 23.

11   *Al-Akhbar*, 24 November 1924; Hawa Idris, *Ana wa al-Sharq*, unpublished, printed in Cairo, 1973, p. 366.

12   *L'Égyptienne*, April 1925, p. 81.

13   Fawzia Zouari, 'Étonnantes Voyageuses' in *Méditerranée*, March 1998, hors-serie, p. 47.

14   Family letter, 24 November 1924.

15   Lord Lloyd, *Egypt Since Cromer*, Macmillan and Co., London, 1933, vol. I, p. 153.

16   Shaarawi, *Mudhakkirat*, p. 335.

Chapter 6

1   Don Peretz, *The Middle East Today*, Praeger, New York, 1994, p. 219; Afaf Lutfi al-Sayyid Marsot, *Egypt in the Reign of Muhammad Ali*, Cambridge University Press, Cambridge, 1984, p. 258; Jawaharlal Nehru, *The Discovery of India*, Meridian Books Ltd, London, 1951, p. 276.

2   Moustafa Kamel, *Égyptiens et Anglais*, Perrin et Co. Éditeur, Paris, 1906, pp. 58–59.

3   Muhammad Husain Haikal, 'Haithiat al-hukm fi qadiat al-jizia, *Al-Siyasa al-Usbu'ia*', 16/6 (1925), Cairo, and in *Assiassa*, 9 June 1925, p. 1.

4   Family letter, 26 June 1925.

5   Kamel, *Égyptiens et Anglais*, pp. 58–59.

6   *L'Égyptienne*, February 1925, p. 14.

7   Ibid., p. 23.

8   *L'Égyptienne*, July 1925, p. 171.

9   *L'Égyptienne*, August 1925, p. 204 and Juliette Adam, *L'Égypte, une leçon diplomatique*, Éditions de l'Égypte, Paris, 1924.

10   *L'Égyptienne*, June 1925, p. 138.

11   *L'Égyptienne*, February 1925, pp. 24–25.

12   *L'Égyptienne*, May 1925, p. 96.

13   Ibid., p. 169.

14   *L'Égyptienne*, September 1925, p. 235.

15   *L'Égyptienne*, December 1925, p. 342.

16   George Antonius, *The Arab Awakening*, J.B. Lippincott Company, New York, 1919, Appendix 6: 'Recommendations of the King–Crane Commission with regard to Syria, Palestine and Iraq (28 August 1919)'.

17   *L'Égyptienne*, December 1925, p. 347.

18   Ibid., p. 338.

19   Ibid., p. 348.

20   Ibid., p. 31.

21   Lord Lloyd, *Egypt Since Cromer*, Macmillan and Co., London, 1934, vol. II, p. 148; Marcel Colombe, *L'évolution de l'Égypte, 1924–1950*, Éditions G.P. Maisonneuve, Paris, 1951, p. 33.

22 *Cinquantenaire de La Réforme Illustrée*, a special 1945 issue that covers 50 years of Egyptian history especially published for the fiftieth anniversary of *La Réforme* magazine, created by Raoul Canivet, p.83.

23 *L'Égyptienne*, February 1926, p.29.

24 *L'Égyptienne*, December 1925, p.328.

25 Ibid., p.329.

26 *L'Égyptienne*, February 1926, p.27.

27 *L'Égyptienne*, January 1926, p.32.

28 *L'Égyptienne*, April 1926, p.86.

29 Jeffrey Abt, 'Towards a historian's laboratory', *Journal of the American Research Center in Egypt*, 33 (1996).

30 *L'Égyptienne*, August 1926, p.203.

31 *L'Égyptienne*, July 1926, p.162.

32 Lloyd, *Egypt Since Cromer*, vol.I, pp.168–69.

33 Ibid., vol.II, p.167.

34 Ibid., p.168.

35 *L'Égyptienne*, p.163.

36 Ibid., p.171.

37 Ibid., p.168.

38 Quoted by Leila J. Rupp, in 'Challenging imperialism in international women's organisations, 1888–1945', *Global Perspectives*, 8 (Spring 1996).

39 Viscount Alfred Milner, *England in Egypt*, Edward Arnold, London, 1904, p.60.

40 Huda Shaarawi, *Mudhakkirat ra'idat al-Mar'a al-'Arabia al-haditha Huda Shaarawi*, Dar al-Hilal, Cairo, 1981, p.354.

Chapter 7

1 *L'Égyptienne*, October–November 1926, p.49.

2 *L'Égyptienne*, January 1927, p.3.

3 *L'Égyptienne*, February 1927, p.59.

4 *L'Égyptienne*, July 1926, p.163.

5 Muhammad Husain Haikal, *Mudhakkirat fi al-Siyasa al-Misria*, Dar al-Maarif, Cairo, 1977, vol.I, p.277; *L'Égyptienne*, August 1927, p.2.

6 Abd al-Rahman al-Raf'i, *Fi a'qab al-thawra al-Misria* (2nd edition), Maktabat al-Nahda al-Misria, Cairo, 1959, vol.I, p.277.

7 *L'Égyptienne*, June 1927, p.10.

8 Jacques Berque, *L'Égypte, impérialisme et révolution*, Éditions Gallimard, Paris, 1967, p.227.

9 Afaf Lutfi al-Sayyid Marsot, *Egypt's Liberal Experiment, 1922–1936*, University of California Press, Berkeley and Los Angeles, 1977, pp.204–5.

10 Haikal, *Mudhakkirat fi al-Siyasa al-Misria*, vol.II, p.231.

11 *L'Égyptienne*, December 1927, p.2.

12   Ibid., p. 2.
13   *L'Égyptienne*, July 1927, p. 28.
14   Personal letter, 11 November 1927.
15   *L'Égyptienne*, March 1928, p. 25.
16   *L'Égyptienne*, September 1928, p. 4.
17   *L'Égyptienne*, October 1928, p. 2.

Chapter 8

1   *Al-Ahram*, 28 December 1928.
2   *L'Égyptienne*, January 1928, p. 2.
3   *L'Égyptienne*, January 1929, p. 5.
4   Ibid., p. 7.
5   *L'Égyptienne*, February 1929, p. 33.
6   *L'Égyptienne*, March 1929, p. 8.
7   Ibid., p. 45.
8   *L'Égyptienne*, May 1929, p. 1.
9   *L'Égyptienne*, October 1929, p. 5.
10   Ibid., p. 30.
11   *L'Égyptienne*, February 1932, p. 19.
12   *Le Progrès Egyptien*, 25 November 1984.
13   See 'Minutes of the 19th meeting of the Board of Trustees of AUC', New York City.
14   *L'Égyptienne*, November 1929, p. 2.
15   Ibid., p. 40.
16   *L'Égyptienne*, May 1930, p. 12.
17   *L'Égyptienne*, December 1929, p. 19.
18   Ibid., p. 22.
19   *L'Égyptienne*, January 1930, p. 5.
20   *L'Égyptienne*, July 1930, p. 14.
21   *L'Égyptienne*, February 1930, p. 36.
22   Abd al-Rahman al-Raf'i, *Fi a'qab al-thawra al-Misria* (2nd edition), Maktabat al-Nahda al-Misria, Cairo, 1959, vol. II, pp. 130, 150; Jacques Berque, *L'Égypte, impérialisme et révolution*, Éditions Gallimard, Paris, 1967, p. 456.
23   *L'Égyptienne*, June 1931, p. 6.
24   *L'Égyptienne*, May 1931, pp. 2–8, 13, 28.
25   *L'Égyptienne*, December 1931, p. 2.
26   *L'Égyptienne*, June 1931, p. 6.
27   *L'Égyptienne*, May 1931, p. 28.
28   *L'Égyptienne*, December 1931, p. 43.
29   Interview with Huria Shafik, 16 April 1997.

~ Notes ~

Chapter 9

1   Margot Badran, *Feminists, Islam, and Nation: Gender and the making of modern Egypt*, Princeton University Press, Princeton, NJ, 1995, p. 100.
2   Family letter, 23 July 1932.
3   *L'Égyptienne*, October 1933, p. 21.
4   Ibid., p. 30.
5   Tom Segev, *One Palestine, Complete*, translated by Haim Weitzman, Metropolitan Books, Henry Holt and Company, New York, 2000, p. 376.
6   *L'Égyptienne*, April 1933, p. 5.
7   Quoted by Leila J. Rupp, in 'Challenging imperialism in international women's organizations, 1888–1945', *Global Perspectives*, 8 (Spring 1996).
8   *L'Égyptienne*, November 1934, p. 43.
9   Letter, Huda to Germaine Malaterre-Sellier, 1939.
10 *L'Égyptienne*, April 1933, pp. 40–41.
11 *L'Égyptienne*, May 1933, p. 7.
12 *L'Égyptienne*, April 1933, p. 415.
13 *L'Égyptienne*, March 1933, p. 21.
14 *L'Égyptienne*, May 1933, pp. 11–13.
15 *L'Égyptienne*, June 1933, p. 42.
16 *L'Égyptienne*, February 1935, p. 8.
17 Jacques Berque, *L'Égypte, impérialisme et révolution*, Éditions Gallimard, Paris, 1967, p. 458.
18 *L'Égyptienne*, December 1933, p. 13.
19 Ibid., p. 7.
20 Ibid., p. 9.
21 *L'Égyptienne*, December 1933, p. 4.
22 Saneya Shaarawy Lanfranchi, 'Un sculpteur égyptien: Abdel Badi Abdel Hay', *Le Progrès Égyptien*, Cairo, 25 November 1984.
23 Badr al-Din Abu Ghazi and Gabriel Boctor, *Mouktar ou le réveil de l'Égypte*, H. Urwand et Fils, Cairo, 1949, p. 86.
24 *L'Égyptienne*, November 1934, p. 2.
25 *L'Égyptienne*, October 1935, p. 5.
26 *L'Égyptienne*, March 1935, p. 24.
27 *L'Égyptienne*, February 1935, p. 3.
28 Charles Crane documents, American University in Cairo Library.
29 *L'Égyptienne*, May 1935, p. 5.
30 Ibid., p. 29.
31 Ibid., p. 36.

Chapter 10

1   *L'Égyptienne*, August–September 1935, pp. 2–3.
2   Royal Institute of International Affairs, *Great Britain and Egypt 1914–1951*, Information Papers no 19, RIIA, Chatham House, London, 1952, pp. 32–36.
3   Jacques Berque, *L'Égypte, impérialisme et révolution*, Éditions Gallimard, Paris, 1967, p. 472: 'Nous avons donné des conseils hostiles à la remise en vigueur de la Constitution de 1923.'
4   *L'Égyptienne*, November 1935, p. 2.
5   Royal Institute of International Affairs, *Great Britain and Egypt 1914–1951*, pp. 36–37.
6   Berque, *L'Égypte, impérialisme et révolution*, p. 478.
7   *L'Égyptienne*, June 1936, p. 8.
8   Ibid., p. 12.
9   Ibid., p. 10.
10 *L'Égyptienne*, July–August 1936, p. 28.
11 Ibid., pp. 28–32.
12 *L'Égyptienne*, February 1936, p. 35.
13 *L'Égyptienne*, October 1936, p. 3.
14 *L'Égyptienne*, December 1936, p. 2.
15 *L'Égyptienne*, April 1937, pp. 2–10.
16 William Stadiem, *Too Rich: The high life and tragic death of King Farouk*, Robson Books, London, 1991, p. 172.
17 *L'Égyptienne*, July–August 1937, pp. 8–16.
18 Ibid., p. 21.
19 *L'Égyptienne*, October 1937, p. 2.
20 *L'Égyptienne*, September 1937, p. 5.

Chapter 11

1   For more information about Muhammad Mahmud and the treaty, see Afaf Lutfi al-Sayyid Marsot, *Egypt's Liberal Experiment, 1922–1936*, University of California Press, Berkeley and Los Angeles, 1977, p. 82.
2   *L'Égyptienne*, April 1938, p. 24.
3   *L'Égyptienne*, May 1938, p. 4.
4   Ibid., p. 6.
5   Ibid., p. 26.
6   Ibid., p. 6.
7   Margot Badran, *Feminists, Islam, and Nation: Gender and the making of modern Egypt*, Princeton University Press, Princeton, NJ, 1995, p. 228.
8   *L'Égyptienne*, July–August 1938, p. 3.

9   *Al-Mar'a al-'Arabia wa qadiat filistin, al-Mu'tamar al-Nisa'i al-Sharqi*, Al-Matba'a al-Misria, Cairo, 1938, p. 26.

10 Ibid., p. 28.

11 Ibid., p. 46.

12 Ibid., pp. 47–90.

13 Ibid., p. 148.

14 Ibid., pp. 161–62.

15 *Al-Misria*, 15 December 1938, p. 18.

16 *Al-Misria*, 15 January 1939, p. 13.

17 *Al-Misria*, 15 December 1938, p. 14.

18 *L'Égyptienne*, May 1938, p. 6.

19 *L'Égyptienne*, March 1939, p. 18.

20 *L'Égyptienne*, August 1928, p. 7.

21 Tom Segev, *One Palestine, Complete*, translated by Haim Weitzman, Metropolitan Books, Henry Holt and Company, New York, 2000, p. 420.

22 Ibid., p. 440.

23 Ibid., p. 426.

24 Ibid., p. 419.

25 *L'Égyptienne*, June 1939, p. 2.

26 *Al-Misria*, 1 June 1939, p. 10.

27 *Dhikra Faqidat al-'uruba sahibat al-'isma al-sayida al-jalila Huda Hanim Shaarawi*, Sharikat Fann al-Tiba'a, Cairo, 1948 (Huda's commemorative publication), p. 167.

28 *L'Égyptienne*, July–August 1939, p. 29.

29 Ibid., p. 5.

30 Ibid., p. 5.

31 Ibid., p. 9.

Chapter 12

1   *L'Égyptienne*, November 1933, p. 32.

2   Muhammad Husain Haikal, *Mudhakkirat fi al-Siyasa al-Misria*, Dar Al-Maarif, Cairo, 1977, vol. II, p. 163.

3   *Dhikra Faqidat al-Adab al-Nabigha Mayy*, Al-Matba'at al-Misria, Cairo, 1941 (Mayy's commemorative publication), p. 2.

4   Royal Institute of International Affairs, *Great Britain and Egypt 1914–1951*, Information Papers no 19, RIIA, Chatham House, London, 1952, p. 68.

5   Abd al-Rahman al-Raf'i, *Fi a'qab al-thawra al-Misria* (2nd edition), Maktabat al-Nahda al-Misria, Cairo, 1959, vol. II, pp. 123–24; Royal Institute of International Affairs, *Great Britain and Egypt 1914–1951*, p. 70.

6   Haikal, *Mudhakkirat fi al-Siyasa al-Misria*, vol. I, p. 205.

7   *Dhikra Faqidat al-'uruba sahibat al-'isma al-sayida al-jalila Huda Hanim Shaarawi*, Sharikat Fann al-Tiba'a, Cairo, 1948 (Huda's commemorative publication), pp. 217–19.

8   Royal Institute of International Affairs, *Great Britain and Egypt 1914–1951*, pp. 79–80.

9   *Dhikra Faqidat al-'uruba sahibat al-'isma al-sayida al-jalila Huda Hanim Shaarawi*, p. 49.

10   The account of the 1944 conference in this chapter is drawn from 'Al-mu'tamar al-Nisa'i al-Arabi bi al-qahira min 12 ila 16 disambar 1944', *Dar Al-Maarif*, Cairo, 1944.

11   Hawa Idris, *Ana wa al-Sharq*, unpublished, printed in Cairo, 1973, p. 84.

12   Jacques Berque, *L'Égypte, impérialisme et révolution*, Éditions Gallimard, Paris, 1967, p. 604.

13   Al-Raf'i, *Fi a'qab al-thawra al-Misria* (2nd edition), p. 153.

14   *L'Egyptienne*, November 1935, p. 32.

15   Interview with Boula Hénein, 1970s.

16   George Hénein, *Le Prestige de la terreur*, Éditions de la Rue Champollion, copied from the original edition published by Éditions Masses du Caire, Cairo, 1945, pp. 2–3.

17   Francisca De Haan, 'Getting to the Source', *Journal of Women's History*, 2004, 16/4, p. 148.

Chapter 13

1   Dame Margery Corbett-Ashby, *Memoirs of Dame Margery Corbett-Ashby*, with additional material by Dr Michael Ashby, M.G. Ashby, Horsted Keynes, 1996, p. 204; Amina al-Said, 'Mu'tamar al-hind al-nisa'i', *Al-Mar'a al-'Arabia*, Cairo, March 1947, p. 10.

2   Royal Institute of International Affairs, *Great Britain and Egypt 1914–1951*, Information Papers no 19, RIIA, Chatham House, London, 1952, p. 80.

3   Karima al-Said, 'Rihlati ila al-hind', Al-radio al-Masri, 4 May 1947, p. 8.

4   Hawa Idris, *Ana wa al-Sharq*, unpublished, printed in Cairo, 1973, p. 84.

5   Ibid., p. 218.

6   Amina al-Said, 'Mu'tamar al-hind al-nisa'i', p. 10.

7   Kamaladevi Chattopadyay, *Outer Space and Inner Recesses*, Navrang, New Delhi, 1986, p. 219.

8   Ibid., p. 218.

9   Ibid., p. 220.

10   Tom Segev, *One Palestine, Complete*, translated by Haim Weitzman, Metropolitan Books, Henry Holt and Company, New York, 2000, p. 412.

Select bibliography

Sources in English and French

Abu Ghazi, Badr al-Din and Gabriel Boctor, *Mouktar ou le réveil de l'Égypte*, H. Urwand et Fils, Cairo, 1949

Adam, Juliette (Juliette Lambert), *L'Angleterre en Égypte*, Imprimerie du Centre, Paris, 1922

— *L'Égypte, une leçon diplomatique*, Éditions de l'Égypte, Paris, 1924

— *Et c'est moi, Juliette: Madame Adam 1836–1936*, Éditions de la Saga, Gif-sur-Yvette, 1988

Ahmed, Leila, *Women and Gender in Islam*, Yale University Press, New Haven, CT, 1992

Amin, Qasim, *The New Woman*, translated by Samiha Sidhom Peterson, American University in Cairo Press, Cairo, 1995

Antonius, George, *The Arab Awakening*, J.B. Lippincott Company, New York, 1919

Badran, Margot, *Feminists, Islam, and Nation: Gender and the making of modern Egypt*, Princeton University Press, Princeton, NJ, 1995

Badran, Margot and Miriam Cooke, *Opening the Gates*, Virago Press, London, 1992

Badrawi, Malak, *Isma'il Sidki, 1875–1950: Pragmatism and vision in twentieth century Egypt*, Curzon Press, Richmond, Surrey, 1996

— *Political Violence in Egypt 1910–1921*, Curzon Press, Richmond, Surrey, 2000

Baron, Beth, *Egypt as a Woman: Nationalism, gender and politics*, University of California Press, Berkeley and Los Angeles, 2005

— *The Women's Awakening in Egypt*, Yale University Press, New Haven, CT, 1994

Berque, Jacques, *L'Égypte, impérialisme et révolution*, Éditions Gallimard, Paris, 1967

Blunt, Wilfrid Scawen, *Secret History of the English Occupation of Egypt*, T. Fisher Unwin, London, 1882

Booth, Marylin, *May her Likes be Multiplied: Biography and gender politics in Egypt*, University of California Press, Berkeley, 2005

Chattopadyay, Kamaladevi, *Outer Space and Inner Recesses*, Navrang, New Delhi, 1986

Clément, Mademoiselle, *Conférences données au Caire chez Madame Ali Pacha Charaoui et à l'Université Égyptienne*, Imprimerie Paul Barbey, Cairo, 1914

Colombe, Marcel, *L'évolution de l'Égypte, 1924–1950*, Éditions de G.P. Maisonneuve, Paris, 1951

Cooper, Artemis, *Cairo in the War (1939–1945)*, Penguin Books, London, 1989

Comte Cressaty, *L'Égypte d'aujourd'hui*, Marcel Rivière et Co., Paris, 1912

Corbett-Ashby, Dame Margery, *Memoirs of Dame Margery Corbett-Ashby*, with additional material by Dr Michael Ashby, M.G. Ashby, Horsted Keynes, 1996

Cromer, Earl of, *Modern Egypt*, Macmillan and Company, London, 1907

Danielson, Virginia, *The Voice of Egypt: Umm Kulthum, Arabic song and Egyptian society in the twentieth century*, University of Chicago Press, Chicago, 1997

Davis, Eric, *Challenging Colonialism: Bank Misr and Egyptian industrialization, 1920–1941*, Princeton University Press, Princeton, NJ, 1983

Devonshire, Henriette, *L'Égypte musulmane*, Livres de France, Cairo, 1982

El-Feki, Mustafa, *Copts in Egyptian Politics, 1919–1952*, General Egyptian Book Organisation, Cairo, 1991

El-Masri Sidhom, Eva, *Memories of a Co-ed at the American University in Cairo, Memoirs of an Egyptian American or the Life Story of the First Co-ed at the American University in Cairo*, Engeltal Press, Jasper, AR, n.d.

Ezzel Arab, Abdel Aziz, *European Control and Egypt's Traditional Elites: A case study in elite economic nationalism*, Edwin Mellen Press, Lewiston, NY, 2002

Fahmi-Wissa, Hanna, *Assiout, the Saga of an Egyptian Family*, Book Guild, Brighton, 1994

Fromkin, David, *A Peace to End All Peace*, Henry Holt and Company, New York, 1991

Gallagher, Nancy Elizabeth, *Egypt's Other Wars: Epidemics and the politics of public health*, American University in Cairo Press, Cairo, 1993

Goldschmidt, Arthur Jr, *Biographical Dictionary of Modern Egypt*, American University in Cairo Press, Cairo, 2000

— *Modern Egypt: The formation of a nation state*, Westview Press, Boulder, CO, 2004

Hénein, George, *Le Prestige de la terreur*, Éditions de la Rue Champollion, copied from the original edition published by Éditions Masses du Caire, Cairo, 1945

Hobsbawm, Eric, *The Age of Extremes: The short twentieth century 1914–1991*, Penguin, London, 1995

Hunter, Robert, *Egypt under the Khedives (1805–1879): From household government to modern bureaucracy*, American University in Cairo Press, Cairo, 1999

Hussein, Taha, *The Future of Culture in Egypt*, Palm Press, Cairo 1998 (first published in English by the American Council of Learned Societies, Washington, DC, 1954)

Kamel, Moustafa Pasha, *Égyptiens et Anglais*, Perrin et Co. Éditeurs, Paris, 1906

Kent, Marian (ed.), *The Great Powers and the End of the Ottoman Empire*, George Allen and Unwin, London, 1984

Lebrun, Eugénie (written as Niya Salima), *Harems et musulmanes d'Égypte*, Felix Juven Éditeur, Paris, n.d.

~ Select bibliography ~

Lloyd, Lord, *Egypt Since Cromer*, Macmillan and Co., London, 2 vols, 1933 and 1934

Lutfi al-Sayyid Marsot, Afaf, *Egypt's Liberal Experiment, 1922–1936*, University of California Press, Berkeley and Los Angeles, 1977

— *Egypt in the Reign of Muhammad Ali*, Cambridge University Press, Cambridge, 1984

— *A Short History of Modern Egypt*, Cambridge University Press, Cambridge, 1994

Madanian, Annie Zarouhie, 'The Emerging of the New Egyptian Woman as Seen in *L'Égyptienne*: The redefinition of Egyptian womanhood', MA thesis, American University in Cairo, May 1975

Mansfield, Peter, *The British in Egypt*, Weidenfeld & Nicholson, London, 1971

Milner, Viscount Alfred, *England in Egypt*, Edward Arnold, London, 1904

Mitchell, Timothy, *Colonizing Egypt*, Cambridge University Press, Cambridge, 1988

Nehru, Jawaharlal, *The Discovery of India*, Meridian Books Ltd, London, 1951

Nelson, Cynthia, *Doria Shafik, an Egyptian Feminist (A Woman Apart)*, University Press of Florida, Gainesville, FL, 1996

Owen, Roger, *The Middle-East in the World Economy 1888–1914*, I.B. Tauris and Co., London, 1981

Peretz, Don, *The Middle East Today*, Praeger, New York, 1994

Raafat, Samir W., *Maadi (1904–1962)*, Palm Press, Cairo, 1994

Ronfard, Bruno, *Taha Hussein: Les cultures en dialogue*, Desclée de Brouwer, Paris, 1995

Roussillon, Alain (ed.), *Entre réforne sociale et mouvement national, identité et modernisation en Égypte (1882–1962)*, CEDEJ, Cairo, 1995

Royal Institute of International Affairs, *Great Britain and Egypt 1914–1951*, Information Papers no 19, RIIA, Chatham House, London, 1952

Russell, Sir Thomas, *Egyptian Service, 1902–1946*, John Murray, London, 1949

Sabry, Mohamed, *L'Empire égyptien sous Ismail et l'ingérence anglo-française*, Librairie Orientaliste Paul Geuthner, Paris, 1933

Scotidis, N., *L'Égypte contemporaine et Arabi pacha*, C. Marpon et E. Flammarion, Paris, 1888

Segev, Tom, *The Seventh Million, the Israelis and the Holocaust*, translated by Haim Weizman, Hill and Wang, New York, 1994

— *One Palestine, Complete*, translated by Haim Weitzman, Metropolitan Books, Henry Holt and Company, New York, 2000

Shafik, Doria, *La femme nouvelle en Égypte, 1919*, Paris, 1920

Shaarawi, Huda, *Harem Years: The memoirs of an Egyptian feminist*, translated, edited and introduced by Margot Badran, Virago Press, London, 1986

Shaarawy Lanfranchi, Sania, 'The Role of Tradition and the Individual Talent in the Love Poetry of Ahmed Shawqi', MA thesis, 1985

Shafik, Doria, *L'Ésclave sultane*, Les Nouvelles Éditions Latines, Paris, 1951

Stadiem, William, *Too Rich: The high life and tragic death of King Farouk*, Robson Books, London, 1991

Tignor, Robert L., *Modernization and British Colonial Rule in Egypt 1882–1914*, Princeton University Press, Princeton, NJ, 1966

— *Egyptian Textiles and British Capital, 1930–1956*, American University in Cairo Press, Cairo, 1989

Van Den Bosch, Firmin, *Vingt années d'Égypte*, Librairie Académique Perrin, Paris, 1932

Vatikiotis, P.J., *The History of Egypt from Muhammad Ali to Sadat* (2nd edition), Weidenfeld & Nicolson, London, 1980

Vatin, Jean Claude (ed.), *La fuite en Égypte*, CEDEJ, Cairo, 1989

Wissa, Esther Fahmi, *He Maketh Wars to Cease: World unrest causes and cures*, printed by Whitehead Morris Limited, Alexandria, 1940

Yeghen, Foulad, *Saad Zaghlul, le père du peuple égyptien*, Les Cahiers de France, Paris, 1927

— *Chants d'un oriental, à l'ombre du sphinx*, Les Cahiers de France, Paris, 1928

— *Une vie de Musulmane*, Imprimerie Paul Barbey, Cairo, 1929

Magazines, articles and speeches in English, French and Italian

Abt, Jeffrey, 'Towards a historian's laboratory', *Journal of the American Research Center in Egypt*, 33 (1996)

De Haan, Francisca, 'Getting to the Source', *Journal of Women's History*, 16/4 (2000)

Hunter, Robert, 'The making of a notable politician: Muhammad Sultan Pasha (1825–1884)', *International Journal of Middle Eastern Studies*, 15 (1983)

L'Égypte: Les évènements d'Égypte, bi-monthly publication by the Egyptian Association of Paris, 9 and 10 (10 December 1919)

L'Égypte et l'Union Inter-parlementaire, conférence du Caire, Ed. al-Hilal, 1947

L'Égypte nouvelle, Cairo, 1 January 1924

L'Égyptienne, monthly, founded by Huda Shaarawi, editor Céza Nabarawi, Imprimerie Paul Barbey, Cairo, 1925–39

La Réforme, special issue, *Cinquantenaire de La Réforme Illustrée*, 1945

Le Progrès Égyptien, 'Cent ans de passion, 1893–1993', Cairo, 1993

Lombardo, Esther, 'Sorelle di terra lontana', *Giornale di Roma*

Nukrashi, Mahmud Pasha, *Statement made by His Excellency the Prime Minister of Egypt before the Security Council, August 1947*, Government Press, Cairo, 1947

Rupp, Leila J., 'Challenging imperialism in international women's organisations, 1888–1945', *Global Perspectives*, 8 (Spring 1996)

Shaarawy Lanfranchi, Saneya, 'Un sculpteur égyptien: Abdel Badi Abdel Hay', *Le Progrès Égyptien*, Cairo, 25 November 1984

The Times Book of Egypt, Times Publishing Company Ltd, London 1937, extracts reprinted in *The Times*, 'Egypt' feature, published on 26 January 1993

Volait, Mercédès, 'Un architecte face à l'Orient: Antoine Lasciac (1856–1946)', in Jean-Claude Vatin (ed.) *La Fuite en Égypte: supplément aux voyages européens en Orient*, Institut français d'archéologie orientale, CEDEJ, Cairo, 1986

Zouari, Fawzia 'Étonnantes Voyageuses', in *Méditerranée*, March 1998, hors-serie

~ Select bibliography ~

Sources in Arabic

Abd al-Nur, Fakhri, *Mudhakkirat thawrat 1919*, edited by Yunan Labib Rizq, Dar al-Shuruq, Cairo, 1992

Abu al-Majd, Sabri, *Sanawat ma qabla al-thawra, 1930–1952*, 3 vols, General Egyptian Book Organisation, Cairo, 1987, 1988, 1989

Alluba, Muhammad Ali, *Dhikrayat Ijtima'ia wa Siyasia*, General Egyptian Book Organisation, Cairo, 1988

Amin, Qasim, *Tahrir al-Mar'a*, edited by Muhammad 'Imara, Dar al-Hilal, Cairo, 1980

al-'Aqqad, Abbas Mahmud, *Rijal 'Araftuhum*, Nahdat Misr li al-Tiba'a wa al-nashr, Cairo

al-Hilbawi, Ibrahim, *Mudhakkirat*, edited by Isam Dia' al-Din, General Egyptian Book Organisation, Cairo, 1995

al-Miliji, Muhammad Ahmad, *Abd al-Khaliq Tharwat wa dawruhu fi al-siyasa al-Misria 1873–1928*, General Egyptian Book Organisation, Cairo, 1989

al-Moti'i, Lami'i, *Safwit al-'asr fi tarikh wa rusum mashahir rijal masr*, Matba'at al-I'timad bi Sharia Hasan al-Akbar, Cairo, 1926

al-Raf'i, Abd al-Rahman, *Mustapha Kamil*, Maktabit al-Nahda al-Misria, Cairo, 1950

— *Fi a'qab al-thawra al-Misria* (2nd edition), Maktabat al-Nahda al-Misria, Cairo, 1959

— *Al-Thawra al-'urabia wa al-ihtilal al-injilizi* (2nd edition), dar al-qawmia li al-tiba'a wa al-nashr, Cairo, 1966

al-Subki, Amal Kamil Bayumi, *Al-haraka al-nisa'ia fi misr ma bayna al-thawratain, 1949–1952*, General Egyptian Book Organisation, 1986

al-Tunsi, Bairam, *Maqamat Bairam*, Madbuli, Cairo, 1985

Fahmi, Abd al-Rahman, *Mudhakkirat Abd al-Rahman Fahmi*, General Egyptian Book Organisation, Cairo, 1988

Farid, Amani, *Al-mar'a al-Misria wa al-barlaman*, Al-Tawakkul Press, Cairo, 1947

Haikal, Muhammad Husain, *Tarajim Misria wa gharbia*, Al-Siyasa Press, Cairo, 1929

— *Mudhakkirat fi al-Siyasa al-Misria*, Dar al-Maarif, Cairo, 1977

— *Zainab* (fifth edition), Dar al-Maarif, Cairo, 1992

Hifni Nasif, Malak, *Athar Bahithat al-Badia*, a collection of essays, poems and letters edited by Magd al-Din Hifni Nasif, with an introduction by Suhair al-Qalamawi, Al-Mu'assassa al-Misria al-'amma li al-ta'lif wa al-tarjama, wa al-Tiba'a wa al-nashr, Cairo, 1962

Idris, Hawa, *Ana wa al-Sharq*, unpublished, printed in Cairo, 1973

Lashin, Abd al-Khaliq, *Sa'd Zaghlul wa dawruhu fi al-siyasa al-Misria*, Madbuli, Cairo, 1975

Lutfi al-Sayid, Ahmad, *Safahat matwia min tarikh al-haraka al-istiqlalia fi-misr*, Maktabit al-Nahda al-Misria, 1946

— *Ta'ammulat fi al-falsafa wa al-adab wa al-siyasa wa al-ijtima'*, Dar al-Maarif, Cairo, 1946

Makhluf, Najib, *Nubar Pasha*, Maktabit Zidan al-'Umumia, Cairo, 1925

Mubarak, Zaki *Ahmad Shawqi*, General Egyptian Book Organisation, Cairo, 1997

Nasralla, Emily, *Nisa' ra'idat min al-sharq*, Al-Dar al-Misria al-Lubnania, Cairo, 2001

Raghib, Nabil, *Huda Shaarawi wa'asr al-tanwir*, General Egyptian Book Organisation, Cairo, 1988

Ramadan, Abd al-Azim, *Al-sira'baina al-wafd wa al-'arsh 1936–1939*, Al-Mu'asasa al-'arabia li al-dirasat wa al-nashr, Beirut, 1979

— *Mustapha Kamil fi mahkamat al-tarikh*, General Egyptian Book Organisation, Cairo, 1994

— *Tatawur al-haraka al-watania fi Misr, 1937–1948*, Markaz al-Tiba'a al-haditha, Alexandria, n.d.

Rashad, Ahmad, *Mustapha Kamil*, Dar al-Sa'ada, Cairo, 1958

Shaarawi, Huda, *Mudhakkirat ra'idat al-Mar'a al-'Arabia al-haditha Huda Shaarawi*, edited with an introduction by Amina al-Said, Dar al-Hilal, Cairo, 1981

Shafik, Ahmad Pasha, *Hawliat Misr al-Siyasiya*, Maktabit Hawliat Misr, Cairo, 1927

— *Mudhakkirati fi nisf qarn*, Maktabit Misr, Cairo, n.d.

Shakir, Safa', *Isma'il Sidqi, al-waqai' al-siyasia fi muwajahat al-haraka al-watania*, Dar al-Shuruq, Cairo, 2005

Sidqi, Ismail Pasha, *Mudhakkarati*, edited by Sami Abu al-Nur, Madbuli, Cairo, 1991

Sidqi-Rasheed, Bahija, Tahia Muhammad Asfahani and Samia Sidqi Murad, *Al-yubil al-dhahabi 1923–1973 (Tarikh mujaz'an al-ittihad al-nisa'i al-misri, jam 'iat Huda Shaarawi li al-nahda al-nisa'ia)*, Dar Ma'mun li al-Tiaba'a, 1973

Silim, Muhammad Kamil, *Azmit al-Wafd al-kubra, Saad wa Adli*, Mu'asasat Akhbar al-Youm, no 157, Cairo, 1976

Subaih, Muhammad, *Kifah shaab Misr fi al-qarnain al-tasi' 'ashir wa al-'ishrin* (second edition), Cairo, 1966

Thabit, Adil, *Faruq al-awwal, al-malik alladhi ghadara bihi al-jami'*, translated into Arabic by Muhammad Mustapha Ghunaim, Akhbar al-yum, Cairo, 1989

Zaghlul, Saad, *Mudhakkirat Saad Zaghlul*, edited by Abd al-Azim Ramadan, 4 vols, General Egyptian Book Organisation, Cairo, 1920, 1988, 1990, 1991

Ziadé, Mayy, *Bahithat al-Badia*, Matba'at al-Muqtataf, Cairo, 1920

Magazines, essays and articles in Arabic

Abd al-Malik, Balsam, *Al-Mar'a al-Misria*, 4 vols, publisher unknown, 1920, 1921, 1922, 1923

Al-Mar'a al-'Arabia, chief editor Amina al-Said, Cairo, 1947

Al-Mar'a al-'Arabia wa qadiat filistin, al-Mu'tamar al-Nisa'i al-Sharqi, Al-Matba'a al-Misria, Cairo, 1938

Al-Mu'tamar al-Arabi li tawhid juhud al-mar'a al-sharqia wa taqrir huquqiha al-madania wa al-siasia wa al-difa' 'an qadiat filistin, Dar al-Maarif, 1944

Al-Misria, founded in January 1937 by Huda Shaarawi and edited from 1937 to 1938 by Fatma Nimet Rashid and from 1938 to 1942 by Eva Habib al-Masri

~ Select bibliography ~

al-Said, Karima, 'Rihlati ila al-hind', Al-radio al-Masri, 4 May 1947

Dhikra Faqidat al-Adab al-Nabigha Mayy, Al-Matba'a al-Misria, Cairo, 1941 (Mayy's commemorative publication)

Dhikra Faqidat al-'uruba sahibat al-'isma al-sayida al-jalila Huda Hanim Shaarawi, Sharikat Fann al-Tiba'a, Cairo, 1948 (Huda's commemorative publication)

Haikal, Muhammad Husain Pasha, 'Haithiat al-hukm fi qadiat al-jizia, *Al-Siyasa al-Usbu'ia*', 16/6 (1925), Cairo, and in *Assiassa*, 9 June 1925

Majallit Biladi (commemorative issue dedicated to Ahmed Mahir), 21 (6 April 1991), Dar al-mustaqbal, Cairo

Ramadan, Abd al-Azim, 'Min tawdhif al-din ila tawdhif al-amwal', *October*, 611 (10 July 1988), Cairo

Index

299

~ Index ~

~ Index ~

~ Index ~